D0560409

UNIVERSITY OF WINNIPEG
LIBRARY
515 Portage Avenue
Winnipeg, Manitoba R3B 2E9

DISCARDED

THE UNIVERSITY OF WINNIPEG

LIBRARY FUND

Presented by

BRENDA MAE SUDERMAN

William Parker
Mounted Policeman

HV
1911
P35
A37
1973
c.3

William Parker
Mounted Policeman

Edited by Hugh A. Dempsey

Glenbow-Alberta Institute, Calgary
Hurtig Publishers, Edmonton

Copyright © 1973 by The Glenbow-Alberta Institute

No part of this book may be reproduced or transmitted
in any form by any means, electronic or mechanical,
including photocopying and recording, or by any information
storage or retrieval system, without written permission
from the publisher, except for brief passages quoted
by a reviewer in a newspaper or magazine.

Hurtig Publishers
10560 105 Street
Edmonton, Alberta

ISBN 0-88830-072-7

Designed, typeset, printed and bound in Canada

Contents

Published with the cooperation and assistance of
The Glenbow-Alberta Institute, Calgary

Introduction

William Parker devoted most of his active life to the North-West Mounted Police, enlisting as a sub-constable in 1874 at the age of twenty-one, and retiring as an inspector in 1912 at the age of fifty-nine. During that time he grew with the West and witnessed many events which became a part of its history. He started on the Great March of 1874, was present at the signing of two Indian treaties, pursued fugitive Indians and criminals, assisted settlers, and performed the countless other functions expected of a pioneer Mounted Policeman.

Unlike most of his comrades, William Parker left a detailed record of his activities. A prolific writer, he sent frequent letters home to his family in England between 1874 and 1882, maintained thorough diaries, and after his retirement from the Force he wrote his reminiscences. The latter were based in part upon his letters and diaries, but expanded considerably upon the numerous incidents and personal experiences of his career.

William Parker was born on August 15, 1853, at New Romney, a short distance from Dover in Kent. He was the son of Reverend Henry Parker and Anne Parker (née Milton). His father was the rector of St. Mary's Anglican Rectory while his grandfather, Reverend Henry John Parker, had been ordained to the ministry in 1795 and had been appointed professor of Divinity at Gresham House, London, in 1801. Reverend Henry Parker had graduated from Cambridge and was one of the most highly regarded ministers of his day.[1] He also was an avid hunter, a love which he passed on to his son, who found the Canadian West to be ideal for the sportsman. William's letters home are filled with glowing accounts of the hunt.

There were six boys and two girls in the Parker family—Arthur, Thomas, Harry, William, Alfred, Julius, Annie and Alice. Although details are lacking, William's letters indicate that his two sisters were considerably younger than him and were still children when he left for Canada. Of the boys, Arthur was an older brother who was working away from home when he died in 1875. Thomas, another older brother, had a brewing business for a time, producing Parker Ale, but went broke in 1876 and moved to London. Harry was two years older than William and came to Canada with him in 1871. After working in Ontario for a number of years he tried unsuccessfully to join the North-West Mounted Police and finally came west with the Canadian Pacific Railway in 1881. By the following year he had joined his more successful brother in Battleford.

Alfred, or Ted, was a younger brother who, during the period of William's correspondence, was living at home. He was involved in a family scandal and tried unsuccessfully to join the Mounted Police in 1878. By 1881 he was still at home and was hoping his brother could find a place for him in Canada. The last brother, referred to in William's correspondence as Julie, Julius or Jue, was Julius Foster Dyke Parker, who became a well-known missionary in Saskatchewan. After his graduation from school he worked for a short time in the British Museum, emigrating to Canada in 1882. There he joined his brother in Battleford where he worked for a short time as a special constable for the NWMP. In the spring of 1884 he joined the Canadian government's telegraph service and operated in that capacity during the Riel Rebellion of 1885. Four years later he became an Anglican missionary, working for many years among the Indians of Fort à la Corne and Sturgeon Lake. When he retired in 1942, he and William were two old veterans of the West. Reverend Dyke Parker died in Regina in 1944.

Of these members of the family, William wrote fairly regularly to Annie, of whom he seemed to be most fond and to whom he liked to describe western life. He also corresponded on a number of occasions with Julius and less frequently with Alice and Harry. Not surprisingly, the bulk of his correspondence was with his parents.

William left home in April 1871 at the age of eighteen, accompanied by his brother Harry. Although he does not specify his reasons for going to Canada, the bleak employment picture was probably the primary cause. The fact that his brothers who remained behind had great difficulty in finding work would seem to support this theory. The destination of the two brothers was southern Ontario where a cousin, Alfred Barber, lived. Upon arrival, the boys obtained work on adjoining farms near Strathallen on "the twelfth line" with William being employed by Joseph Plaskett.

The brothers were laid off after the harvest in 1872, at which time they visited their cousin in Sarnia in an attempt to find work. When they were not successful, William returned to the Plaskett farm while

Harry remained in town, hoping for something better. William's decision to return was based partly upon the kind treatment he had received from the farm family.

As the end of 1873 drew near, William again was concerned about his employment. He had found the work to be gruelling. Feeding cattle in all kinds of weather, planting, harvesting and numerous other activities so exhausted him that Saturday nights were sometimes spent just resting. By this time William was prepared to remain, "but . . . he [Plaskett] has to give me more for the month than he has been doing or else he will not get me, for the winter work is just as bad or worse than the summer."[2]

However, no agreement could be made with the Plasketts, so William went to Sarnia. By this time he had saved enough money to start farming on his own, and in the spring Bishop Helmuth offered to lease some land to him. William visited the place early in March 1874 but he turned it down when he found it was partly unfenced and had poor buildings. He went on to the Plaskett farm, hoping to find something in that region but returned without success.

While in Sarnia William saw an advertisement announcing that men were being interviewed in London, Ontario, for the North-West Mounted Police. He took the train to the nearby city and was one of twelve candidates selected by Commissioner G.A. French from the crowd of young applicants. On April 4, he took the oath of allegiance and was sworn in as a sub-constable, with regimental number 205. This was later changed to 252 and, when he arrived in the West, changed again to number 28.

The North-West Mounted Police had been formed a year earlier by the Conservative government. Concerned about the need for law enforcement in the northwest after the acquisition of Rupert's Land from the Imperial government in 1870, Sir John A. Macdonald had first planned that a force would be raised at Red River. However, the onset of the 1870 rebellion under Louis Riel had resulted in the organization of a military expedition under General Garnet Wolseley which took charge of the Red River area. After the withdrawal of the British troops, a Canadian militia remained behind to maintain law and order. In the rest of the northwest, the Hudson's Bay Company continued to enforce government regulations.

The introduction of the whiskey trade from south of the border brought pressure upon the government to extend its legal jurisdiction to the western prairies. As a result, on May 3, 1873, Macdonald introduced a Bill "for the establishment of a Police Force in the North-West Territories."[3] Upon its passage three weeks later, the prime minister had the authority to launch the new police body. It provided for a police force of 300 men who would be signed on for a period of three years.

By this time Macdonald was becoming politically embroiled in the Pacific scandal, and it was not until alarming reports of a massacre of Canadian Indians by Americans in the Cypress Hills reached him that the prime minister was spurred into action. Responding to pleas from Red River, Macdonald authorized the engagement of 150 men who were sent to the West before the onset of winter. In the meantime Lieutenant-Colonel George Arthur French was appointed the first Commissioner of the Force and arrangements made for him to recruit a further 150 men in the spring.

In the federal election of the fall of 1873, the Pacific scandal drove the Conservatives out of office, and the Liberal government of Alexander Mackenzie took control. However, with a police force already committed to the northwest, no effort was made to change the Conservative plans. Instead, the new government was receptive to the needs of the northwest in suppressing the whiskey traffic.

In the spring of 1874, Commissioner French and other officers toured Ontario, Quebec and the Maritimes, interviewing candidates for the remaining 150 vacancies on the Force. In London, Ontario, William Parker was one of the fortunate ones to be selected from the large number of applicants.

At the time, Parker saw the appointment as only a temporary one; there was speculation that the Mounted Police would deal with the whiskey trade and then be disbanded. He told his parents that he might come home in the following year "if the government find it a pretty expensive thing keeping up a North-West Mounted Police."[4] His only disappointment was that he had to postpone his plans to visit his family in England during the autumn of 1874.

After a brief training period at New Fort, Toronto, Parker was posted to "D" Division and on June 6, 1874, he was part of the contingent that departed for the West. Travelling by rail through Chicago and St. Paul, they reached the end of the steel at Fargo, in Dakota Territory, and travelled overland to their temporary quarters at Dufferin, Manitoba.

There, on July 8, the original three troops joined with the new recruits and set off into the "great lone land." Travelling a short distance north of the international boundary, the Force reached Roche Percée, located in what is now southern Saskatchewan. By this time the inexperienced travellers were suffering from sickness and lack of water. The fact that the Force ignored the usual trade routes to the

West was coupled with a severe drought which left scanty supplies of water and grass.

At Roche Percée, the Force split into two groups, one under French, continuing west towards Blackfoot country, the other under Inspector W.D. Jarvis proceeding north to the Saskatchewan River, from which point they were to travel upstream to Fort Edmonton.

Parker did not accompany either party. Struck down by typhoid fever, his role in the Great March ended at Roche Percée and he was returned to Dufferin where he languished near death for several days. Then, recovering from his illness, he left Dufferin in October with a number of other police for the new headquarters at Swan River, 250 miles northwest of Winnipeg. In the meantime, Commissioner French had left part of his Force in the Milk River country of southern Alberta, and had returned with "D" and "E" Divisions to winter at Swan River. There, he was chagrined to discover that the contractors had not yet completed the fort and that the location was entirely unsuitable for a police headquarters and capital of the North-West Territories.

Leaving part of "E" Division to winter at the barracks, French turned south with the rest of his men, and was met by Parker and his group coming up from Dufferin.

Turning back with the Commissioner, the men went to Dufferin where they remained for the winter, and by the spring of 1875 Parker had become a seasoned westerner who devoted much of his spare time to hunting. At the same time he was unhappy about some of his officers and commented that he was "in good quarters but sick of the police force. If the management does not improve I shall skin out."[5]

However, on March 14, 1875, Parker was promoted from sub-constable to acting constable and reported that he was "quite swellish now, with two very pretty gold stripes on each arm."[6] The promotion also changed his attitude towards the Mounted Police, for he observed that "I like the Force much better since I have been promoted. It is much better than being a sub-constable."[7]

In spite of the promotion, his problems with some of his officers continued. When his friend, Sergeant-Major A.H. Griesbach, was transferred to Winnipeg, Parker found that "Dufferin was getting pretty warm for me."[8] He was placed under arrest twice for minor infractions and was almost reduced in rank. Finally, in May 1875, Griesbach arranged for Parker to be transferred to Winnipeg where he assisted the sergeant-major in recruiting. In the following month, he joined the rest of the Division en route to the nearly completed Swan River barracks.

Parker remained at Swan River for the next year, performing routine duties, carrying mail, and so forth. During this period, the Mounted Police were expanding their activities in the West. The Force which had been housed in the Hudson's Bay Company post at Fort Edmonton moved downstream to construct Fort Saskatchewan. In the south Fort Macleod became the centre of activities on the prairies, while Fort Calgary and Fort Walsh were established. Good relations had been fostered with the Indians and the whiskey trade had been virtually eliminated.

At the same time, Commissioner French was under increasing criticism from the Liberal regime in Ottawa. His outspoken criticism of the "barracks swindle at Swan River"[9] and of the delays in paying his men did not endear him to the politicians. "The actions of Colonel French from first to last," commented a cabinet minister, "appear to be in defiance of the wishes of the government."[10] Finally, in the spring of 1876 relations between the Commissioner and Ottawa became so poor that French requested permission to visit the capital "to discuss this and many other important matters."[11] When the request was refused, French resigned.

William Parker carried the mail sack which contained the acceptance of the Commissioner's resignation. "We are very sorry to lose him," wrote Parker when he heard the news, "& we non-commissioned officers presented him with a splendid gold watch and a beautiful address. He made us a splendid speech & at the latter part of it I was quite overcome."[12]

This was in August 1876, and events were moving quickly on the frontier. General Custer and his men had been wiped out by the Sioux on the Little Big Horn and rumours were rampant that the hostile tribe was coming to Canada. Colonel James F. Macleod, a great favourite of his men and popular with the Indians, was appointed to replace French and immediately made plans to reinforce the border posts at Fort Walsh and Fort Macleod. In the meantime, the Crees and Assiniboines of the central prairies had agreed to negotiate a treaty and a Mounted Police escort was required for the government party.

Combining the immediate needs of the Force, Macleod withdrew most of his men from Swan River and sent them as an escort to the signing of Treaty No. Six at Fort Carlton and later at Fort Pitt. Once this was successfully concluded, the Force marched south across the prairies to Fort Walsh, and west to Fort Macleod.

Although Parker had been in the Mounted Police since 1874, this expedition was his first venture into the far West since his near fatal typhoid attack. At Treaty No. Six he was impressed by the plains

Indians, some of whom "were dressed most hideously & looked more like devils than men."[13] A few days later he observed that "I saw my first buffalo the other day; they are hairy monsters & look awfully fierce." To add to his excitement, he was promoted to the rank of sergeant on September 20 while the Force was camped at Battleford.

Upon his arrival at Fort Macleod on October 23, Parker noted that the new headquarters was "the worst Fort I have been into yet for comfort. The buildings are miserable, mud floors & mud roofs, so when it rains there is a devil of a mess."[14]

By this time Parker had become a confirmed member of the Force and when his father suggested that he resign at the end of his three-year term in the spring of 1877, the sergeant argued that "under the circumstances, I think I cannot do better than take on again, as I hear times are pretty tough all over."[15]

Three weeks after his arrival at Fort Macleod Parker was sent upstream with a party of men to cut wood for the winter. They built a small cabin near the banks of the Oldman River and remained in the area until June of 1877. Three months later Parker was part of a troop which accompanied the treaty commissioners to Blackfoot Crossing for the signing of Treaty No. Seven.

Parker had been due for a furlough at the time he rejoined the Force in April 1877, but he was not allowed to leave Fort Macleod until May of the following year. By that time he had been in the Force for more than four years and had not seen his parents in seven years. En route to England, he escorted a convicted horse thief, "Slim Jim" Brooks, across the prairies to Stony Mountain Penitentiary in Manitoba. This trip of 1,000 miles was made by four-horse team with the prisoner driving most of the way.

From Manitoba the sergeant continued on to England for a happy reunion with his family. This three-month leave was his only extended furlough to Britain during his active service in the Force.

Upon his return to the West, Parker was posted to Shoal Lake, 150 miles northwest of Winnipeg. By this time, changes were beginning to take place in the land, settlers were arriving in larger numbers and increasing attention was being given to the needs of these "pilgrims." By the time Parker was transferred to Fort Qu'Appelle in May 1879, the Indian supremacy of the West was at an end. At Fort Qu'Appelle, forty-five miles northeast of the present city of Regina, Parker had ample evidence of the change. With the buffalo virtually destroyed, starving Indians came to the post begging for food and asking for help. No longer were they the lords of the plains. Instead, they were beginning the unsettled years of poverty and near starvation on their reserves. This resulted in a number of incidents, culminating in the Riel Rebellion.

William Parker was transferred to Battleford in 1880 and remained there until 1882. During much of this time he was involved in an on-again, off-again romance with a Métis girl named Mary Margaret Calder. They were married in August 1882 and began a long, happy life together, which ended only with her death on November 30, 1944. There were three children from this marriage, Maude, Gordon Sinclair and Reginald John.

Parker's mother was apparently opposed to the marriage and perhaps for this reason William's letters home terminate in that year. If any were written after 1882, they were not returned to his possession, nor do they appear to have been available to him when he wrote his reminiscences.

Shortly after his marriage Parker was transferred to Fort Saskatchewan, arriving in October 1882. He remained there for two and one-half years, paying treaty money, arresting bootleggers and performing other duties. At the outbreak of the Riel Rebellion in 1885 he volunteered and was accepted as a member of Steele's Scouts, who saw action against Big Bear.

Before leaving Fort Saskatchewan, Parker was severely reprimanded for his relations with the militia. As the officer in charge of the fort was absent when the 65th Montreal Regiment arrived, Parker called his police on parade and had them inspected by the militia officer. Such subservience to a military force was greeted with anger by his superior officers and as a result, Parker did not return to Fort Saskatchewan after the rebellion. However, he did see action with Steele's Scouts at the Battle of Frenchman's Butte and aided in the rescue of prisoners who had escaped from Big Bear's camp.

Parker was discharged from Steele's Scouts in Calgary and, after brief assignments in that city, in Regina and in Battleford, he was posted to Prince Albert in October 1885. There he began the longest residence of his career, remaining in that Saskatchewan centre until 1903. During this time he was involved in a number of cases, including the tragic Almighty Voice affair in 1897. He also took a leave of absence in February 1900, joining Lord Strathcona's Horse in the Boer War. He enlisted as a lieutenant and was promoted to captain while in South Africa. His participation in that war resulted in him receiving two nicknames—"Cap" and "Old Hardface." On his way back to Canada, his regiment was presented to King Edward VII in London.

Parker was promoted to the rank of sergeant-major on May 1, 1902, and was made an inspector a year later. At that time he was transferred to Battleford where he assisted a large number of English settlers known as the Barr colonists. These people, many of whom were inexperienced as farmers, had come to Canada to establish an agricultural colony and needed help in travelling to their allotted lands. Parker was of great assistance to them, both on their trip and in their newly formed village of Lloydminster.

In June 1905 Inspector Parker was transferred for the last time, taking charge of a large district in southern Saskatchewan and southern Alberta, with headquarters at Medicine Hat. There, as magistrate and officer commanding, he was responsible for maintaining law and order among the ranchers, settlers and miners.

By this time Parker was already a thirty-year veteran of the Force. He had seen the country change from a wilderness to a land of ranching and agriculture. Only sixty miles north of Medicine Hat he had helped to capture four wanted Assiniboines in 1881. Forty miles southeast, he had ridden into the palisaded walls of Fort Walsh when Sitting Bull was still a free man.

As a result of his colourful life, Parker became a popular raconteur in Medicine Hat. He was able to regale his friends for hours with stories of the "old west" and sometimes became more interested in the events of the past than the problems of the present. This created a number of problems for those administering the Force, but on October 31, 1912, Inspector Parker decided upon an early retirement after more than thirty-eight years of service.

By this time he had become fond of Medicine Hat, so he opened a real estate and insurance business which he operated until 1938. He was frequently visited by old friends and comrades and was widely recognized as one of the "originals" of the North-West Mounted Police. He was one of the few survivors of 1874 to attend Calgary's jubilee celebration in 1925, and in 1939 he was presented to the King and Queen during their royal visit. In the same year, when a small memorial chapel was erected at Regina barracks, William Parker was the sole "original" to be present and, as guest of honour, he unveiled the memorial plaque.

"An excellent raconteur," observed a police historian, "Parker could tell endless stories of the early days, and with his special brand of humour he could make drab details of pioneer life in the Territories seem interesting and entertaining."[16]

Partly because of his storytelling abilities, Parker had a number of friends who persistently requested him to write about his experiences in the Mounted Police. When he did so, he remarked that the first six years of his account were based on "extracts from my old diaries that were lost in England some thirty years ago and, with about one hundred of my old letters to my parents, recently recovered by my brother, Rev. Canon J.F. Dyke Parker, of Regina."[17]

This comment would seem to indicate that William Parker wrote his reminiscences between the time that Canon Parker retired to Regina in 1942 and the missionary's death in February 1944. At that time the ex-policeman was between eighty-nine and ninety-one years of age. He was living with his daughter Maude in Medicine Hat, and was alert in mind and body until his death on May 16, 1945. Three days later he was buried beside his wife in Medicine Hat's Hillside Cemetery with six Mounted Police acting as pallbearers.

After his death, Inspector Parker's papers and memorabilia were inherited by his children, Maude and Reginald. Upon their deaths, Mrs. Reginald Parker had the material and it was passed on to her son, Captain William Parker, Canadian Armed Forces Base, Vancouver. In 1970 the manuscripts and artifacts were acquired by the Glenbow-Alberta Institute, Calgary.

Although a major portion of the papers are published in this volume, they do not constitute the entire collection. The published and unpublished material may be summarized as follows.

Reminiscence: originally entitled "Thirty-Eight and a Half Years' Service and Experience in the Mounties," the reminiscence is published virtually intact. A considerable amount of minor editing was required, particularly in punctuation, paragraphing, sentence structure and the division of chapters. However, there are no major deletions and the style has been carefully preserved. Footnoting has been limited primarily to the identification of persons, explanation of events, and the correction of errors.

Letters: the letters have been heavily edited to remove extensive salutations, paraphrasing of news from home, ephemeral comments, general comments about the family in England which had no direct bearing upon Parker's own experiences, and subjects covered in his reminiscences. Such deletions constitute more than half of the original contents.

Diaries: because of the repetition of most of the diaries when compared to the reminiscence and letters, none of these has been reproduced. Pertinent excerpts have been used as footnotes where appropriate. However, the diaries do form an excellent source of primary data on minor activities, weather, visitors, etc., which are not found in this published work. Parker's diaries cover all or a portion of the years 1874 to 1897 and 1905.

The place of Parker's writings in Mounted Police and western Canadian history is worthy of examination. Parker was not a senior officer of the Force during his active years and it is apparent from his work that he was not a party to important discussions or decisions. For these reasons he cannot be compared with officers who wrote their reminiscences. Cecil Denny (*The Riders of the Plains, The Law Marches West*) was an inspector in 1874, while Samuel B. Steele (*Forty Years in Canada*) was a sergeant-major. A decade later, R. Burton Deane (*Mounted Police Life in Canada*) was a superintendent. The only police-author of that period with whom Parker might be compared is Jean d'Artigue (*Six Years in the Canadian North-West*). Like Parker, d'Artigue joined the Force as a sub-constable in 1874. Unlike Parker, however, he remained in the Force for only six years.

Almost all other police authors, for example Turner, Longstreth, and Haydon, were historians rather than autobiographers; later authors such as Kemp, Harvison and Rivett-Carnac dealt with an entirely different period of history.

With the paucity of published primary data on the North-West Mounted Police, Parker's writings are important because of his role as an observer. His letters to his family often contain valuable glimpses of daily life or of routine activities which would not be found in annual reports or official papers. For example, in his letter from Swan River barracks to his mother on December 9, 1875, he says, "I think you would like to take a peep at our room at the present moment. It looks very clean & nice, the beds are arranged on each side, the bed tick neatly rolled up & the blankets folded on top & over each of the beds a buffalo robe is spread. In the centre of the table, it is so clean & white that it is like the snow. I see that the table is laid out, the plates, cups & saucers are enamelled blue on the outside & white inside. The knives & forks are clean & there are four plates of bread all ready [*sic*] cut in the centre of the table. Our fare is very simple, bread & coffee for breakfast, generally roast beef & potatoes for dinner, bread & tea for tea."[18] Parker also provides some of the barrack-room gossip, speculation about police movements, complaints about discipline, loneliness and homesickness and comments about problems in the Force.

His direct involvement in Treaties No. Six and Seven, the Riel Rebellion, and the Almighty Voice affair, also enable him to provide eyewitness accounts of some of the most important events of western Canadian history.

Although Parker had the reputation of being a raconteur and teller of tall tales, he apparently recognized his responsibility for veracity, both in his letters and his later reminiscence. In his introduction to the latter work he stressed that "There is no fiction, all being a true account of what took place, including the different stories and jokes."[19]

Because he had his diaries and letters to guide him, Parker was easily able to keep his reminiscences factual and yet still retain a lively and interesting account. Only on a few occasions do his favourite tales creep into the account and any that depart from fact are duly footnoted. The general level of accuracy, however, is quite high, both in the letters and reminiscence.

From his papers, William Parker emerges as very British, a lover of sports and hunting, and a man who had strong family ties. The fact that three of his brothers tried to follow him into the North-West Mounted Police is tangible evidence that he was considered to be the successful one in the family. His enforced separation from his family was a source of great sadness to him during his first few years in the Force. The recovery of his letters and diaries several years later gave him the raw material to transform his colourful storytelling into a valuable source of history. Although he had planned to have his reminiscence published, it has remained in manuscript form until the printing of this work.

Hugh A. Dempsey
Glenbow-Alberta Institute
Calgary, Alberta

The Reminiscences of William Parker

"Thirty-eight and a half Years' Service
and Experiences in the Mounties"

Chapter One

1871-74. Arrival in Canada—farm work—enlist in NWMP—New Fort—on to Dufferin—horse stampede—looking for the Sioux.

After reading several books on Canada, my brother Harry and I decided to emigrate to Canada, for the purpose of learning to farm, neither of us knowing the first thing about the subject. Harry was twenty years old and I was eighteen. We decided to hire out for wages and would, by this means, have to work and learn the business, instead of paying the farmer as a lot of Englishmen did, with the result they learned very little about it.

Just before leaving England the Bishop of Dover gave us letters of introduction to Sir John A. Macdonald, the Prime Minister of Canada, but we never used them.

It was on about the 17th of April, 1871, that we sailed on the S.S. *Peruvian* from Liverpool to Canada. There were large numbers of emigrants aboard, most of them like ourselves were dreadfully seasick for about half the voyage. There was great excitement aboard on land being sighted and coming up the St. Lawrence River we all liked the look of the country. Although there was plenty of snow on the ground, the stately trees and snug villages spoke volumes.

We arrived at Quebec on the 25th of April, 1871, going right on by rail to Woodstock, Ont., where I met Joe Plaskett, a farmer, and applied for work. He said, "What work could you do with these two little white hands of yours?" I replied, "I could try." He then offered me six dollars a month, all found for one year, which I accepted, Harry having hired to a farmer just across the road from me.

The Plasketts were lovely people. The work was long and tough, but it made me strong and healthy. Mr. Plaskett found fault with me only once. With my old team, Buster and Damsel, I had been rolling different fields of the farm that day, being delayed a lot by picking up stones and rocks. On his return in the evening he said as much as if I had been loafing. The next day when he went to town, I rolled pretty nearly his whole farm all over, both horses being used right up. He never complained again. I had made up my mind that unless he more than doubled my wages the second year, I would quit. He offered $12.00 and when he saw me packing up my trunk he said, "All right, I will give you $13.00," so I stayed another year.

In the spring of 1874 I left for Sarnia and on the way stopped off at London, Ont., to look over the farm of Bishop Helmuth,[1] as he had offered to lease it to me. The farm was close to the edge of the city and, unbeknown to me, there had been several fires in that vicinity, farmers losing their barns, etc. On looking over the different fields, I noticed a woman advancing on me with about six men armed with pitch-forks, scythes, etc.

"There he is! That's the man," she called. As they rushed at me I said, "Hold on, I am a friend of the Bishop. Take me to him to prove it." The Bishop's house and ladies college were only one hundred yards away. On arrival there at the end of the pitch-forks, the Bishop came out and exploded with laughter, while I felt greatly relieved.

After a chat about the farm, the Bishop asked if I would like to look through the ladies college. I said yes and on going inside he took me down a long, wide corridor with rooms on both sides. Young ladies were peeping out from the doors and as we went along they fairly made me blush by saying, "Oh, isn't he nice!" "A regular peach," and so on. At the same time the Bishop was chuckling away to himself, evidently enjoying the scene. I was dressed in top boots, cord breeches and peajacket, which probably took their fancy.

While in Sarnia at the end of March 1874, I saw an advertisement of Colonel G.A. French,[2] calling for recruits for the NWM Police. He would accept twelve recruits from London, Ont., and would be there at the Tecumseh House on the 4th of April to receive applications. On deciding to apply, I arrived early at London on the 4th and went to the Tecumseh House where a waiter informed me he expected the colonel down to breakfast any minute. I then told him I wanted to enlist. He said to take to a chair and I would see the colonel come down the stairs. If a chance occurred he would put in a good word for me. In five minutes the colonel came down twirling his black moustache, and as he passed into the dining room I saw him eyeing me. In a short time the waiter came out and said the colonel was asking about me and that he had been told I wanted to enlist. The colonel then asked if I could ride and the waiter replied that I could ride anything with hair on it. This waiter must have been after a tip, as I never said such a thing.

There was quite a large bunch waiting at the door of the recruiting room. Then about two hundred strapping men from Stratford turned up. They were mostly six feet tall and I thought there was no chance for me. After a long time I got in and after answering a lot of questions, the colonel asked for my character reference. I said I had quite overlooked bringing one. He asked for my nearest relation and I told him it was my first cousin at Sarnia. Then he replied, "I will give you two hours to obtain a character by wire."

The wire was sent and the answer came in about fifteen minutes before the two hours were up. I said to the operator, who was smiling, "Let me see it." He said, "No, it is addressed to Colonel French, but you can take it in to him," which I did after quite a struggle. The crowd was so great that I had all the buttons on my peajacket torn off. The colonel opened the telegram and started to frown and then smile. He repeated this two or three times then he looked up and said, "I will give you a note to the doctor, and if you pass I will accept you." The doctor passed me flying. I was then told to report to the New Fort, Toronto, on the 10th of April.

On my return to Sarnia I asked my cousin Alfred Barber what kind of a character reference he had given me as the colonel seemed puzzled over it. The following was the wire he sent and the character I was accepted on: "I have known William Parker ever since he was a kid. He has been well brought up, and he is a beggar on the fight, and a good judge of whiskey."[3]

At the New Fort the two hundred of us got along splendidly

with the different duties and drills. On arrival I had a free kit given me and had to go and fill my bed with straw. The riding school was the most interesting, as the sergt. major standing in the centre of the circle with his long whip would drive us around bareback and when the command trot was given, quite a few would tumble off into the sawdust. Then the sergt. major would shout out, "Who told you to dismount!" After a few days we got our saddles, but at first we were not allowed to use the stirrups, which were crossed over the horses' withers. In about ten days, with two or three exceptions, we could all ride fairly well. Our Commissioner, Col. French, was present at the first riding lesson of the sixteen London recruits and showed his wonderful gift of memory by calling out half a dozen or more of our names after seeing us only a few minutes when he engaged us.

At Toronto on the 6th of June, all dressed in civilian clothes, we marched to the Union Station and entrained on two special trains for the West. A very large crowd gave us a send-off.

The marching out state showed sixteen officers, two hundred and one non-commissioned officers and men, and two hundred and forty-four horses. Being an armed force, we had to wear civilian clothing going through the States. By telegraphing ahead to towns and cities we received splendid meals, with handsome girls to wait on us which was most appreciated. On arriving at Chicago the horses were unloaded for twenty-four hours and fed; this was repeated at St. Paul. On the 12th of June we arrived at Fargo, the end of our railroad journey, and everything was dumped off on the bald-headed prairie. Covering acres of ground were all our uniforms, arms, ammunition, provisions, bedding, saddles, harness, wagons, hay-rakes, ploughs and harrows.

The two hundred sets of harness, three hundred saddles, and seventy-five heavy wagons were all new, and in separate pieces, and had to be put together. It looked as though it would be a week before we could get away but every officer and man pitched in and worked steady all afternoon and far into the night. Reveille was at 4:00 A.M. and at 5:00 P.M. "D" Troop pulled out with about twenty-nine loaded wagons and a complement of mounted men, "E" Troop following at 7:00 P.M., the two camping six miles out. "F" Troop, after delivering unwanted stores to the river steamer and cleaning up camp, joined the other two troops the next morning.

The 14th, being Sunday, we stayed in camp all day. Horses and all of us had a good rest. It was a lovely day and a wonderful sight to look west over the flowers and grass-covered boundless prairie that stretched a thousand miles to the foot of the Rocky Mountains. On Monday, the 15th, we were up at 4:30 A.M. and left camp at 6:30 A.M. We followed the mail coach trail, which was heavy from recent rains, and led straight north, close to the west side of the Red River. The banks of the river were lined all the way with oak, elm, poplar and birch trees, as well as wild berries, black currants, raspberries, gooseberries and others. We made twenty-seven miles that day. On the second night we had a lovely camp, our tents being pitched on heavy grass amongst wild rose bushes and prairie flowers. On getting up at 4:30 A.M. we were greeted with a glorious sunshiny day. This, with the perfume of the flowers, was quite intoxicating; then finding a prairie chicken's nest full of eggs settled it. I was one hundred percent for the West.

Nothing particular occurred during the rest of the march, except that nearly all the team horses had their shoulders badly chafed. The flies were exceptionally bad, torturing both man and beast the whole march.

On the 19th of June, towards evening, we passed the village of Pembina which was close to the boundary line. A complement of U.S. Infantry were quartered there. Then we crossed the boundary into Manitoba and went two or three miles to Dufferin, where we met the assistant commissioner, Col. James F. Macleod,[4] with "A," "B" and "C" Troops. They were encamped there waiting for us to join them. About a hundred strong with sixty-five horses, they had been assembled in October 1873, and had been quartered . . . at Lower Fort Garry, where they were instructed in mounted and foot drills.

The second night after the arrival at Dufferin a big stampede of about two hundred and fifty of our horses took place. It was during the greatest thunderstorm that Manitoba had ever seen, lasting eight hours, from 10:00 P.M. to 6:00 A.M. The horses had been put in a large fenced field of the Boundary

Commission to the west of us. It was not fenced on the east end where we were camped and our heavy wagons were placed along this part, with a two-inch rope being strung along through the wagon wheels to keep the horses from getting out. Then the rain started coming down in torrents and the thunder and lightning was most terrific.

I was sleeping in a square tent with twelve men when I felt the ground trembling. As I jumped outside, it was like day with the continuous lightning. Then I saw a terrifying sight. The two hundred and fifty horses, with their eyes like fire, tails straight up in the air, and what looked like steam coming from their nostrils, were charging down on top of us at breakneck speed. In an instant they struck the heavy wagons and big rope, knocking over several of the former and breaking the latter. I know my hair stood on end as I stood at the corner of the tent. As the horses flew by me I hit two or three of their sides with my fists.

The tent was torn down but none of us were hurt. Our herd of cows and calves were about one hundred yards in the rear of our tents and as the horses struck them we heard them bellow. Then there was a human scream and we could also hear a tin pail being carried along by the horses' hooves. We secured a lantern and going to the place where the cows had been, we found a constable lying unconscious with his collar bone broken. He was one of the night guard who had been getting some milk for his coffee. Corp. Bill Latimer,[5] who was in charge of the guard, was quite badly injured by a horse trying to jump over him when he was standing upright. It struck him on the top of his skull with its shod hoof, tearing two holes in his head. They both recovered but Corp. Latimer was never quite the same man. Four others were less seriously hurt.

Major Walsh,[6] officer commanding "D" Troop, had us fall in and detailed us off in parties to look for the horses. I was in Inspector Jack French's party[7] and we went down to the river amongst the bushes and trees where we stumbled across a burly half-breed lying flat on his back. We thought he was dead but when the inspector knelt down and smelled his breath, he jumped up and gave him a kick, saying, "Drunk, by God!" Then he wished he had half of the man's complaint. All this time the rain was coming down in buckets full. It was then found that the horses had taken our trail back to the States. Insp. Walker,[8] with two other men, left right away and returned in about four days with the horses. Only one was missing. I was informed the horses had gone back about seventy-five miles towards Fargo. In stampeding through the small town of Pembina, what with the storm and the noise of the horses' feet, they had terrified the inhabitants and two women were prematurely confined. It was also reported that six or seven persons in different parts of Manitoba were killed by the lightning.

After the storm, and until we started West, we had a very busy time with constant fatigue parties preparing for the big march. Besides our large number of heavy wagons we had over one hundred Red River carts and oxen, with half-breeds to drive them. The horses had to be shod. All food supplies, oats, bran, coal, charcoal and other government stores had to be unloaded from the river steamer and moved to camp. My job was hauling enough water from the Red River with two barrels, Red River cart and pony, to supply the six troops. It kept me busy for the river was in flood and the water was thick with mud. The weather was extremely hot and I drank quite a lot of water, and I blame this for the serious illness which I subsequently had.

After being in camp about ten days the colonel received a despatch from the American authorities that the Sioux Indians in Dakota, just across the boundary line, were on the rampage and killing the settlers. He had the assembly sounded and gave orders for the whole force to mount in full dress, fully armed with carbines and revolvers. The horses were brought in on the gallop and the whole six troops were mounted and ready in half an hour, with the two nine-pounder guns. This was the first and last time the whole Force paraded together. It was a great sight, the long red line, white helmets and white gauntlets. The four-year-old horses were in fine fettle, each troop having its own coloured horses—"A" Troop, white, "B" Troop, dark brown, "C" Troop, chestnut, "D" Troop, dapple gray, "E" Troop, black and "F" Troop, bay. We marched off and halted close to the boundary line where we waited about one and a half hours. Then, as there was no further despatch from the Americans, we returned to camp. We were all disappointed in not being in a scrap with the Indians.

Chapter Two

1874–76. The Big March—typhoid fever—back to Dufferin—to Swan River—meet Col. French's party—to Dufferin again—accident with the Bishop—promoted to corporal—sent to Swan River—not finished—trip to Winnipeg and return—to Shoal Lake in winter for oats—fire at Commissioner's house—brass band organized—mail to Shoal Lake and terrible trip back—Col. French leaves the Force.

On the 7th of July, 1874, all being ready for the big march, Colonel French had the whole Force on parade. He made a speech to us, stating that great hardships might have to be endured on the long march west and if anyone thought he would not be able to stand it, they could have their discharge. Only about half a dozen took advantage of this.[9]

The next evening, the whole Force pulled out for the West. The marching out state was as follows: staff 4, superintendents 4, inspectors 1, surgeon 1, veterinary surgeon 1, sergt. majors and sergeants 30, corporals 20, constables 204, for a total of 265. Horse-public 308, private 2; guides and half-breeds 20; working oxen 142; cows and calves 93, wagons 73, oxcarts 114, field guns 2, and mortars 2. To this must be added a party to be picked up at Fort Ellice who had been sent ahead from Winnipeg: inspector 1, sergeant 1, corporal 1, constables 12, for a total of 15. Horses 17. Left behind at Dufferin: staff 2, superintendents 2, sergeants 5 and constables 14.

At the last moment, much to my disgust, I was detailed to drive a yolk [sic] of oxen pulling a covered heavy wagon loaded with ammunition. The oxen were enormous beasts; when standing beside them I could not see over their backs. I had had no experience driving oxen but they told me there was nothing to it. If I wanted them to go to the right, I was to shout "Gee," and to the left, "Haw." They also gave me a stick with a small spike at one end to prod them with. I had to sit on a cramped narrow seat in front just behind the oxen and there was no way of getting off when moving.

Just after starting, we had not gone very far when the oxen ran away at full gallop over the rough prairie. I was sure I was going to be killed as there was no way of getting out of the seat and jumping for it. Luckily, some of the half-breeds in front spotted the runaway and two of them ran out on the prairie and caught the oxen. The half-breeds took them over while I hoofed it to camp and got my charger back.

During that night I was quite sick and in a fever. The next morning just before pulling out, a team of horses from "F" Troop ran away with a mowing machine. It was lucky they took to the open prairie, but the machine was badly damaged. The colonel got after Supt. Richon about it; they had some hot words and the colonel placed him under arrest. The superintendent then went back to Dufferin and that was the last heard of him. He had disobeyed orders in not putting a quiet team of horses on the mower.[10]

It was a beautiful day and quite hot, which kept the mosquitoes down. The prairie, with its black loam, good grass, millions of wild flowers, an ideal lake or two teeming with wild fowl, was all quite enchanting to us. We made about thirty miles during the day.

Resuming the march the next day, the Pembina Mountains and a vast plain extending south, west, and north came into view. The so-called "mountains" should be called hills, as they are very low. In passing over the north side of them we were engulfed by a flight of grasshoppers which darkened the sun and sky, eating up everything green in sight. They were about two or three inches deep on the ground and the wagons passing over them on a slanting hillside slid right around from the grease of their crushed bodies. By evening we had left them behind and had an excellent camp by a good-sized lake full of wild ducks. The men soon waded in and gathered a large number of eggs, and killed quite a number of flapper ducks with clubs. As I could not eat the government rations of soggy bread and salt bacon, my comrade made duck soup for me which was good.

It was at Roche Percée, or near it, that I had become very ill and quite helpless. I was sent back to Dufferin and on arrival there was put in a small hospital where I lapsed into unconsciousness, remaining that way for a week. The American army doctor, who came over from Pembina once a day, afterwards told me I had typhoid fever and he thought that Mrs. Almon,[11] the wife of a member of the Boundary Commission, had saved my life by coming to the hospital every day and feeding me a teaspoonful of sherry at different intervals.

On recovering my health and strength again, I had about one month of excellent sport, shooting prairie chickens and ducks. Not being able to finish in the march west was a keen disappointment to me, but afterwards my comrades told me I was lucky, having missed lots of walking and severe hardships.

On the 4th of October, under instructions, I left Dufferin for Winnipeg with two horses, arriving there on the 6th. I then joined Inspector Dalrymple Clark's[12] party of nine other constables about to proceed to Swan River barracks for the winter.[13] We pulled out on the 24th, and after going about two hundred miles we met, to our great surprise, the Commissioner, Col. French, with "D" Troop coming in from Swan River. The barracks there were not completed, but "E" Troop had been left there for the winter.

The column was a wonderful sight to see, straggled out for two or three miles. Nearly every man was walking; horses were like laths, swaying and wobbling from side to side; an odd team of horses every once in a while fell down, to be replaced by saddle horses. The men appeared rosy and in the best of health, but oh, what a sight! All were virtually in rags, no hats, most of them with no boots and several wearing their own makes of moccasins made from the rawhide of buffalo. Nearly all were growing beards. They said they had passed through great hardships and nearly starved at times until they struck countless thousands of buffalo about five hundred miles out. The water was mostly alkali which gave them dysentery. When they were suffering badly from it they came across a big patch of chokecherries in a deep coulee, so Doctor Kittson ordered a halt for two days and told all ranks to eat all the cherries they could. The result was they were all cured. To save the horses, every man had to take his turn at walking.

The Commissioner made us turn about and go back with them to Winnipeg. That evening in camp was a joyous one. They had not heard anything from the outside nor received any mail for months and we had brought a heavy mail for them. It was amusing to see them get supper by making slap-jacks [pancakes], which were as black as a hat, but good eating at that. They said they had not seen butter for months and had to use axle grease to fry them with. We built big campfires and for two hours sang most of our favourite songs. One composed by a Mountie was:

Pass the tea and let us drink
To the guardians of our land,
You bet your life it's not our fault
If whiskey is contraband.

Others were, "My Heart Still Bends to the Good Old Friends," "Tenting on the Old Camp Ground," and "'Tis Growing Very Dark, Mother."

On the 7th of November we arrived in Winnipeg, stayed a week there, then marched sixty miles to Dufferin where we occupied the Royal Engineers' barracks for the winter. There was about six inches of snow on the ground, twenty-five below zero, and most of us got frostbitten.

It got much colder in December, January and February, sometimes forty and fifty below zero, but generally with bright sunshine. We had about sixty horses and about twice a week we had to haul hay by four-in-hand teams a distance of eighteen miles and return over the bare plain. It was a cold job. The Commissioner stayed in Winnipeg, Inspector Walker being in command.

One day two wild and woolly constables, Mike Slevin and Pat Wheeler,[14] imbibed in some Red River whiskey and quarrelled. Pat had left Mike and was having his hair cut by the troop barber when in rushed Mike who threw an adze and broad axe down in front of Wheeler and shouted, "Choose your weapons!" Wheeler took one look, sprang from the barber chair and scooted outside for his life with Mike after him. Just outside the door Mike grabbed a heavy iron crowbar, whirled it around his head, and let it go. It fell right at Wheeler's heels. Just then the sergeant of the guard appeared and put them in the guard-room. They both drew stiff fines.

On the 15th of February, 1875, I was detailed to take a cutter and horse named "Jackson," and drive across the Red River to Emerson to pick up Bishop Machray of Rupert's Land. I was to drive him to Scratching River, half way to Winnipeg. The snow was fairly deep with the temperature about twenty below zero. The Bishop got in and we started off. The horse was in high spirits and hard to hold; then suddenly he bolted off the trail in a straight line to Dufferin. I was powerless to stop him as he had placed his underjaw with the bit on his breast. In a few seconds we reached the river bank, which had a twelve foot straight drop to the ice; the horse flew into space and we landed on the ice with a crash. The cutter was smashed to smithereens and the horse went galloping off with the shafts down the river to Dufferin. I got to my feet and was swearing and shaking my fist at the fleeing horse when a voice exclaimed, "My good man, do not swear." It was the Bishop, lying amongst the fragments of the cutter. I apologized and asked if he was hurt. He said his left side pained him but on helping him to his feet he said he would be all right. I told him there would be another horse and cutter sent to us in about twenty minutes, which turned out to be correct, and we resumed our journey. About five miles from Dufferin there were a couple of settlers and the Bishop had a christening there. The men were away and there was nobody for godfather, so I offered to stand. His Lordship said, "Oh, no you don't." He had heard me swearing! We arrived safely at Scratching River that evening. Next day a blizzard raged all day and nobody could travel, but we were comfortable in the hotel. Afterwards we heard the Bishop had two ribs broken in the runaway.

Our principal amusement was boxing in the large black-smith shop. Lectures were given on our police duties and towards spring, when mild enough, both mounted and foot drills were held.

On the 14th of March, 1875, I was promoted to corporal,

and on the 16th of May I left Dufferin for Winnipeg on the new steamer *Manitoba*. There I joined Regimental Sergt. Major Griesbach[15] to help him in recruiting. To show how the great West was starting to forge ahead, the steamer for Winnipeg had aboard three hundred passengers and three hundred and seventy-five tons of freight.

Winnipeg was a mass of mud when "D" Troop arrived from Dufferin. On the 28th of May, the whole of us, including about thirty recruits, went into camp on the western outskirts of the town close to the old Pacific stables. It turned cold and rained continuously, with the result that all the tents were flooded. It was miserable and after four days of it we moved three miles further west to higher ground. Inspector Dickens[16] joined us there.

On the 1st of June we pulled out for Swan River barracks, a march of three hundred and fifty miles. With the exception of bad roads and mosquitoes, we got along splendidly. The recent heavy rains caused several wagons to become mired and one heavily loaded wagon which went down to the hubs took nearly two hours to get out. The mosquitoes and flies never let up, torturing both man and beast, and we had to keep smudges going all night for the horses.

On arrival at Shoal Lake, halfway to Swan River, we camped three days to let the horses rest. The prairie grass was up to our knees and the horses sure enjoyed it. While there I went for a long walk and noticed an eagle's nest at the top of a poplar tree, so I climbed up to get an egg. I carried a club with me for protection. On peeping over the side I got quite a start for instead of eggs, I saw two fierce-looking birds with large hooked beaks and fierce eyes. I decided they were young birds so with the club I managed to push one off the nest and it fluttered down to the ground. He put up a fight and as I reached to grab him he struck out with one claw and cut my hand badly. However, I finally caught him and in three or four days in camp he grew very tame and friendly. Afterwards, at Swan River barracks, he grew to be about two and a half feet tall and stalked about the barracks like a man. He was christened "General" and seemed to understand the trumpet calls, as he attended all means regularly.

One day I heard a great commotion amongst the small herd of cows just outside the barrack fence and on going over I found General lying on his back, with the cows charging him with lowered heads to gore him. With his talons he cut big gaps in their noses and the smell of their own blood made them frantic with rage. I did a foolish thing by rushing into their midst and seizing General by one wing. I ran back to the fence, threw him over and got over myself just as the bellowing cattle reached the fence.

A detachment of one sergeant[17] and eleven men were left at Shoal Lake for duty there while the rest of us resumed the march. We passed a beautiful part of the country, the soil a rich clay loam with clumps of trees, waving grass and gorgeous prairie flowers. We then crossed Bird Tail Creek and went into camp. The following day we arrived at Shell River, a small stream winding through a lovely valley three or four hundred feet below the level prairie; the view was a perfect one.

After that we crossed the Assiniboine River on a ferry installed by the Public Works Department. Two constables[18] were left there to build a log cabin and to look after the ferry. The next eighty miles to Swan River was easy travelling. Nine miles from Swan River we crossed the Assiniboine River, again by a good ford, and four hundred yards up a green slope we came to the H.B.Co.'s Fort Pelly. That evening, 6th of July, we arrived at Swan River barracks, which for a time was called Fort Livingstone. It was no fort, as the buildings were strung out in a long line about a quarter of a mile in length. There were two large stables at the west end and the Commissioner's house at the east end. In between was a building for the men; it was of an enormous size, two stories, 140 feet long by 40 feet wide, and would hold four troops.[19] With the exception of the hospital, very few of the buildings were completed. Plastering was the principal delay. It was the middle of October before we finally got inside our quarters which was a great comfort as it was very cold in the tents at night. We did move into the uncompleted barracks temporarily for about two months on our arrival but moved out again for the plastering.[20]

In August, the Commissioner chose me to take a party to Winnipeg. It included his two young sons who were going to St.

John's College, Winnipeg; an inspector's wife who was going east;[21] a sergeant of "E" Troop going on sick leave to Hamilton;[22] and one constable. On August the 8th we pulled out with two light wagons. After lunch at Fort Pelly the sergeant could not be found, so I let the other team go ahead and waited for fifteen minutes for him. There was still no sign of him so I drove the four hundred yards to the ford, crossed the river and tied my team behind some bushes. This had the desired effect for I soon saw our brave Romeo with his lady love coming slowly down the green sward to the ford. They would stop and embrace each other, the last embrace being a tight one. As the sergeant tore himself away and coming running [*sic*] to the ford, I was standing on the opposite side and gave him fits for the delay. He was wearing a new pair of pure white riding breeches made of antelope skin. He ordered me to drive over and bring him across and that if I did not he would punch my head good and plenty. I replied that two could play at that game, that I had quite a wallop myself, and if he did not come across in two minutes he would be left behind. He then waded across and instead of punching my head he offered an apology. On overtaking the others we went into camp, the sergeant looking dreadful as his beautiful riding breeches were ruined with the wetting they got. Mrs. S——and the two young boys teased him incessantly and kept it up for two or three days. The whole trip was most enjoyable, the roads having dried up and the weather being perfect. We averaged forty miles a day, arriving in Winnipeg on the 15th of August.

I was delayed two weeks in Winnipeg awaiting orders to leave and on the return journey, having heavy loads, we made shorter daily drives. The result was that in the long evenings I had splendid shooting; in fact, we lived on ducks and prairie chicken. After fourteen days we arrived back at Swan River and found it very quiet and deserted. Both "D" and "E" Troops, in full marching order and with extra ammunition, had left for Fort Carlton where a large number of half-breeds and Indians had met. They were making fiery speeches against a new Act passed by the North-West Assembly which protested the ruthless killing of buffalo; the matter ended peacefully by the government withdrawing the Act.

In September we built a snake fence a mile square around the barracks, and during the first week in October we banked up all the buildings. Winter set in about the 15th of October and we found it awfully cold under canvas until we moved into the barracks on the 20th of October.

We spent a merry Christmas, the barrack room being decorated with evergreens and we had a big dinner in the evening. Afterwards there were speeches, toasts and songs; they made me open the singing with the "Roast Beef of Old England." The "wee drappie" for the occasion was sadly missed as we had nothing stronger than coffee.

About the middle of January 1876, I received orders to take charge of six constables,[23] eighteen horses and sleds and to proceed to Shoal Lake to bring back a supply of oats, as the stock in hand was getting low. It took six days to get there in bitterly cold weather and we lost one horse that died on the way down. On the return journey we had 9,000 lbs. of oats and 1,000 lbs. of freight, besides carrying a large quantity of hay for the horses. The snow was three feet deep and we had to break a trail ahead with a saddle horse. The cold was intense; about forty below zero all the time. Twice we struck big dry wood bluffs and warmed ourselves and horses with huge fires. The cold was so intense and the snow so deep that at one time I thought we could not make Swan River. During the last few days we all were getting snowblind for we never thought of taking goggles along. I was not as bad as the men, as I rubbed charcoal around my eyes. Besides this, all of us suffered from severe frostbites. On the 10th, about noon, we were overjoyed to arrive at Fort Pelly where we got a hearty welcome and a good warming up. In the afternoon we made the barracks quite easily as the road was good. The Commissioner complimented us on the trip we had made. The six constables all went into the hospital with snowblindness.

In the middle of March we had nice mild weather, just mild enough not to thaw. Then one day we were startled by the trumpet sounding the assembly, which meant fire. I grabbed the Babcock fire extinguisher and as I rushed outside I found the roof of the Commissioner's house all ablaze! There were men on ladders throwing pails of water on the fire, so I went inside and up to the loft. From there the Babcock did good work and in half an hour we had the fire out.

About this time our beef supply was running low and we had no more cattle to kill, so for two days a week we had to eat pemmican, made of dried buffalo meat. Most of us liked it but a few would rather starve than eat it, and preferred the rancid bacon.

Early in the winter, a dramatic club was formed and once a week they put on some capital plays. A minstrel troupe also performed once a month and we got a good kick out of them both. They sure helped to pass the long winter away and were well attended.

In addition, "D" Troop subscribed for a brass band and the instruments arrived the first week in March. In a month's time the members played very well. It was the first band west of Winnipeg[24] and the Indians thought it wonderful, especially the big drum which they often wanted to buy.

By the 27th of March the weather was excellent and snow was disappearing fast so our spring drill commenced. We had five hours a day, both foot and carbine drill.

Queen Victoria's birthday on the 24th of May, 1876, was a gloriously fine day, not a cloud in the sky. At reveille, 5:30 A.M., the band paraded and played "God Save the Queen." All forenoon there was a carbine shooting match with three cash prizes. There were fifty entries and I came in fourth. At noon a salute of twenty-one guns was fired. In the afternoon athletic sports were held and I captured first prizes in the high pole jump, broad jump, and the three-legged race. We finished up in the evening with a smoking concert.

During the first week of July, a report was received that a Cree Indian had murdered his wife. A sergeant and constable were sent out to investigate and found that a very fine-looking Cree Indian named Little Weazel had killed his wife in a jealous rage. He was arrested without any trouble and lodged in the guardhouse.

Our chief recreation in the long evenings was cricket, a constable having made two splendid bats and a set of wickets out of birchwood. Although a bit heavier than willow, the bats did not break so easily.

In summer we carried our own mail to and from Shoal Lake and, being very short-handed, I was elected to make the round trip of two hundred and eighty miles. I left about the 15th of July, driving a buckboard and single horse. Having no load I had no trouble in doing the eighty miles to our two-man detachment at the Assiniboine River ferry, arriving there the same evening. Leaving next morning with a change of horse, I made the sixty miles to Shoal Lake by early afternoon. Then I had to stay for a week, waiting for special official letters from Ottawa, so I enjoyed myself boating and fishing. Sergt. Bob Wild was in charge of nine constables, all under canvas. It was an important place, as all the traffic coming west had to pass the narrow strip of land between Shoal Lake and Raven Lake. It was the duty of the police to search everything going west for liquor. Any liquor found without a permit was seized and confiscated and the owner arrested. The searching was a long tedious job as hundreds of Red River carts and wagons would arrive during day and night. To expedite matters, the sergeant used a fencing foil to probe into crates, sacks, etc. This proved disastrous in one instance when I was present. A train of about fifty carts had arrived and five constables and the sergeant were searching them. The sergeant used his foil on several crates and sacks and as no liquor was found, the train was allowed to proceed to Edmonton. Then, about two months later, a complaint came in from the Hudson's Bay Company that a dozen of their felt hats had been pierced through by the foil and ruined. The hats were in a crate with others done up in rolls of a dozen each, so the foil got the whole dozen in one thrust.

On the seventh day of my wait, the mail arrived in the evening. It was a heavy load, for besides a separate sealed bag from Ottawa for the Commissioner, there were several hundreds of letters and over three hundred pounds of newspapers and magazines. I was instructed to take the mail through with the utmost speed and not take anything else on the buckboard. When I left that evening at 10:00 P.M. it was very dark. On my arrival at Bird Tail Creek I loaded the mail into a boat that was suspended to a hauser across the creek. Just then, my dog Spot tried to get into the boat and pushed it right out into midstream. I had to strip off and swim out to recover it. The mosquitoes nearly ate me alive; in fact they were so bad that after leaving the crossing, the horse almost went crazy with them. They [sic] were plunging and kicking so bad that I stopped for an hour and built a smudge. Later, when a nice breeze got up I was able to go on. Just at break of day, when driving through a slough, the whiffletree [whippletree] broke. But by jumping out quickly into the water and mud I was able to hold on to the horse. Then I had to carry the mail to dry ground, which was some job wading through mud and water nearly to my hips. It was there the mosquitoes did their work; there were millions of them and they were so bad that I rubbed mud all over my face, neck and hands, to relieve the torture. By lengthening out the reins and with a small piece of rope, the horse could stand on dry ground and pull the buckboard out. About 6:00 A.M. I arrived at the Assiniboine River and found the ferry on the other side. In spite of shouting and firing off my revolver, I could not make the two constables hear me, so I stripped and swam across. Then I brought the ferry over for the horse and buckboard; being naked all this time, the bulldog flies and mosquitoes sure punished me. I stayed half an hour for breakfast, then pushed on with a change of horse. At the one hundred mile mark from Shoal Lake, my dog Spot could not run any further and had to be left behind. When within twenty-six miles of the barracks, a wheel of the buckboard broke off, so I cached all the heavy mail in a bluff, tied the letter bags around the horse's neck and finished the twenty-six miles riding bareback. I arrived at the barracks at midnight, having travelled the one hundred and forty miles in twenty-six hours without any sleep.

Staff Sergt. Frank Norman[25] took the mail, the guard looked after the horse, and I went straight to the barrack room, threw myself on my bed without undressing, and slept until 4:00 P.M. the next day. The men said I never moved once during my long sleep.

The mail disclosed that the government had accepted the resignation of Colonel French and that Assistant Commissioner Macleod had been appointed Commissioner. It appeared that Col. French had previously written the government requesting greater powers to be given him in dealing with the North-West

Territories or he would have to resign.

We all were deeply sorry to lose Col. French for although he was very strict, he was impartial, treating officers, non-commissioned officers and men all the same.[26] The non-commissioned officers presented him with an address and a gold watch costing $150 and the men presented Mrs. French with a solid silver tea set valued at $300.

Chapter Three

1876. Goodbye to Col. French—march to Fort Carlton—Treaty No. Six— on to Fort Pitt—further negotiations—to Battleford—across the plains—South Saskatchewan crossing—Fort Walsh—death of Const. Maloney—on to Fort Macleod—Peigan buffalo hunt.

On the 8th of August, 1876, Colonel Macleod, Superintendent Herchmer[27] and Capt. Dalrymple Clark arrived at Swan River barracks. A report had been received that the Indians had threatened to stop the lieut. governor from crossing the South Saskatchewan River to make a treaty[28] so a general order was issued that "D" Troop was to parade right away in heavy marching order, and leave for Fort Carlton. Under the command of Superintendent Jarvis[29] we marched off at 11:00 A.M., the strength being forty-six of all ranks, thirty-seven horses, and several wagons. Just before leaving, Col. French came and shook hands with all of us and said goodbye; he looked very sad.

Here I quote from my diary of the march to Carlton. The first night we camped at Fort Pelly and next morning reveille sounded at 4:30 A.M. We marched at 6:00 A.M. and after an hour on the road it started to rain, and rained all day and night. Having only two tents, nearly half of us had to sleep outside or under the wagons.

August 10th. We left camp at 6:00 A.M. and four wagons got mired in marshy ground. We passed numerous lakes, mostly alkali, with thousands of ducks on them. In the evening a heavy thunderstorm took place, raining nearly all night.

August 11th. We marched at 6:00 A.M. Observed a flight of grasshoppers flying northeast; better roads today. We marched about thirty miles and camped five miles west of Quill Lake trail near two large salt lakes.

August 12th. We marched at 6:00 A.M.; raining from 7:00 A.M. to 11:00 A.M. Camped for the night twelve miles from Touchwood Hills. Obtained a quantity of dried buffalo meat from the Indians.

August 13th. We marched at 6:00 A.M., travelling over very hilly country till we hit the Carlton Trail about a mile from the Hudson's Bay Company post at Touchwood Hills. We passed Constable Chasse[30] who had lost his horses; he reported that Lieut. Governor Morris of Manitoba, and escort, had passed him on the 10th. We went into camp for the night at the old Touchwood Hills post.

August 14th. We marched at 6:00 A.M. and passed Corp. Welsted.[31] This part of the country is very pretty with rolling prairie, hills and clumps of trees and bushes. We secured and loaded dry wood for cooking and started to cross the Big Salt Plain at 9:00 A.M., camping for the night seven miles from the north side of it. We made thirty-five miles today.

August 15th. We left camp at 6:00 A.M. Prairie fire on distant hills ahead of us. We camped at 3:30 P.M. and had band practise in the evening.

August 16th. We marched at 6:00 A.M. and reached the forks of the road, then passed under the new government telegraph line at 8:45 A.M. We tapped the wire without results and then went on through a bare, hilly and rocky part of the country till reaching Mount Carmel. We camped at 5:00 P.M. One horse died today.

August 17th. We marched at 6:00 A.M. Passed numerous alkali lakes; ducks very plentiful. We camped for the night six miles from the South Saskatchewan River.

August 18th. We left camp at 5:45 A.M., arriving at the South Saskatchewan River about 7:00 A.M. The river is 300 yards wide with trees and bushes along its banks. With a ferry boat, crossed the whole outfit in three hours, then passed the small trading post of Duck Lake with our band playing and arrived at Fort Carlton in the evening, where we joined up with "E" Troop.

August 19th. A mounted parade was held at 9:30 A.M. and

we marched off to the council tent in following order: the band, followed by "D" Troop, then the lieut. governor and his staff, including Hon. William Christie (one of the commissioners), followed by "E" Troop. We paraded past the big Cree Indian camp and they were quite excited, never having seen or heard a band before. A number of squaws were running into their teepees crying, "We are losing our country."

At the council tent the lieut. governor made a long speech to the Indians, stating the Great White Mother had sent him to make a treaty with them, and explained that they would be fed by the government during the time of treaty making. He also said he was informed that the Indians had spoken of stopping him from crossing the South Saskatchewan River. He said they might as well try to stop the running waters of the river, as the Queen's soldiers were as thick as the grass on the prairies. He then said that the next day, being Sunday, they would not meet again until Monday. In the meantime he wanted them to meet together and decide what they wanted to do about the treaty.

In the evening the Indians held a big pow-wow, the dance lasting all night. On Sunday morning both troops paraded for church, the service being held in the open air inside the fort. The service, conducted by a Church of England minister,[32] was an impressive one and was attended by a lot of Indians and half-breeds. After the service a lot of us had a swim in the river. We found the water very cold, the river being about 400 yards wide with a number of sand bars and islands in it.

Fort Carlton, one of the Hudson's Bay Company posts, was quite large with high, log stockade and bastions, loopholed for defense. The dwelling houses, warehouses, etc., were all inside the four walls.

Early Monday morning the Indians sent word that the previous day being Sunday they hadn't had their meeting and wanted to hold it that day. The lieut. governor gave his consent.

On Tuesday, August 25th everyone gathered at the council tent. The chiefs and head men had some great speeches and the lieut. governor told them he did not want them to beat about the bush, but to tell him all that was on their minds. They replied they would put their wants in writing. The meeting was then adjourned.

On Wednesday the 23rd they all met again, the Indians making great speeches. They wanted pretty nearly everything required to stock a good farm, as well as nets, hooks and twine to fish; powder, shot and bullets for hunting; clothing; all kinds of grub; money; and a large reserve of land to each tribe. The commissioners granted most of their requests. The Cree chiefs said they would sign the treaty, but a small band of Saulteaux said they would not. Some bitter and angry words passed between the Crees and Saulteaux. I think it was the Cree chief, Sweet Grass,[33] who said he would not go back on his word if he died for it, and called on the redcoats to help him.

On Thursday at 9:30 A.M. the proceedings were continued and the treaty was signed by the Crees. The Salteaux refused to sign, saying the white people were cheating the Indians. The lieut. governor gave them a great talking to about using the word cheating and of their loyalty to the Great White Mother. The Saulteaux left in a very sullen mood. The chiefs that signed were given silver medals, also long scarlet coats trimmed with gold lace, and black trousers. Then Hon. William Christie started to pay the Indians their first treaty money. It was a long, trying day on both men and horses.

He finished paying the Indians the next day, and in the afternoon a great horse race took place. The half-breeds and Indians challenged the NWMP to race their best horse for one mile against their best buffalo runner and champion of the prairies. The racetrack was on top of the bench above the fort where it was as smooth and level as a billiard table. Half an hour before the race, hundreds of Indians, whites and half-breeds lined the two sides of the course and did their betting. I saw an Indian saddle and bridle bet against a beaded deerskin coat; a rifle against a horse; a four-point blanket against a pair of leggings and moccasins; money against a pony; and a set of harness against money. Oxen and Red River carts also were bet. There were a hundred or more of these kinds of bets piled up separately on both sides of the one-mile course.

The big crowd gathered at the winning post and as the two horses came thundering down it was plain to see that "Kangaroo," the police horse, was leading;[34] he won the race by three or four lengths. In many cases our men returned their winnings to the Indians and half-breeds, the former exclaiming in Cree, "Ke-manas-ko-motin" meaning "soldiers." This made us quite friendly. For the rest of the afternoon the Indians and half-breeds had horse races and kept it up till sundown. They have a great craze for horse racing and gambling, the latter being a game similar to the "crook's pea skin" game.

Returning to my diary, on August 26th, Saturday, "D" Troop was busy crossing the river to the north side. It was hard work, using an old water-logged scow; after each crossing it had to be pulled upstream about two hundred yards, as the swift stream would carry it down that far before reaching the other side. We finished crossing at 5:00 P.M. and went into camp on the high prairie bank opposite Fort Carlton.

In the afternoon the Indians in a body, headed by their chiefs, fired off their guns, marched to the fort and said goodbye to the governor, giving cheers for the Queen and governor.

August 27th. We were in camp all day. "E" Troop crossed the river.

August 28th. The lieut. governor went to Duck Lake to see the Indians there who would not come to the treaty at Fort Carlton. "E" Troop supplied the escort for him. The sand flies were very bad so we had to make smudges for the horses.

August 29th. In early A.M. both troops pulled out for Fort Pitt to make a treaty with the Plain Crees. The lieut. governor and his party caught up to us in the late evening, having enrolled the Duck Lake Indians in the treaty.

August 30th. It rained all day, making it hard on the team horses. We passed the Big Muskeg where wild ducks were very numerous. We camped for the night at Lizard Lake. Nearly all the lakes are alkali and dry wood is scarce. We marched thirty-six miles today.

August 31st. Marched at 5:45 A.M., travelling through stony land where the prairie is all burnt. At noon we arrived opposite Battleford. Spelled for noon and met Inspector Frechette[35] with supplies for us. On my charger I chased a bunch of antelope, but could not get a shot. Camped for the night at Jack Fish Creek.

September 1st. We left camp at 5:45 A.M., passing through very pretty country. There were poplar bluffs and the odd pine trees, with an abundance of grass and wild vetch for the horses. Prairie chicken were very plentiful and I shot several. Bush rabbits were numerous in the bluffs. We camped for the night at Turtle River.

September 2nd. We travelled four and a half hours when we reached Pine Creek at 10:30 A.M. and decided to remain there all the following day to rest the horses. I visited a beaver dam down the creek and saw a black bear which retired gracefully. Ducks were plentiful and I shot several. The mosquitoes and sand flies were very bad and we had to make the smudges for the horses.

September 3rd. Stayed in camp all day.

September 4th. We started to march at 7:00 A.M.; went about thirty-six miles and camped ten miles from Fort Pitt.

September 5th. We went shooting in the morning and bagged eleven mallard ducks. At 11:30 A.M. we left camp and about 2:00 P.M. paraded into Fort Pitt in the following order: the band, "D" Troop, the lieut. governor, "E" Troop, the governor's transport, police transport consisting of about fifteen wagons, a sergeant and four mounted men as rear guard.

The Indians had a very picturesque camp consisting of one hundred and seven teepees, a large number of horses and pinto ponies, and untold numbers of dogs of many colours. The Hudson's Bay Company fort consisted of seven large buildings and several smaller ones. . . . the stockaded fort had been pulled down some years ago. We had fresh buffalo meat for dinner.

The next day we remained in camp, cleaning up and preparing for the treaty. During the night the Indian dogs stole forty pounds of our bacon.

At 10:00 A.M. on September 7th, with the lieut. governor and his staff, we marched to the treaty grounds. The two troops of about eighty mounted men were formed in two facing lines from the council tent, leaving a lane for the Indians to come to the front of the tent. It was a great sight to see the Indians as they came forward. In front were fifty mounted Indians in full war paint of the most hideous colours. One of our constables remarked, "They look like devils." They circled us to and fro at the gallop, shouting their war whoops and firing off their guns. When within about fifty yards from us, two riders met in a collision and both horses fell to the ground. Each horse had a leg broken and both had to be shot. The two riders were badly bruised and one had some ribs broken. Our doctor and veterinary surgeon attended to them.

The chiefs and head men in full regalia then came along on foot, followed by a large body of warriors, women and children. They all were singing and chanting in Cree as they moved up between the two lines of the Mounties and squatted down in front of the council tent. The lieut. governor told them what he was here for, and explained to them what the Great White Mother would give them if they agreed to sign a treaty with her. He said he wanted them to talk the matter over amongst themselves and let him know what they wanted. They requested all the next day to hold council together and decide what they would do. This was granted.

On September 8th we remained in camp all day. There was a heavy frost during the night but this did not deter our adjutant, a blooming Englishman,[36] from taking his usual cold bath in a small rubber tub. His "A" tent was too small so he took his bath in the open air. By this time we had just finished grooming and feeding our horses and had gone into our tents to clean up for breakfast. Then we heard the adjutant shout out, "Commissioner, come and look! I have got quite an audience this morning." We put our heads out of the tent and saw the adjutant having his bath while seven or eight women were lined up, and making great exclamations of surprise, like "Watch-she-gat!" and "Wah-waw-waw!" When he plunged back into his little tent, they made a clicking noise with their tongues, which is an exclamation of great surprise and wonder. The whole troop got a good laugh out of the incident.

The next day the treaty-making was resumed. The chiefs and headmen made long speeches, generally about the great deeds they had done, and hoped the Great White Mother would have pity on them and give them all they were asking for. Suddenly one Indian jumped before the council tent stark naked and said, "Here I stand just as God made me. I hope the Great White Mother will keep the promises made to us." The governor told him that as long as the grass grew and the water ran, they would be kept. Then they signed the treaty.

The next day, being Sunday, a church service was held in camp. Three Indian chiefs and their families attended and Rev'd. John McKay took the service.

"D" Troop crossed the river on September 11th, and we had a hard time of it, as the old leaking scow would nearly sink at every loaded trip. "E" Troop crossed the next day[37] and about 4:00 P.M. we started for Battleford, arriving there on the 16th. We found the Department of Public Works erecting a barracks for the Force on the high bench between the North Saskatchewan and Battle rivers, about two miles west of the confluence. It was the best site in the west for a fort. There were large government buildings being constructed on the high bench south of the Battle River and it was rumoured that Battleford was to be the headquarters of the NWT government.

During our stay, our new Commissioner, Col. Macleod, put us through mounted and foot drills. Supt. James Walker had arrived from the East with a number of recruits, some being drafted to our two troops.

On the 20th of September I was promoted to the rank of sergeant.

After a five-day halt at Battleford, "D" and "E" Troops resumed the march south across the big plains to Fort Walsh and on to Fort Macleod. Col. Macleod was in command, with Capt. Clark as adjutant and in command of "D" Troop and Insp. Frechette in command of "E" Troop. On the second day out we had a big prairie fire, evidently started by the advance guard of sixty mounted men. They had to back fire to save the teams and wagons from being caught in it. We passed several dead buffalo, and at Sixty Mile Bush we loaded up with dry wood, as there would be none for the next hundred and fifty miles. The dry wood was used principally for lighting the buffalo chips (dry buffalo manure) which, when piled in heaps, made a very hot fire and was good for baking bread.

On the third day out, a good joke was pulled off on Const. Joe Kenny,[38] while he was riding on advance guard with about fifty men in half section. It was a cold, blustery morning and we were all wearing cavalry cloaks with helmets. Kenny was riding "Montana Jack," a spirited horse. It always carried its tail projecting out, so Const. Frank Carruthers[39] ran up alongside and slipped a large cactus under the horse's tail. In the next instant Kenny was up in the air about fifteen feet, and when he came down the horse was not there. Luckily he came down in a sitting position but with the jolt he got, his helmet was forced down over his ears and the broken stem of his Irish clay pipe was still between his teeth as the horse went bucking over the prairies.

On the fourth day out, we travelled two hours after dark hoping to find water, but finally had to make a dry camp. We just had the water that was carried in the water-cart, enough to give each of us a cup of tea. On the next day we marched at 5:30 A.M. and found water so the horses had a big drink. We passed over a vast plain with rocks and boulders and saw our first four head of buffalo. As we proceeded the buffalo became more numerous, and towards evening we came to a small slough with hundreds of buffalo standing in it. The water was of a thick, chalky colour and the cooks used it to make tea right away. What a distressing cry went up as we started to drink it! We had to hold our noses and gulp it down quickly, at the same time swearing at the buffalo and country. There was no other water for miles so the buffalo had collected there in the thousands and had contaminated the water with their droppings. We went to work right away and made shallow wells around the edge of the slough, and in about two hours we got good filtered water. The buffalo had eaten all the grass, so the horses only got a feed of oats. That night the guard had to be doubled to keep the buffalo off.

The next day, September 27th, the prairie was black with herds of buffalo and numerous bands of antelope. In the evening we camped at Egg Lake which was covered with ducks and geese; we shot over fifty of them. When travelling across this vast plain we would see a ridge ahead of us and wondered what we would see on the other side of it. On arrival, there was nothing but another similar ridge ahead, and this went on day after day.

We did see some wonderful mirages in the sky. One especially was like a large city upside down, showing houses, large buildings and churches, even to the spires. Another showed beautiful trees. Then there a ground mirage showing lovely lakes of water in the distance; these have fooled many a traveller who, in driving to the place, discovered there was no lake or water to be seen.

On the 28th our Indian guide and two officers on horseback wounded a buffalo. With its tail straight up it was standing at bay, charging at odd intervals at them. I called to some of the recruits who were riding in the wagons and told them to come along if they wanted to see a buffalo before it was killed. Half a dozen of them joined me and we ran ahead of the column and were within about seventy-five yards of the buffalo when he turned and charged after us. It was then a case of letting "the devil take the hindmost" and you bet I wasn't last! We tore back to the wagons, 200 yards away and there was no looking back. Just as we neared the wagons there were great shouts of laughter and on looking around, the buffalo was seen to be still standing at bay, having charged only about thirty yards towards us. We felt quite cheap about it.

On September 29th we arrived at the South Saskatchewan River, at the place where the Red Deer enters it, and went into camp. We had to cut the bank down to get the horses to water. It was quite a treat to see the trees and good water again.

The next day being like summer, we crossed the river in our wagon boxes by tieing [sic] two together and putting tarpaulins underneath and around the sides. Two men baled out the water and on several occasions they sank on nearing the other shore. Luckily they were in fairly shallow water. Most of us got some good duckings, the water being very cold. In the afternoon a large party went to work building a large, dry wooden raft. It was very hard work cutting the logs from old, dead cottonwood trees. Early next morning the raft was loaded up with heavy stuff, such as sacks of oats, wagon wheels, ammunition, etc., and the first trip caused quite a sensation. As it came around a bend of the river in sight of the camp, the huge load was piled high to a peak, topped by the Union Jack, and the boys gave three lusty cheers. There were four men with heavy sweeps rowing like mad as the raft, being too heavily loaded, was sinking fast. It did sink about twenty-five feet from the shore, but fortunately the water was fairly shallow and all the men got was a good ducking. The next day, by not loading it so heavily, and using a sail, the raft worked much better.[40] We also had to swim the horses across and had some trouble, as they galloped back on us a couple of times. By two men swimming ahead with their horses the big bunch followed and they got across all right.

While at the crossing, a heavy wind arose which blew all night, drifting the sand so that we could not sleep. We remained in camp for two days while twenty-four men helped the bull train cross the river. They had a hard time of it because the sand was drifting so badly.[41]

On October 4th we left the camp and crossed an area where the soil was very light and sandy, with mostly cactus and not much grass. In the afternoon we had a big buffalo hunt. A bunch of buffalo, about a hundred, were seen a mile ahead and did not observe us. A dozen of us rode off and by keeping to the lower ground we got within four hundred yards of them. I was riding a cream pony from Montana, said to be a good buffalo runner. As we topped the rise, the word "charge" was given and I noticed the bulls swing quickly around the cows and calves, with their horns lowered. My pony went off like an arrow ahead of the other riders and made straight for the lowered horns. I was sure I was going to be killed, but when some of those behind me fired at the herd, they broke just as I landed in the thick of them. My pony brought me alongside a fat three-year-old cow and, firing just behind the shoulder, I killed my first buffalo, then I went right on and wounded another. We must have chased them five or six miles until they came to a deep coulee and disappeared.

I rode back, looking for the column, but I could not see it anywhere; in fact, I was lost. Luckily, our Indian guide, who was in the hunt, rode up to me. I was parched for a drink and made signs to him what I wanted. He nodded his head and rode on. We passed two dead buffalo bulls and stopped at a three-year-old cow which looked like the one I had shot. The Indian jumped down, took his sheath knife, and made a circular hole in the sod. Then he partly skinned the animal, placing the skin on the hole and pressing it down to make a good basin. Then he stuck his knife into the cow's udder and a good two quarts of milk flowed into the basin. He had a good drink and said in Blackfoot, "Oxee," meaning good. The milk looked dreadful with blood streaking through it, but I was so parched that I went to it and found it good as the Indian had said. On looking up, I found that Capt. Dalrymple Clark had arrived on his pony "Minnie" and saw me drinking.

"Captain," I said, "come and have a drink." "Parker," he replied, "I always thought you were a beast, and I know it now." Then he put his spurs to "Minnie" and galloped off.

The next day, when passing a small rush lake, a large animal with two young ones ran out on the prairie. We thought at first it was a buffalo, but [it] was a grizzly bear. The Indian guide and two of the officers gave chase but each time they got fairly close the bear would turn around, stand up on her hind legs with front paws extended above the head, and show her enormous teeth. She evidently did this to let the cubs escape.

During the second stand up, she was shot in the abdomen but ran along on three legs, at the same time pushing the projecting entrails back into her body with the remaining front paw. On the third time standing up, one of the riders got off his horse and shot her through the head. The Blackfoot said it was "bad medicine" to kill the cubs so they were not molested. The mother bear weighed about 900 lbs. and we had bear steak for supper that night; it was good eating. The skin was given to Col. Macleod. For the past three days we had seen thousands upon thousands of buffalo, as well as numerous antelope.

On October 6th, when we approached Many Island Lake, the ground around it looked all white. We thought it was snow but it turned out to be thousands of wavey geese. Several of us turned out with shotguns and had wonderful sport. At the first shot the birds rose up by hundreds of thousands, making a noise like thunder. They included swans, different kinds of geese, sand hill cranes, pelicans, all kinds of ducks, snipe and plover. They made such a noise through the night that we got very little sleep.

The next night we camped six miles from Fort Walsh and the next morning we left at 3:00 A.M. and ascended a long steep hill and down to a beautiful valley to the banks of Battle Creek.[42] We then arrived at Fort Walsh and received a roaring welcome from our comrades of "B" Troop, under command of Supt. Walsh. We camped outside near the front entrance. Next morning, a large number of recruits arrived from eastern Canada, via the United States. We stood close by, watching them as they marched mounted into the fort; they had the new

Hussar uniform, yellow facings and pill box caps. I called out, "Sammy Cartwright," and sure enough it was him, a schoolmate of mine from Bristol, England. We had many good chats about our school days during my six-day stay at the fort. The most interesting sight there was a party of American cowboys breaking fifty wild broncho horses for the police; the bucking was terrific.

It was very cold in our bell tents at night, generally from twenty to twenty-five degrees of frost, but it was warm in the day time. On the third morning, while we were feeding and grooming our horses, a strange-looking mounted man emerged out of the fog, his whiskers all white frost and a buffalo tongue hanging to his saddle. He turned out to be Sergt. Major Frances[43] who, on returning from Winnipeg with a party bringing four seven-pounder guns to Fort Walsh, had gone buffalo hunting and was lost several days on the prairie.

About this time Goodwin Marchand, a half-breed who had left Battleford with Constable Mahoney with our excess baggage a few days after we did, arrived and reported the tragic death of Mahoney. It appears that they arrived at the same crossing as we did on the South Saskatchewan River and built a small boat of willows with buffalo skin around it. When about one hundred yards or so out from the shore the boat upset and floated away from them. Marchand, having moccasins on, managed to struggle to shore, while Mahoney wearing police top boots, was caught in the quicksand and the more he struggled the worse it became. Marchand claimed he had no rope to throw to him and could do nothing to save him. Mahoney, as he was sinking, made his will by telling Marchand to say goodbye to his wife and children in Battleford and that she was to have his farm in Manitoba and any other property he owned. Marchand was arrested but subsequently released.[44]

After six days at Fort Walsh, "D" Troop pulled out on 13th of October for a two hundred mile march to Fort Macleod, leaving "E" Troop at the fort.[45] Our troop consisted of three four-in-hands, seven teams and wagons, two carts, fifty-one horses, and about seventy men of all ranks, including our famous scout and guide, Jerry Potts.[46] The country which we passed through had very dry, light soil, with short buffalo grass, sun cured in the autumn, which is splendid for feed in winter.

On the second day, when passing down a very steep hill, we had to lock both back wheels of the wagons and one turned completely over, breaking the axle. The third day, we crossed several dry river beds and camped north of the Three Buttes.[47] In the forenoon, when riding in the advance guard with Jerry Potts, he said to me, "Like antelope for dinner?" I said, "Very much, Jerry." He then said, "You guide the column and keep straight towards Chief Mountain," which he pointed out. Then he galloped off with just his revolver. It was nearing noon when we came on him with two antelope he had shot with his revolver.

On the 18th of October, although the night horse pickets were doubled on account of the buffalo being so numerous, seven horses were missing in the morning. We later found them but on this account we did not leave camp until 7:00 A.M.

Inspector Frechette, who always rode his private blood horse, was sick in the morning, so his batman, a recruit named Christie,[48] rode the horse alongside the wagons. I was in the advance guard and noticed an enormous buffalo bull standing alone on our right flank, about five hundred yards away. Then I saw Christie, with his Snider carbine in his right hand, galloping straight for the buffalo. When within fifty yards, he fired at the bull and the horse stopped suddenly, throwing Christie over its head. He came down in a sitting position, facing the buffalo, which immediately charged for him. As the carbine was a single shot rifle, we held our breaths as we watched Christie take out the empty cartridge and put in a loaded one. When the animal was within eight or ten yards of him, coming with its head lowered, Christie fired and the big brute fell dead right at the constable's feet. The whole column whipped off their helmets and cheered him to the echo. This was short-lived as the sergt. major rode out and placed Christie under arrest for disobedience of orders, as no buffalo were allowed to be shot without permission. He received no punishment except a calling down. It turned out that Christie was an excellent rifle shot.

About noon, on cresting a ridge, a wonderful sight was disclosed. A band of Peigans[49] were having one of their large buffalo hunts to provide meat for the winter. There were about one hundred mounted Indians, stripped to the waist, chasing and shooting down the buffalo in a vast circle. They were on a beautiful, level prairie, about ten miles in diameter. A number of mounted Indians kept the buffalo in this circle and we could see numerous dead buffalo scattered over the ground, with women and children skinning the animals and cutting up the meat. As the column had halted and we were looking on, two exhausted buffalo calves, which had escaped out of the circle, tried to pass the wagons. Three or four constables jumped down and caught them, tieing [sic] them to the end of the wagon; later, when we halted to camp, the two constables untied them, when the calves politely butted the two men head over heels and scampered off, amidst great cheers and laughter.

On our fourth day, we pulled out at 6:15 A.M. and marched through snow and rain for most of the forenoon, passing through thousands of buffalo. As far as one could see, the country was black with them. We shot three cows and a year-old bull as we were out of meat.

The next day was very wet and cold as it had rained all the previous night. We had just enough dry wood to make a cup of tea for breakfast and, as buffalo chips would not burn when wet, we had to drink water for the rest of the day. The country was still black with buffalo.

October 21st dawned as a damp, cold morning which was made worse when we had to drink water for breakfast as the cook had mistakenly put salt into the tea instead of sugar. He was cussed plenty. At 1:30 P.M. we arrived at Fort Whoop-Up at the confluence of the St. Mary's and Belly rivers. The historic fort looked quite formidable, with its high stockade of heavy logs which enclosed numerous buildings and stables. Skeletons of odd Indians that had been shot down by the American whiskey traders were still laid about in the bushes and grass.

The next day, the 22nd of October, we forded the St. Mary's River, then the Belly River, and arrived at Fort Macleod. All the civilians and Mounties turned out in full force and they sure gave us a great welcome, cheering us time and again. The one street was decorated with flags and evergreens. The fort, adjoining the town, was also decorated, including a magnificent arch over the main entrance. This latter was in honour of our new Commissioner, Colonel Macleod who, two years ago with his men, had built the fort.

Chapter Four

1876-77. Fort Macleod—arrest of whiskey trader—upriver to wood camp—Blackfoot tree burial—breaking a horse—off to Blackfoot Crossing—Treaty No. Seven.

Fort Macleod in 1876 consisted of log buildings, mud floors and mud roofs. If it rained, especially at night, many a sleeping man got a daub of mud in his face. The large stables on the west side were well-built and warm. Also on that side were the saddle and harness rooms, carpenter shop and quartermaster stores. On the north side were four barrack rooms and blacksmith shop. On the east side, officers' quarters and mess room, main gate and guard room. On the south side, hospital, four barrack rooms, sergeants' quarters, mess room and kitchen. The men's cook house, mess room, and a small gate were in the southwest corner adjoining the town. On the large square and parade ground stood two nine-pounder field guns and two mortars, with the flagstaff and flag in the centre.

One non-commissioned officer and nine constables mounted guard every twenty-four hours. Discipline was strict at all times, as we were governed under the Queen's Regulations, as well as the NWMP Act.

Some four months before we arrived at Fort Macleod, a wealthy American whiskey trader named Weatherwax, in defiance of the police, had gone out with a large outfit of ponies, carts, etc., to trade with the Indians. An information and complaint having been laid against him for supplying the Indians with whiskey, a party of Mounties was sent out. They returned in three days with Weatherwax a prisoner, and with all his outfit, including several hundred buffalo robes seized and brought in. At his trial he was found guilty, fined four hundred dollars and six months' imprisonment, and all his carts, ponies, and outfit confiscated, including all the buffalo robes.

On hearing the sentence, Weatherwax, in a most indignant voice, cried out, "Hold your horses there! When the wires get a-humming between Uncle Sam and Queen Vic there will be war sure." It turned out there was no war. Weatherwax paid his fine, did his imprisonment and lost all his trading outfit.

The robes saved the government many hundreds of dollars as the Commissioner ordered them to be made into winter coats for the Force. A supply was given to each of the six troops and their tailors turned out useful and warm coats, being made pea-jacket shape, with a good high collar, suitable for both riding and walking.

After doing general duty for about three weeks, I took a contract to supply the fort with four hundred cords of dry wood. I was allowed three constables[50] to do the chopping and two with their teams and wagons to haul the wood to the fort. On the 17th of November, we went six miles up the Old Man River to a bottom full of dry wood, where we went into camp.[51] We started using a teepee for a tent but it smoked so badly that after three days we decided to build a log shack. We put one up, 10 x 12 feet, finishing it in one and a half days. It was snug and warm. The three men worked hard and well, always keeping a good supply of cordwood ahead of the two teams.

At Christmas we all went into the fort, and had a glorious time feasting on roast buffalo, venison, and plum pudding; then there were speeches, stories and songs galore. The Commissioner and officers visited the different mess rooms and wished us all a merry Christmas; we followed by singing "For They are Jolly Good Fellows," and did not break up until 3:00 A.M.

At the wood camp one afternoon, as I was going to visit the three men chopping in the bush, I took my twelve-bore shotgun along thinking I might see a prairie chicken or a partridge. On nearing a point of the woods that ended in a patch of open prairie, a fine specimen of blacktail deer sprang up to its feet about thirty-five yards away. Before it could run off, my gun touched my shoulder and on firing, the deer dropped in its tracks. As the cartridge used was No. 6 shot, I could hardly believe the deer was dead and for a couple of minutes I kept it covered with the other barrel. Then, on going up to it I found it stone dead. The men would not believe I had shot a deer with my gun and thought I was trying to fool them. On telling them to put up their axes and call it a day's work, they came along and were delighted to see the deer, which when dressed was found fat and weighed two hundred pounds.

On the first of February, 1877, having cleaned out all the dry wood at our camp, we said goodbye to our shanty and moved about six miles farther west along the river to Lime Kiln Bottom. We went into camp and by the following evening had built a larger shack, 12 x 16 feet. The weather was like summer; one day it was so hot that the three men chopped in their bare skin from the waist up. On some days we had snowstorms but the chinook winds would blow from the west and take the snow off in an hour or so. There being no game laws, on Sunday we all used to go shooting and generally got a few ducks and an odd goose; one of the men also killed a white-tailed deer. In the evenings I used to troll in the river and caught a good many fish. There was a very tall cottonwood tree not far from the shanty with an enormous eagle's nest at the top. A wild goose had taken possession of it and we observed it sitting in the nest several times.

The Blackfoot Indians buried their dead in trees. There was one about four hundred yards from our shanty, the corpse being rolled up in a buffalo robe and resting on some low branches. It looked as though it had been there for twenty-five years or longer. At this time I was sending to my parents in England a large packing-case of Indian curios, so I thought it was a good chance to obtain one or two small, carved images of animals that were generally placed around the shoulders or neck and buried with the Indian. It was late in the evening when I approached the burial and by standing on my tiptoes I could just reach the buffalo robe at the neck. With the end of my fingers I was just loosening it up to find the images, when suddenly the corpse collapsed down on me, knocking me flat with the bones rattling all around me. It was most weird. I jumped to my feet and ran to the shanty as if the devil was after me. The men were there and gave me a great laugh but the

UNIVERSITY OF WINNIPEG
LIBRARY
515 Portage Avenue
Winnipeg Manitoba R3B 2E9

worst was yet to come. The dust of the remains had gotten into my mouth and nostrils and for three days I could hardly eat or drink anything, as everything tasted of the corpse.

On the 14th of June, 1877, having completed the wood contract we were called into the fort for duty.

During the winter of 1876–77 the boys at the fort had been quite busy getting after the whiskey runners, capturing and arresting four or five different parties. They were generally convicted, as quantities of liquor were generally found with them. They were never fined less than $200 or six months' imprisonment.

As the treaty with the Blackfeet was coming off in September, about one hundred horses from our herd were brought in so that we could have fresh ones to drill with. I chose a beautiful looking horse named "Fox" and the next morning took him out for mounted drill. I had no sooner gotten into the saddle when he bucked me off. I mounted again and he went all right. He threw me pretty regularly for seven or eight days, then I beat him to it a couple of times and thought he was conquered. One day, there being no mounted drill, I took "Fox" out for exercise. On leaving the stables to cross the square to the main gate, he tried his best to buck, but I held his head up tight with the bit. Just as I got outside the gate, without any warning, he suddenly stood straight up and threw himself backwards on top of me. I evidently was stunned and on coming to, I found the guard putting water on my face.

"Where is Fox?" I asked.

"Gone back to the stables," he replied.

"Bring him out," I responded, which they did, and on mounting I rode him six miles out and back at a gallop. When he wanted to slacken up, I jabbed the spurs into him and on dismounting I found my spurs covered with blood. We understood each other better after that and although not cured of bucking, he never turned over backwards again.

On the 12th of September, 1877, "C" and "D" Troops, nearly one hundred strong, with the two nine-pounder guns, marched out for Blackfoot Crossing on the Bow River to make a treaty with the Indians. The distance was about eighty miles and we arrived there on the 15th. We descended from the high prairie into a beautiful, spacious valley where we went into camp, close to the mouth of a large coulee. The Indians were camped about six hundred yards from us in the same valley. There must have been nearly five hundred teepees, most of them brand new and made with white buffalo hides, painted around the outsides illustrating the different fights and horse-stealing raids they had been in.

Early the next morning we noticed there was quite a stir in the Indian camp. Women were working on horses which were tied up here and there at their teepees, and parties of two and three warriors kept riding up the hill to the prairie bench above. Then we heard shouting and fierce Indian yells. We all turned out and lined the south side of the camp as Indians galloped from the coulee in two and threes, mounted on their painted horses. The riders were all naked except for breechcloths and were painted in the most hideous colours from head to foot. Some had yellow and black spots all over; others, white spots; still others, the body was half black and half white. As they passed us at full gallop, they would lie alongside their horses on the opposite side with just their foreheads showing over the horse's mane. They would shoot off their rifles under the horse's necks right over our heads and after firing they would come to an upright position on the horse. Then, as they galloped off, with hand to mouth they would yell out their shrill war cries. They circled the entire valley and finally wound up at their own camp.

Having sent word that they would hold a sham battle between the Crees and themselves, everyone with the exception of the camp guard, went over to see it. It was a hair-raising affair. They had a big circle about two hundred yards in diameter; the Indian onlookers, including all the women and children, were on the north side, and the lieut. governor and Mounted Police on the south side. A hundred mounted Blood Indians, divided fifty on each side, went at it. Several times an Indian, being shot at, would fall off his horse and the attacking Indian instantly dismounted and rushed to his fallen enemy. He fired a shot close to his head, whipped out his knife and scalped his foe, then tucking the imaginary scalp under his belt, let out his war cry. Several Indians got unhorsed and there were many fights on the ground with knives. As the Indians were firing ball cartridges it was a miracle nobody was hit. The sham fight lasted about half an hour, the Blackfeet being declared the winners, as they had the most scalps to their credit. This affair, and the galloping parade of the two hundred Blood Indians, was all most thrilling and we would not have missed it for the best farm in Manitoba.

The next day the treaty commissioners, Lieut. Governor Laird and Col. Macleod, met most of the leading chiefs. They fully explained the terms the government was prepared to offer them if they would make a treaty with the Great White Mother, Queen Victoria.

The following day at two o'clock the treaty proceedings opened, the two commissioners being in a small square tent, the front being open. There were two interpreters, one on each side, Jerry Potts from Fort Macleod, and Lavallee from Fort Walsh. About seventy Mounties on their horses were formed in two lines facing each other in front of the council tent and about forty feet apart. This made a passageway for the Indian chiefs and head men to come right to the council tent and make their speeches. A vast crowd of women and children followed behind the chiefs.

Crowfoot was the first to speak; he was very brief, stating that the police were his friends and their advice was always good, that they were thankful for the police being sent out to them. He would sign the treaty as long as the sun shone and water ran. Chief Old Sun of the North Blackfeet was next; he said Crowfoot had spoken well, that they wanted money, cattle, etc. Bull's Head, chief of the Sarcees, also agreed to sign, as did Rainy Chief of the North Bloods, Eagle Head[52] of the Peigans and several other minor chiefs.

An amusing incident occurred about this time. All Indians, before addressing the commissioner, had to have their names interpreted into English. An Indian stepped up to make a speech and Lavallee interpreted his name as Horse's Tail. Jerry Potts got very mad and yelled out, "You son of a bitch, you lie. I tell you it is Horse's Ass." I saw the lieut. governor hold his hands up in horror. He was a very religious man and probably had not heard such choice prairie language before. The treaty was then signed, after which two Mounted Police officers started right away to pay the Indians their first treaty money; it took the best part of three days. We then marched back to the fort.

While at the treaty, every morning early and again in the evening, we would hear a head chief call out in Blackfoot, "Pox-o-put, Kab-ba-nis-ky, Ak-ki-am Siks-a-kum-ee Nap-i-am, Yo-ho," meaning in English, "Come quick, plenty of tea and bread." This was to call the whole camp to breakfast and supper.

Crowfoot was a very fine man and most observant. At reveille one morning he came into the fort, squatted down in a corner and watched everything that went on until the guard mounted at 7:00 P.M. At noon the Commissioner took him to lunch.

We had found that the Blackfeet were much superior to other Indians and had strict moral laws. One was if a young maiden went wrong before marriage, they would cut off her nose. I saw one such case at Fort Macleod; it was a terrible disfigurement.

All Indian parents are exceedingly fond of their children. One instance I observed myself. After dark one evening, I had gone out of the fort to shoot jack rabbits. It was a bright moonlight night in winter, but there was no snow on the ground and, as the rabbits had turned white, they were easily seen. I had shot several and was returning to the fort when piercing screams rent the air. I made for the place of two or three cottonwood trees and perceived a Blackfoot woman kneeling under them, looking up and screaming out, "Mis-to-put! Mis-to-put," then the third time raising her voice to a blood curdling scream. ("Mis-to-put" means gone.) In seeing a bundle fastened up in the tree, I knew then she was mourning for her dead child buried up there.

After our return from the treaty, having noticed some cutbanks and deep water down the Old Man's River, a mile from the fort, I took my twelve-foot rod to troll for pike. On the first throw something big took the spoon and the hundred feet of line was running out at terrific speed. I repeated reeling up the fish about fifty times, and in about half an hour managed to get him to the edge of the river. There I was surprised to see such a large head. I pulled out my hunting knife and drove it through the fish's head with both hands as he lashed water all over me. It was a muskellonge, four feet long and must have weighed between thirty and forty pounds. I threw my spoon in again and in a few minutes caught another nearly as large, weighing between twenty and thirty pounds.

Chapter Five

1878–80. "Slim Jim" to Stony Mountain Penitentiary—home to England—back to Shoal Lake—escape of Ko-wee-ta-ass—prisoner to High Bluff—transferred to Fort Qu'Appelle—capture of Ko-wee-ta-ass—stolen horse—bad winter.

One day in the early spring of 1878, a report came in about midnight to the fort that "Slim Jim," a notorious horse thief, had run off about thirty head of the best horses in Macleod.[53] Supt. Winder and three constables were sent in pursuit. Just at daylight they saw Slim Jim and the horses on the opposite high bank of the Belly River, a good mile away. He evidently saw the police at the same time, as he was seen to lasso the best horse in the bunch, change his saddle onto it, and gallop off. The chase was on, the police being delayed in having to ford the river, and after chasing him for fifteen miles or so, Slim's horse commenced to tire. The police were all strung out, with the superintendent nearly a mile in the rear. Constable Ed Wilson got within about a hundred yards of Slim who started to throw his rifle to and fro as if intending to shoot. Wilson opened fire on him, the second shot passing between Slim's bridle arm and body. He then halted his horse and said, "Well, I guess you have got me, but who is that policeman away back there?" Wilson replied, "That is Supt. Winder."[54]

"I thought so," said Slim. "I wish he had been up here so as I could have had a shot at the old baldheaded son of a bitch just to see how he would have acted." When the superintendent rode up, Slim cussed him in dreadful language. It appeared that in 1876 Slim Jim had been held in the Fort Macleod guard room for six months on another horse stealing charge but the

Indian witness could not be found, so Slim had to be discharged. During his confinement he had taken a great dislike to Supt. Winder.

At the trial after his capture, Slim Jim was found guilty and sentenced to five years' imprisonment in the Stony Mountain Penitentiary. Sergt. Lake[55] and I, together with four constables,[56] were detailed to escort the prisoner to the penitentiary near Winnipeg, a journey of one thousand miles. There were no bridges across the rivers and the only roads were at the eastern end. Three of the constables were leaving the Force and although I had re-engaged for another three years, I was given a three months' furlough providing we got our prisoner safely into the penitentiary. We left Fort Macleod on the 7th of May, 1878, with four saddle horses and a four-in-hand team which was driven by the prisoner. He was an expert driver and was wonderful with the long four-in-hand whip. If requested, he could hit any spot on the four horses, making the hair fly and the blood spurt out. Two constables rode in the wagon with the prisoner, who was dressed in prison uniform. Each night before dark, a ball and chain was put on his leg and a constable was posted to watch him. Sergt. Lake and I divided every night into two shifts, sitting up to see that the constable did not fall asleep. This was an arduous duty after riding forty and fifty miles every day for a month in all kinds of weather. This precaution had to be taken as Slim Jim could pick the locks of any of our out-of-date irons. The ball and chain was not used on him when he was baking bread or wanting to go to the toilet, when two constables were detailed to guard him. It was taken off every morning just before we started to pull out to allow him to drive the four-in-hand.

On the 12th of May we arrived at Fort Walsh, stayed there two days, and pulled out on the 15th.[57] The next day we crossed the White Mud River, which was about thirty yards wide, the four-in-hand getting badly mired. Later we came across the remains of two of Sitting Bull's warriors buried on the prairie, about two miles apart. The first was in a good teepee and tucked up in a bed of blankets, buffalo robe and pillow; for his nose having been eaten away by wild animals, the body seemed in good condition. His dead horse with the saddle was lying at the teepee door, and his rifle and provisions were by his bed to be carried by him to the Happy Hunting Grounds. The second warrior was wrapped in a buffalo robe on a six-foot platform.

The same evening we arrived at East End Detachment, where Sergt. Kennedy was in charge with three constables. There were several log buildings there; the one we occupied had sleeping cots and an open fireplace to cook with. After supper, Slim Jim baked a supply of bread, under escort of Const. McLeod, who was very short-sighted; on that account he was to take his discharge in Winnipeg. The other escort and I were lying on the cots, reading newspapers, as we had not seen any for weeks. McLeod then addressed me, saying the prisoner had finished baking the bread and wanted to go to the toilet outside. I said all right and they were gone for only a few seconds when a strange feeling came over me. When I jumped up, I noticed that the second escort, a lazy beggar, was still lying on the cot and had not gone out with McLeod.

I grabbed my revolver and rushed outside, shouting, "Where are you?" It was very dark and I couldn't see them. McLeod said, "Here." I pointed my revolver in that direction and ran towards him and was relieved to find that Slim Jim was still there. I had expected he would have jumped into a deep ravine which was near them. Afterwards Slim told me he had the mistake of his life in not jumping from McLeod right away, but in the darkness he could not locate the ravine. Then he saw me plainly in the light of the open door pointing the revolver straight at him.

The next morning we pulled out at 6:00 A.M. for Fort Qu'Appelle, a drive of three hundred and fifty miles over bare prairie with no road. That night it started to rain and it kept it up for two and a half days. We had taken only a small quantity of dry wood along, as we depended on buffalo chips, but they got wet [and] we could not use them. The dry wood lasted only a day and a half, so we did not have any tea or coffee for two days, till the chips got dry. In passing Old Wives Lake, swarms of flying ants beset us and the horses and men were nearly driven crazy from their stings. At last we drove into the water along the edge for about a mile, until they left us.

Buffalo were seen every day. In the Dirt Hills I chased one

and wounded it badly, but could not get my horse, "Fox," close enough to finish him off. Sergt. Lake shot an antelope and our half-breed guide shot a buffalo, so we had lots of fresh meat.

We generally got up at 4:00 A.M. and travelled ten miles before breakfast. On the 21st, we spelled for dinner on the Souris River, a beautiful part of the country abounding with ash, poplar, and wild plum trees. After shooting a two-year-old buffalo cow, we passed Moose Jaw Creek and camped. On the 22nd, when we spelled for dinner, a bad thunderstorm came on and lasted for most of the afternoon. We did not get very wet, however, as we pulled the tent over the wagon and got under it.

The next day three horses played out and two of them had to be left behind about eight miles from Fort Qu'Appelle. We arrived at the fort late that evening and put up at the detachment. It consisted of three constables, with Corporal Borrodaile[58] in charge.[59] We stayed there three days to rest the horses, having recovered the two we left behind. We left on the 27th, and between Fort Qu'Appelle and Fort Ellice we had lots of rain, which was hard on the horses as it made the roads very bad. We had to cross over a muskeg a quarter of a mile across and there Slim Jim showed his skill with the four-in-hand. He stood up alone in the wagon and as a horse went down to its belly in the muskeg, the whip would catch it, and it would instantly recover itself. It was truly a wonderful performance.

On the 30th it rained all day and in the afternoon we arrived at Fort Ellice, a Hudson's Bay Company post on the Assiniboine River. The next day we laid over, drying our clothes, cleaning our arms and saddlery, etc. We also had the horses shod at the fort and purchased provisions and oats, the latter costing twenty-five cents a bushel.

On the 1st of June, after crossing the Birdtail Creek, we arrived at Shoal Lake and put up at the detachment there, Inspector Jack French being in command. This officer was a fine, brave man. Poor fellow, he was shot through the heart by a Métis sniper at the battle of Batoche in 1885, just when the battle was won.

In speaking to several new settlers along the way, they said they liked the country and that a large number would be following them. We stayed over only one day at Shoal Lake to rest the horses. Here we purchased our first butter at 35 cents a pound and splendid oats at thirty cents a bushel.

We left on the 3rd of June, had a fairly good road, and camped at Little Saskatchewan River. Next day the wheel horses of the four-in-hand got badly mired, the wagon going down to the hubs. We had a hard job digging it out and were covered with mud from head to foot. Passing some fine fields of grain, we met a large number of new settlers from Bruce, Ontario, having their breakfast. As we went sailing past them, they gave us three hearty cheers. Further on we noticed a lone man coming towards us with a beautiful black team of horses and wagon. He drew off to the side of the road and stopped and as we were passing him at a sharp trot he looked up to Slim Jim and said, "I guess you are fixed now." Slim hauled the four-in-hand back on their haunches to a dead stop and said, "What's that you say, you son of a bitch?" The man, evidently a newcomer, replied, "I guess you are fixed now and will not steal any more horses."

Slim Jim in a towering rage cursed him again, saying, "If I was only let loose, I would get down and kick the stomach out of you, you dirty son of a bitch," which was followed by other terrible oaths. The stranger sat there staring with his mouth wide open without uttering another word; Sergt. Lake then ordered Slim to drive on, which he did.

I rode up to the fellow and said, "You must be very ignorant. The prisoner has received his punishment and it is not up to you to rub it in. For two pins I'd get the ball and chain off the prisoner and put it on you, and take you along." He never moved and when I joined the party half a mile down the trail, he was still sitting there with his mouth wide open staring after us. Slim then said, "Sergeant, that son of a bitch has a fine team of horses, and I am a son of a bitch; if I ever get out of the penitentiary, I will make it a point to steal the son of a bitch's horses."

As the main road was just about impassable, we were advised to take a side road which ran through some farms, where some of the farmers charged a toll on horses and wagons. We took this side road which soon brought us to a farm yard which had a padlock on the gate. On requesting the French-Canadian farmer's wife to let us through, Sergt. Lake gave her all the change he had, which was not quite enough, and she let us into the yard. Suddenly her husband appeared from ploughing, carrying whiffletrees over his shoulder. He asked his wife in French if we had paid all the toll. She replied, "Not quite all." He then threw down the whiffletrees and grabbed our lead horses by the bridles. When Lake ordered him to let go of them, he still held on and told his wife, who was standing crying at the shanty door, to bring his gun. Lake spurred his horse up to the man, drew his revolver and, pointing it at the farmer's head, said, "I'll give you three chances, I warn you; let go of the horses at once." The Frenchman held on and looked straight at the revolver. Then Slim Jim said, "Sarge, let me have a crack at the son of a gun's ear. I'll make him let go of them horses." He would have done it too, and at the first crack of the whip he could have split his ear in two. Lake evidently did not hear him and, as he was giving the man his second warning, I spurred my horse to the woman, saying, "If you do not take your husband from there, he will be a dead man in a minute." She rushed and grabbed her husband and he then let go of the horses. He was sure game. After being told who we were and that when conveying a convict to prison we could not be stopped by anybody, he said he was sorry. Afterwards we found out he was a justice of the peace for Manitoba.

The next day, June 8th, we left Silver Heights and, instead of going straight on to Winnipeg, we took a short cut northeast to the penitentiary. Luckily we met the missionary, Father Lacombe, who showed us how to circumvent an enormous swamp that seemed to surround the penitentiary. We arrived there all right and handed over the prisoner to Warden Sam Bedson. We were afterwards informed that Slim Jim was a model prisoner and got a good slice off his five-year sentence for good conduct. On being released he went right back to Montana, started stealing horses again, was caught by the vigilantes, and hanged by them from a branch of a tree.

After two or three days' rest in Winnipeg, I took my three months' furlough, which, with my brother Harry, was spent at my old home in England. My parents did not know me at first for I had changed much in seven years' absence. This was the happiest period of my life and the time passed so quickly that I applied for a month's extension of my furlough. No answer being received, I took a chance and stayed the extra month. On my return back to Canada, I went straight to the comtroller [sic], Col. Fred White, at Ottawa, and explained matters. He said, slapping me on the back, "It's all right, Parker. We are glad to have you back."

As it was too late to return through the United States to Fort Macleod, I was sent to Shoal Lake for the winter. I had not been there very long when, with a Métis driver and police dog team, I left to take a census of all new settlers between east of Shoal Lake and the western boundary of Manitoba. The winter was a severe one, with snow two feet deep; with settlers located in all directions, it made it a hard trip. I found all the settlers including those at the new village of Rapid City, in good health and pleased with the country.

One day, soon after my return to Shoal Lake, we were sitting in the barrack room when we heard a roaring noise from the chimney. In looking out of the windows, we could see nothing but whirling snow. It was one of the worst blizzards that the North-West Territories and Manitoba had seen for years and [it] made the blood run cold to see it and listen to the roar. People who were travelling and were not near shelter had a real chance of freezing to death. Their only hope was to turn their horses or oxen loose, get under all the robes and blankets they had with them, and wait until the blizzard let up.

Later, we had a Saulteaux Indian prisoner named Ko-wee-ta-ass[60] doing six months for stabbing a trader of the Hudson's Bay Company. Every morning, when being taken out to work on the woodpile, he would stop and do his war dance, finishing with a war whoop. I warned the men that the Indian was very hostile and would try to escape. In the spring, when I was in Winnipeg, I heard that he had successfully escaped custody.

A very prominent government official, having been arrested for supplying intoxicating liquor to an Indian in Manitoba, had to be taken to that province for trial. In the middle of April 1879, we left Shoal Lake with the prisoner, and a party consisting of Supt. W. Herchmer, and me (as escort to the prisoner), one constable, a four-in-hand team and a democrat wagon. The spring break-up, having arrived earlier than usual, made the roads really impassable; there was ice, snow, water and mud the whole way. In crossing the creeks the ice would break in the centre and we would have to wade in and chop the ice away to get the four-in-hand out.

On the sixth we arrived at High Bluff where the trial was to be held, but found we were a day late. The law called for the trial of the offender to be held within three months from the time the offense was committed, so the official[61] got off. From High Bluff we went to Winnipeg and a short time after our return to the post, I was transferred to Fort Qu'Appelle.

I left Shoal Lake on the 27th of May, 1879, with two constables,[62] a team of horses and buckboard. The journey of one hundred and fifty-four miles took us four days and was a most enjoyable trip. In the long evenings I had some splendid duck and prairie chicken shooting along the road. The country we passed through was most enchanting and ideal for farming. There was good soil, heavy grass, and good water although wood was scarce for about one hundred miles.

On the 31st of May we arrived at Fort Qu'Appelle. It was situated in the valley between two large lakes, with a small river between them, a most beautiful spot when viewed from the high banks above. The Hudson's Bay fort was on the south side, right opposite the NWMP post which was on the north side. Inspector Griesbach was in command, with one non-commissioned officer and five constables.

In the third week of June 1879, Inspector Griesbach received a letter from the Hudson's Bay Company post at Touchwood Hills,[63] saying that Ko-wee-ta-ass, the prisoner that had escaped from us at Shoal Lake, was in camp there. He had stated he would not be taken alive by the police, but would fight first.[64] Insp. Griesbach asked me what was the best way to get him. I suggested that four of us travel all night and arrive there shortly before daybreak. The Indians would have been dancing and drinking tea and tobacco nearly all night and would be very confused and stupid at daybreak. He approved of this plan, so with the inspector and me in the buckboard, and with two mounted constables, we left that same evening. About half way there we spelled out for an hour to light a smudge and feed the horses. Going on we arrived at a mail shack about four hundred yards from the Indian camp. It was occupied by two young English half-breed lads. We left the two constables there, Insp. Griesbach and I going on and arousing the Hudson's Bay officer, who stated that the Indian was there but he did not know what teepee he was in. The Indians had been drinking a lot and were talking of a fight. The camp consisted of twenty-five or thirty teepees in a circle about one hundred and fifty yards away. The officer[65] said that an English half-breed named Daniels[66] lived just outside the circle and pointed out his teepee to us. We both knew Daniels as once he had been our interpreter.

We then returned to the mail shack and the two of us crept up to Daniel's teepee. He was astonished to see us and said, "How did you come in? The Indians have a sentry posted, watching the trails from Shoal Lake and Qu'Appelle." On peeping outside he said, "Oh, the sentry missed you. He is just returning from visiting the Indian horses behind that big bluff of trees."

We peeped out and saw the sentry, with his rifle over his arm, come to a knoll in the centre of the camp and lie down with just his forehead and eyes showing over the top of the grass as he watched the trails. Daniels, in answer to our question, declared he did not know which teepee Ko-wee-ta-ass stayed in, but that the Indians were all excited and talking bad. They would fight rather than let the police take the fugitive.

At Insp. Griesbach's request, Daniels got Chief Yellow Quill[67] to come over to the teepee. After the pipe had been passed around to us all, Insp. Griesbach asked the chief to surrender Ko-wee-ta-ass to us. The chief replied that Ko-wee-ta-ass was in camp and he knew that he was a bad man, but did not want any bloodshed. He said he would not surrender him and washed his hands of the whole affair. He then walked off to his own teepee.

I was the only one in the party who knew the Indian so it was proposed that we raid the camp and search every teepee around the circle. We wanted Daniels as interpreter, but he said four of us was not enough and would not go unless we had more help. He was asked if he would go if we had two more and he consented, so I crawled out the back of the teepee and ran down to the mail shack. I took the two carbines from the constables, handed them to the two half-breed lads, at the same time placing my hand on their shoulders, and called on them in the name of the Queen to assist us in the arrest of Ko-wee-ta-ass. They willingly agreed.

It was becoming quite light as we came running to join Insp. Griesbach and Daniels. We then rushed to the nearest teepee in the circle and, on jumping inside I found about a dozen Indians all asleep. Pulling the blanket off the first one, he jumped up in terror [sic]. He looked very much like Ko-wee-ta-ass so I sent him outside, telling the others to hold on to him. I then went on pulling the blankets off the faces of the others; they woke in terror on seeing the red coat over them. When about half a dozen had been uncovered, Daniels called, "Come quick, Sir." On jumping outside [sic], Daniels said, "This is a brother of Ko-wee-ta-ass and he is pointing out the teepee of his brother across the circle close to the big bluff of trees." I dashed across to the teepee and on entering it, I found two Indians asleep, one on each side. On pulling the blankets off them, I found they were two women. I then noticed where a third Indian had been sleeping so I jumped outside and just caught sight of him disappearing in the bluff, making for the horses.

I shouted, "The Indian is in the bluff! Surround it!" At the same time I ran with all my might around to the other side. By this time it was quite light and young warriors were running with their rifles and bridles to get their horses. Women with their children were making for cover in the bushes, dogs were barking and the horses were neighing, all making quite a din. I got around the bluff just in time to see Ko-wee-ta-ass about twenty feet away, with a blanket on and his rifle over his arm. I pointed my revolver at him but he turned and went back into the trees so I shouted to our party, "He is going back to his camp."

I started to run towards Insp. Griesbach and Daniels, to get around to the camp side of the bluff, when I heard the inspector say, "Daniels, is that the man?" Daniels did not answer, so the inspector swore at him and repeated the question and, as I was nearing them, I saw Daniels point his finger and nod his head. The inspector shouted out, "Seize him, Donaldson!"[68]

It appears that Donaldson was posted close to where Ko-wee-ta-ass came out, but the constable could not tell if he was the right man or not, so he took the precaution of following him. When Insp. Griesbach called out, Donaldson seized both arms of the Indian and held on.

I was running hard to help Donaldson and when about thirty yards away, I saw one of the two half-breed lads run up, grab the Indian's blanket and throw it over the Indian's head. At the same time, a large sheaf [*sic*] knife was thrown up in the air, followed by the Indian's rifle; it was all done so quickly that the two weapons were up in the air at the same time. Thus did the lad disarm the Indian in a few seconds. At this instant I came running up, saw that the Indian was Ko-wee-ta-ass and slapped the handcuffs on him.

With Donaldson on the left and me on the right, both with drawn revolvers, we started to hustle the Indian out of the camp. He was very hostile, kept pushing backwards and shouting out in Saulteaux to his companions to shoot us down. I fully expected to get a bullet in my back any minute but they did not shoot, and we got him down to the mail shack. There we were hurrying to hitch the team to the buckboard when fifty or more mounted Indians led by Chief Yellow Quill galloped up fully armed and surrounded us, demanding the release of Ko-wee-ta-ass. This Inspector Griesbach refused to do and after they had argued for about an hour, the chief finally gave way and told the Indians to let us go. We went right away and, with the prisoner, arrived safely back in Qu'Appelle the same afternoon, having travelled ninety-six miles and made the arrest within twenty-four hours.

About the middle of August 1879, an English half-breed named Charles Favell complained that a large party of French Canadians and some nuns under a French half-breed named Lepine[69] were on the road to Prince Albert with a stolen horse of his in their possession. He had applied to Judge Ryan[70] for a warrant but had been refused. Favell gave me a good description of the horse and so with the buckboard and team, Const. Donaldson, Favell and I left in pursuit. With the exception of stopping to feed the horses two or three times, we travelled all night and early next morning overtook the party. Lepine, a very husky man and afterwards one of Riel's lieutenants in the rebellion of 1885, was quite insolent when told our errand, stating there was no such horse in his possession. Favell pointed out the horse and in examining him for different white marks we could not find any. During this examination Lepine and about fifteen young men were smiling and passing nasty remarks. I then ran my hand down the back of the horse to his tail, which I suddenly raised straight up in the air. The hair fell back exposing the bone of the tail with about four inches of the bone cut off. The smiles of Lepine and his crowd disappeared as I said, "This is the horse, Donaldson. Tie him up at the back of the buckboard." Turning to Lepine I said, "You ought to be thankful that I am not taking you back to Qu'Appelle as a prisoner." He replied, "I would go." I replied, "You bet you would go."

On returning across the Salt Plains, Donaldson was taken very ill with cramps in his stomach. We heated rocks, rolled them up in our shirts and placed them on his stomach, but with no effect. Spotting some newcomers about two miles away, I took one of the team horses and galloped over; luckily they had a small quantity of brandy and kindly gave me two or three ounces. The brandy gave Donaldson quick relief and in an hour we were able to proceed. The man who gave me the brandy was John McFadden of London, Ontario, who with his family was going to Prince Albert to take up land to farm.

The winter of 1879–80 was a bad one, often forty and fifty below zero, with several nasty blizzards. Some Indians nearly starved to death, as they could not hunt. On some of the coldest days, I used to take my gun and on snowshoes, trail prairie chicken that had gone to roost under the snow. As I advanced, one or two would pop up out of the snow about twenty or thirty yards away; this made great sport and I often obtained three or four, right and left. The gun when fired sounded like a gun cap going off, caused by the intense cold.

Chapter Six

1880–84. Trouble with Beardy at Duck Lake—on to Battle-ford—barracks not ready—to Turtle Lake to make an arrest—prepared bridge timbers—fire in stables—Marquis of Lorne's visit—arrest of Stonies—close call—transferred to Fort Saskat-chewan—Christmas journey—Edmonton bootleggers—paying treaty money.

Sometime in August 1880, Supt. Herchmer with Insp. Antrobus[71] and twenty-two other ranks arrived from Shoal Lake en route to Battleford and picked me up, the superin-tendent making me his acting sergt. major. On the fourth day after leaving Qu'Appelle, we arrived at Duck Lake about noon. The place was just a small trading post of Stobart & Co., with a few buildings, Sheriff Hughes[72] being in charge. At this time Chief Beardy of the Cree Indians had been making a lot of trouble. He had erected a fence with a padlocked gate across the Carlton Trail, charging the travelling public a certain fee before he would allow them to proceed. He was in a large Indian camp about one mile north so Supt. Herchmer, with Insp. Antrobus and six constables, all on foot, marched over to arrest Beardy. They left me in charge of our camp.

After a short time we heard quite a din and, on looking over, saw an imposing sight. Along the road leading from the Indian camp, which was fenced on each side, walked Chief Beardy with a red-coated constable on each side of him, followed by Chief One Arrow with a constable on each side of him, followed by Beardy's head man[73] between two constables, the two officers walking behind as a rear guard. They were followed by about seventy-five or more Indians who were shouting and firing off

56

their guns over the heads of the police. Seeing this, I ordered my seventeen men to fall in with loaded arms in front of the main log building. As the party came up, the three prisoners were marched into the building, the mob of Indians squatting down in front of my party about fifteen yards away. The preliminary hearing lasted an hour or so, the three prisoners being committed for trial at a higher court. When they were brought out handcuffed for removal to another building, the armed Indians all sprang to their feet very excited. The police party was ordered to bring their rifles to the ready position until the prisoners had entered our small police detachment building, when the Indians started to go back to their camp. "The police will have to pass our camp to Battleford," they said, "and we will then rescue our chiefs."

But Supt. Herchmer fooled them, for a short time later when there were no Indians about he, with two light wagons, the inspector, four mounted constables, and the three prisoners, left in the opposite direction for Prince Albert.[74] He left me in charge and we laid all that night under arms as we thought they might attack us. They sure made enough noise in their camp that night, but they never molested us. The next day Supt. Herchmer and party returned and the whole of us pulled out for Battleford. On arriving at Beardy's big gate, close to the Indian camp, a dozen of us were ordered out with axes to destroy it, which we did without interference from the Indians. The two chiefs and head man were all convicted at Prince Albert, receiving only light sentences.[75]

On arrival at Battleford we found the barracks were not yet finished so we had to live in tents until the 26th of October when we moved in. It was a great relief as the nights were very cold and our blankets did not keep us warm.

Our chief occupation that autumn was erecting a log stockade around the whole barracks which included two very large stables. We had to dig a trench about three and a half feet deep, then place heavy pine logs upright in the trench, forming a wall about twelve feet high. The logs, being green and a foot in diameter, were fearfully heavy to handle. It was a fine job when completed.

During the fall I managed to enjoy some good shooting,

obtaining several large bags of ducks and prairie chicken. I also bagged several geese on our oat stubble. It was that fall we heard of the death of Captain Dalrymple Clark, who died suddenly at Fort Walsh. He was a splendid officer, always looking after the comfort of his men. About the same time we heard of the death of Constable Bill Hooly at Fort Macleod, he and his four-in-hand team all being drowned in the Belly River.[76]

Three days after Christmas we put on a minstrel show and concert, which was a great success. We had a full house in the council hall of the NWT government. Lieut. Governor Laird attended; he was six foot four inches tall and I thought he would break in two, he laughed so heartily.

In February, 1881, I was sent with one constable and interpreter to arrest a half-breed for cruelly beating his wife. It was a tough trip. On the first two nights we had to sleep out in the open, making our beds in the snow; the cold was intense, dropping to forty below zero. On the third day we arrived at Turtle Lake,[77] a beautiful sheet of water about twenty miles long and ten miles wide, surrounded by stately pine trees and full of three or four different kinds of fish. We camped that night in an Indian teepee and had skunk for supper; it tasted like young chicken. Next morning we arrested the wanted man, but found that the chief witness against him was away hunting thirty-five miles further on. Leaving the prisoner with the constable, the interpreter and I went on and found it was the hardest and longest thirty-five miles we had ever travelled. We went up and down hills, through heavy woods, and had no trails or roads, but we did get the witness. We returned safely back to Battleford after a round trip of two hundred and thirty-five miles.

In the beginning of April 1881, the authorities began building a bridge over the Battle River and wanted four long, squared timbers to complete it. They could not get anybody to go for them, so I agreed to get them on a payment of twenty dollars apiece for four of us. Then three constables and I, with wagons, left for Pine Island in the Saskatchewan River sixty-five miles west. We arrived there on the second day and, driving over the ice to the island, camped among the pine trees. Most of these trees were two feet in diameter; it took us about three days of heavy work cutting to get four large trees down and squared into timbers of the required dimensions, 48 feet long, by 10 inches by 11 inches square. A still bigger job was getting these timbers out on to the ice, which now had a foot of water on the top of it, and to make a road up the steep bank to the bench above. We ran out of rations on the last two days, but having my shotgun along I managed to shoot about two dozen prairie chicken which did us very well until we arrived back on the eighth day. We were complimented on the success of our trip.

On the morning that we were camped on the high bench above Pine Island, I got up at daybreak and observed prairie chicken flying in from every direction and alighting on a high knoll about a hundred and fifty yards from our camp. I realized it was their dancing grounds and mating place, so I crawled up to within seventy-five yards of them. It was a most interesting sight; there must have been five hundred of them dancing around in a large circle. They stood up straight like a penguin, then with feathers all ruffled up, especially around the neck, they would bend down, drawing their open wings swooping on the ground, and with their native call, "chuckle, chuckle, chuckle," made a loud noise. The orange mark on each side of the head was very much enlarged and puffed out. After a while I noticed odd pairs leaving the circle and flying off in different directions. On visiting the knoll afterwards, I found willow hoops with horse hair snares stuck in the ground all around the circle, evidently put there in former years by Indians to catch the birds.

In this same month of April, one of our corporals[78] was leaving the Force so we all got up a dance as a farewell to him. Just as we had finished supper, about midnight, there was a cry of fire. We all rushed out and found a large 40- by 60-foot building on fire; part of it was the officers' stables containing some of our best horses, one private and six government ones. The rest of the building consisted of carpenter and blacksmith shops, saddle and harness rooms. On throwing open the stable door, we could see the fire right under the horses' noses; they were squealing and kicking so wildly that it was impossible to rescue them. Nothing was saved except a valuable box of taps and dies that I managed to get from the blacksmith shop.[79]

During the first week of May, 1881, I contracted to plough, harrow and sow with oats, sixty acres of land just outside the fort. I was allowed two constables and three teams of horses to help me. I sowed the sixty acres by hand and it turned out to be a good crop, there having been plenty of rain that summer.

June of the same year was a very wet month and in places the prairie was white with mushrooms. There were wagonloads of them, some as large as soup plates. The grass and wild vetch was waist high and the mosquitoes and sand flies were very bad. All kinds of small fruits were in abundance, such as high bush and low bush cranberries, wild gooseberries, black currants, raspberries, blueberries, and strawberries, the latter being sold by Indian women at fifty cents a pail.

On the 30th of August, the Marquis of Lorne, governor-general of Canada, arrived in Battleford, accompanied by a large escort of NWM Police, commanded by Supt. William Herchmer. He held a big pow-wow with the Indians, Chief Poundmaker[80] being the principal speaker. Afterwards His Excellency inspected our barracks and, on going through the barrack rooms, recognized a cousin of his, Corporal MacNeil;[81] they had a great handshake and chat. Before leaving Battleford he gave every constable one pound of tobacco and each non-commissioned officer two pounds of tobacco. Several correspondents of English and other papers, including Sydney Hall of the *Graphic*, accompanied the party.

On the 1st of September, His Excellency, with a mounted escort of fifty NWMP and about eighteen wagons, nearly all four-in-hands driven by police constables, left Battleford for Fort Macleod. They went via Sounding Lake, Red Deer River, Blackfoot Crossing and Fort Calgary, arriving at Fort Macleod on the 17th of September. On the following day, he left for Fort Shaw, USA, and on crossing the boundary, was escorted by United States Infantry.

About the 10th of September, 1881, I took a contract for $150 with the government to harvest and put in stook the oats that I had planted in the previous spring. The government supplied the reaping machine and horses, while I supplied the labour, which cost twenty cents an hour. It took us just one week to do the job with three men helping; it was a very good crop, between fifty and sixty bushels to the acre.

Towards the middle of October, I received instructions to proceed south to the confluence of the Red Deer and South Saskatchewan Rivers to arrest four Stony Indians for horse stealing. My party consisted of three constables, a half-breed guide and interpreter, five horses and one wagon. The weather was fine when we left but at our first camp it turned cold, with six inches of snow falling; this made it hard going for the horses. On arrival at the forks we found the river partly frozen over and heavy ice running in the current. As we went into camp a big Indian came up and wanted to know where we were going. While talking, he was handling the shackles and logging chain lying in the wagon. We told him we were going to Fort Walsh. The interpreter said he was one of the wanted four Indians and his camp was not far down the river. The other two wanted men had crossed the river and were camped on the other side while the fourth was on this side.

I decided not to arrest the two on this side until I returned from the opposite shore, as the women could call across and warn the others. There was no boat on our side, so next morning I called over to a large camp of half-breeds for help. They tried to bring a boat across, but owing to a big wind and floating ice they were nearly swamped and turned back. I then decided to wait until the next day. Instead, I took my shotgun and, seeing half a dozen swans on the edge of the ice in the river, I crawled on my stomach through the snow on a long sandbar and was rewarded by shooting two of them. They fell in the open water and, rather than lose them, I waded in up to my waist and got them. They were magnificent birds, pure white and weighing about twenty pounds each; we found them very good eating. Afterwards I shot a wolf and some prairie chickens.

The next morning a boat was brought across and, taking one constable and the interpreter with me, I got over and went straight to the half-breed camp. There I met a Mr. Lavielle[82] and his brother, both of whom had large families. They had sold their farms in Manitoba and had located here. They had splendid, large tents with floors carpeted and stoves burning. The children all looked rosy and healthy. They had all kinds of farming implements, horses, cows, oxen, geese, chickens, ducks and dogs, with provisions to last them two years. They also had three huge piles of fresh buffalo meat weighing about ten tons.

Mr. Lavielle informed us that one of the wanted Indians, Thunder Horse's son, was in camp a short distance away and that the other, Little Buffalo, was out buffalo hunting and would be back in about an hour and a half. On my request, Mr. Lavielle sent for Thunder Horse's son and on his arrival in the big tent I at once arrested him. When he started to bawl and shout, I showed him the handcuffs and through the interpreter told him to sit down on the chair and not to utter a word until we were ready to go. If he didn't do as I said, the irons would be put on him. He never moved a muscle after that.

After a long chat and a nice cup of tea with Mr. Lavielle, the other Indian returned. We went to his teepee, leaving the constable outside with Thunder Horse's son. I then arrested Little Buffalo who, while buffalo hunting, had gotten his feet wet; through the interpreter he asked if he could put on a dry pair of moccasins before we left. I consented but just then I heard the constable outside calling for help. With the interpreter I jumped outside and found the two wives of Thunder Horse's son trying to tear him away from the constable. Just as we pushed the women off and put the handcuffs on the Indian, I heard a voice from the teepee say in English, "Look out, mister, or you will be shot."

I jumped in and found Little Buffalo putting a cartridge into his rifle. In an instant I grabbed him, threw his rifle out of his hands, caught the collar around his neck, jerked him up in the air and landed him on his head. He went through the round teepee door and landed at the feet of the other prisoner. I knew what would happen then. As he jumped up he wanted to shake hands with me but instead, the handcuffs which had been hanging on my belt were snapped on him.

I then thrust my head back into the teepee and asked who had given me the warning. An old gray-headed woman sitting close to the door said in good English, "I am Mrs. McKenzie, widow of an old Hudson's Bay officer." I thanked her and as there was not a minute to lose, I gave the order to run for the boat. We drove the two prisoners ahead of us and were chased by the two wives who quit when we went out on the ice. The prisoners were placed in the bottom of the boat and told to lie flat. As there was a large cut-bank on the opposite side about a hundred yards down, our boat had to be hauled up the river nearly two hundred yards to avoid being carried against it by the running ice. I took the tow line, the two men in the boat helping to keep it off the ice; twice I broke through, the second time nearly up to my armpit. As we pushed off it was just about dark and by the time we reached in midstream it was quite dark. It was an anxious time, as the running ice kept smashing against the boat. The two Indian prisoners fairly shook the boat with their trembling, for being handcuffed they would have had no chance if the boat upset. Coming opposite to where I thought we should land, I called out and luckily the two constables were down by the river and directed us where to come in. We got ashore all right, the two constables taking the prisoners to our camp, while we went after the other two.

On entering the Indian camp we got the big Indian who had visited us on arrival. He was very indignant. On leaving him with Const. Hanafin,[83] the other constable, and I went inside a teepee close by to arrest the fourth man, when we heard a big scuffle and yelling outside. On jumping out, we found that the constable had the Indian down, holding him by the throat, with his left hand, and was giving him some blows with his right fist. The Indian, with his mouth wide open, was roaring like a buffalo. At my suggestion the constable let the prisoner get up and he sure was a tamed Indian. It was a well-known fact in those days that Indians never used their fists but always used a billet of wood or a club to beat their wives with. Const. Hanafin explained that the prisoner had tried to escape from him.

We took the prisoners to camp, got out the logging chain and, with handcuffs put one cuff on the right leg at the ankle and the other was fastened to the chain. The fourth prisoner was an old man and was really only required as a witness. This practise had to be resorted to in those days, owing to long distances and the probability of never finding the witness again. On explaining that he would be coming back again, he consented to our taking his large teepee along. We found it a great comfort in going back to Battleford, as there was still four or five inches of snow on the ground. We had a small fire in the centre of the teepee all night, with the prisoners chained around it and a sentry on duty. The rations were getting low when, on the second day after pulling out, we spotted seven buffalo ahead of us. The interpreter, the old Indian prisoner and I gave chase and after running them about five miles we managed to kill a two and a half-year-old bull. The prisoners were made to butcher it, and during the process they astonished us by eating parts of the meat raw. They cut off about six or eight inches of the entrails at a time, and munched it down with great relish. The blood smeared around their mouths made a revolting sight.

Owing to the horses being pretty well played out, having been used on the governor general's escort, I could take along only about two hundred pounds of the meat, the head for the colonel, and the heart and tongue for the sergeants' Christmas dinner. On arrival back at the fort the colonel was highly pleased and complimented me on the success of the trip.[84]

During the summer of 1882, I took a contract with the NWMP to put up seventy tons of hay.[85] I was allowed two constables, two teams of horses, two wagons, a mowing machine and a rake. We got the hay from a large duck marsh in the flat below the barracks. By digging a long ditch from the east end of the marsh into the Saskatchewan River earlier in the season we drained part of the water off and got splendid grass three feet high. We completed the contract by the middle of September. During the same summer, I was married to Miss Mary M. Calder, granddaughter of Chief Factor William Sinclair of the Hudson's Bay Company.[86]

In October I was transferred to Fort Saskatchewan as acting sergeant-major. The fort was situated on the south side of the Saskatchewan River, about eighteen miles east of Edmonton and had been built in 1875 by "A" Troop, under Superintendent Jarvis. It was a stockaded fort with three bastions.

In December of the same year there were two Indians to be arrested at Frog Lake, two hundred miles east and, if arrested, they were to be taken to Battleford.[87] Superintendent Gagnon,[88] who was in command, asked me to go, as he did not know who else to send. I said I would go if he allowed my wife to accompany the party so we could spend Christmas in Battleford. She would drive my private horse and jumper-sleigh. The superintendent consented and gave me permission to stay in Battleford a few days on leave of absence. We had no difficulty in arresting the two Indians and on arrival at Fort Pitt we met three Mounties who took charge of them. While my party of two men and four horses returned to Fort Saskatchewan, my wife and I, with my horse and jumper, went on to Battleford, arriving there a couple of days before Christmas.

On Christmas Day a big football match was arranged between the civilians and the Mounties, and Col. Herchmer, against my will, made me play. It was a tough game, played in snow a foot and a half deep at ten below zero. There was a mixed crowd of about two hundred whites, Indians and half-breeds looking on. As I expected, the civilians made a dead set against me, tore my shirt clean off, kicked me in the nose until the blood was flowing freely, and at the end of the game I sprained my ankle. But we had the satisfaction of winning the game.

Just after celebrating New Year's Day, 1883, my wife and I, with only my private horse and jumper, pulled out on our return to Fort Saskatchewan, a distance of three hundred miles. We left in the afternoon with the thermometer about forty-five below zero and snow two feet deep. We camped that night in an empty log shack. The next day was intensely cold and the trail was difficult to follow, being obliterated with new snow. We made about forty miles and just before dark camped in the snow beside a small bluff that had dried wood in it; having no tent my wife slept in the jumper. It had gotten still colder, sixty below zero, so I kept a big fire burning. The poor horse, with two blankets on him, hugged the fire all night shivering; in fact, I was afraid he would burn his hooves, he got so close to the fire. It kept me busy bringing out dry wood from the bluff and I was getting played out. Finally, at 2:00 A.M. I awakened my wife and said, "We must travel on or be frozen to death."

We went on and after stopping a couple of times for meals and to feed the horse, we arrived on the third day at Fort Pitt, where the factor, William McKay,[89] and his good wife welcomed us and made us stay two days. We still had two hundred miles before us, so we took the north side of the river, which was more sheltered with woods, and had the odd place where we could stay at nights. On the first night after leaving Fort Pitt, we stayed at Frog Lake with the government farm instructor, Mr. Delaney,[90] and Mrs. Delaney. Afterwards, Mr. Delaney was one of nine men cruelly murdered by the Indians in 1885. After leaving Frog Lake, the weather got somewhat milder and eventually we reached Fort Saskatchewan, both in good health. The trip demonstrated that I had the best of wives who never once complained.

In the winter of 1883, Bishop Grandin[91] of Saint Albert, eight miles north of Edmonton, complained that his people, mostly French half-breeds, were being demoralized and made poor by illicit liquor traffic. He thought the liquor was being made in the woods around St. Albert so I was detailed to take one constable and proceed there. In calling on the Bishop, who was one of the finest gentlemen one could meet, he suggested that we ascend the high tower of the church at night and watch for lights in the woods. The first night was most comfortable but nothing was gained. The second night was not so clear, but again no lights appeared, so at midnight we called it off. All this time the Bishop had put our horses and us up, and we lived like fighting cocks, the good nuns being very kind to us.

We then mounted our horses to return to Fort Saskatchewan and, on going down to the Sturgeon River to water the horses, we heard a great noise of shouting and yelling, coming up the river. It was a party of drunken men, in a heavy sleigh and team of horses. We ordered them to stop. They jeered and drove on at a gallop. Constable Curran[92] was ordered to overtake them, which he did, but when they did not stop on his first order, he put his revolver to the driver's head, which had the desired effect. On my coming up, I arrested the whole bunch, about six of them.

The next morning they were all convicted before a justice of the peace, all having pleaded guilty. Before passing sentence, I demanded that the prisoners reveal where they got the liquor from, and they said it was from a man keeping a hotel or saloon in Edmonton and that it was white liquor kept in a jar under the back stairs. I then requested the magistrate to hold the prisoners and all spectators in the courtroom for one and a half hours, which he did. We galloped the eight miles into Edmonton and went to the hotel. Const. Curran was sent to the back door and as I entered the front I saw a man with a large stone jar open the back door. There he found Curran who said, "Thank you, I will take that." It was half full of alcohol. The man was promptly arrested.

A cutter was procured and I drove the prisoner the eighteen miles to Fort Saskatchewan. To my question, he said he bought his liquor from a certain man living in a swell brick house in Edmonton. After putting the prisoner in the guard room and reporting to the officer commanding I returned to Edmonton that same evening with a heavy sleigh and two constables and raided the brick house. The man was not at home but on going upstairs we found one room full in intoxicating liquors put up in different sized bottles, mostly flasks, and all ready for sale. We seized the hundreds of them and filled the sleigh. The owner was later arrested and he, with the other man, were each fined two hundred dollars. Both fines were paid and the seized liquor destroyed.

In the autumn of 1884, I left with one constable and interpreter for Lac La Biche and intervening points to pay the Indians their annual treaty money. The first place we visited was Saddle Lake, where a few Cree Indians were paid and some government presents given them—twine to make fishing nets and powder and lead for hunting. The next place was White Fish Lake where Chief Pakan (The Nut) and his tribe of Cree Indians were paid. The usual presents, including a blue cloth coat trimmed with gold lace for the chief, was given them. The chief, hearing I was a good shot, challenged me to a rifle match, ten shots at 200 yards. I beat him.

On arrival at Lac La Biche, we found the Chipewyan Indians holding sway. I do not remember the name of their chief but their language is hard to understand, being a conglomeration of guttural sounds and grunts. Harrison Young,[93] officer in charge of the H.B. Co. post, kindly put us up and, as I had not sufficient money to pay the unexpectedly large number of Indians present, he advanced me $1,000 which did the trick.

These Indians lived principally on fish. I was told to go and see them eat, which I did. They would put the end of a whole fish in one side of their mouth and as they chewed rapidly, the bones came flying out the other side until the whole fish was eaten up. It was a marvellous performance. The Indians gave no trouble. They told the interpreter that they wanted the government to send me again the next year.

Chapter Seven

1885. Riel Rebellion—warning settlers—broke through the ice—with Steele's Scouts—Frog Lake—Fort Pitt—Battle of Frenchman's Butte—meet escaped prisoners—Loon Lake—to Cold Lake—disband—In Calgary—arrest of whiskey vendors— back to Battleford.

On March 27, 1885, at 3:00 A.M., we were called out of bed, as news came over the single telegraph wire of a fight at Duck Lake. I was ordered to proceed south of the river from Fort Saskatchewan towards Edmonton, warning all settlers and their families to come to the fort if they wanted protection. After this was done, I began to cross the North Saskatchewan River on the ice at Clover Bar when suddenly I broke through, the horse going down under me. For some reason unknown to me now, I had put my sword on, and it caught across the hole in the ice. I am sure it saved my life, for I scrambled out quickly with the bridle rein still in my left hand. Then the thought struck me that the horse would come up with a rush which he did, with his head high in the air. At that moment I gave a mighty pull on the rein and he slid out on his side on to the ice. Lengthening the rein to lead him well behind me, we got across the ice all right. It was then getting dark and freezing hard and I still had nine miles to go. On arrival at Ross's Hotel in Edmonton, my clothes were frozen stiff, and two men had to pull me out of the saddle.

From that time on we were kept on the jump. Settlers kept pouring in for protection and under instructions from the officer commanding, I worked with the settlers and a few constables to put the fort in a good state of defence. We built a new log bastion, reconstructed the stockade, and cut down all the brush surrounding the fort for three hundred yards.

On about the 23rd of April, the Alberta Field Force arrived at Edmonton under General T.B. Strange. It consisted of part of the 65th Battalion of Montreal, Major Steele's Scouts, Alberta Mounted Rifles, about fifty Selkirk redcoats and twenty Mounties with a nine-pounder field gun. I asked the O.C. [officer commanding] to allow me to see some active service, and to join Steele's Scouts. He consented and in two or three days the column, about three hundred and fifty strong, pulled out for Frog Lake. We were in pursuit of Big Bear and his six or seven hundred Indians. After making nearly two hundred miles, we arrived at Frog Lake on the afternoon of the 25th of May. The whole village was virtually burned and destroyed. I helped to recover four burned bodies out of the basement of the Roman Catholic Church. They were burned to a crisp and could not be recognized. In scouting around I found the body of young Gilchrist lying on his face along a footpath from his shack. Evidently he had been running away in his underclothes from mounted Indians, and had been shot at close range in the back; his undershirt was all black from the powder. As he fell on his face in his death agonies, he had bitten a mouthful out of the prairie sod. We accounted for nine men that had been murdered and they were given decent burial.[94]

On the morning of the 26th, the column left for Fort Pitt, arriving there at 4:00 P.M. It was burned to the ground, deserted, and there was no trace of the Indians. We found the body of Constable Cowan who, with Const. Loasby,[95] was returning from a patrol and had charged through the Indians in an endeavour to get into the fort. Cowan was shot dead but Loasby, although severely wounded in the groin, fell off his horse and under heavy rifle fire from the fort, managed to crawl in. At 5:00 P.M. Steele's Scouts were ordered north to try and find the trail of the Indians, which we did find just before dark. This trail was followed until about midnight, when we ran into an outpost of Indians and a brisk fight took place in the thick bushes. Tom McClellan[96] killed a big Indian named Marmaluke;[97] another Indian was badly wounded. There were no casualties amongst the Scouts. We went into bivouac at this spot and I was put in charge of the night guard with double sentries all around.

Early next morning, the 27th of May, General Strange arrived from Fort Pitt with about two hundred and fifty men, consisting of part of the 65th Battalion; two companies of redcoats from Kildonan, Manitoba; the Alberta Mounted Rifles, about sixty strong; one Mounted Police nine-pounder gun; and Steele's Scouts, about eighty strong. We moved forward after the Indians. About 10:00 A.M., on a high knoll ahead, several mounted Indians were observed riding frantically around in circles, evidently making signs to their main body. The general ordered the nine-pounder gun up to disperse them. The first shell was low but the next one burst right over their heads, and one Indian was seen to fall from his horse. The order was then given to advance through thick bushes and up an incline, and several shots were fired down at us. On arrival at the crest there was not an Indian in sight, they having retreated through the thick woods. We followed them for several hours with no opposition. Towards evening the column went into bivouac in quite heavy bushes and trees. Luckily it was a warm night as we had no blankets or bedding of any kind.

On the following morning, the 28th of May, with Steele's Scouts in advance, the column marched forward. Here and there we found camping places and an amount of discarded loot, so we knew the Indians and their prisoners were quite close. About 10:00 A.M. we arrived at a valley cutting across our front, with a bad muskeg between us and the opposite bank. The banks on each side were quite steep, thirty or forty feet above the muskeg. We were at the west side, which was covered with brush interspersed with trees; the east bank was clear of brush but fringed all along the top with heavy poplar trees.

I was one of the advance scouts and we had just started to ride down the slope when our interpreter and guide, Alec Rowland,[98] said he was sure the Indians were on the opposite side. The interpreter said, "The Indians are there, sure." General Strange said, "We will find out," and ordered the nine-pounder gun up and to fire a shell across.

It was no sooner fired than the engagement was on as the Indians poured a heavy fire into us.[99] The 65th Battalion, with the Kildonan redcoats and one troop of Steele's Scouts, were fighting down the bank in the heavy brush while the nine-pounder was firing over their heads, shelling the Indian position. Steele's Scouts were on the left flank and the Alberta Rifles on the right. On the first shell bursting in the heavy fringe of woods in the Indian position, several shrieks and screams were heard, evidently from the prisoners, so the General ordered the gun not to be fired again in that particular spot.

After about two hours of steady fighting by both sides, Steele's Scouts were ordered to go further to the left flank to try and find a crossing over the muskeg. We proceeded there, and I was detailed to take two men and find a crossing. Leaving one man to hold the horses under cover, the two of us started on foot and when about half way over, fired at an Indian pony standing at the edge of the muskeg on the opposite side. There was no return fire, so we went to the other side and found a fairly good crossing. This was reported to Major Steele who sent a message to General Strange.

While waiting, I asked permission of Major Steele to climb a very tall pine tree that overlooked the Indian position. He consented and, on going up about sixty feet, a clear view over the position was obtained. As I suspected, the Indians were getting out in twos and threes and treking in a northerly direction. A message having arrived from the general, I was called down, and was informed by Major Steele that the general had decided to retire two or three miles back from the position to more open ground and to bivouac for the night. The Alberta Rifles had reported that the Indians were getting around our right flank. Steele's Scouts covered the retirement which was carried out without further fighting.

All ranks behaved splendidly. The 65th Montreal boys were very keen to make use of their bayonets and clamoured more than once to be led across the muskeg in a bayonet charge against the Indians.

At daylight the next morning the column moved forward again, with Steele's Scouts in advance. On arriving at the Indian position we found it unoccupied. They had had excellent rifle pits all along the top of the bank just inside the fringe of trees, and had dug a large cellar with logs over the top in which they kept the prisoners. Evidently this was the place where the screams had come from. The campground in the rear of the position was a wonderful sight, being covered with bales of prime furs, valued at between forty and fifty thousand dollars, as well as an enormous quantity of household furniture, ornaments, silverware, cook stoves, bedding, etc.

In the fight we had only three casualties, two privates of the 65th Battalion, one shot through the chest, the other through the shoulder, and Constable McCrae of the Mounted Police and Steele's Scouts, very badly wounded in the leg.[100] This man refused to be brought out by the stretcher bearers until he had fired away all his ammunition. As he was liable to bleed to death, it was reported to General Strange who said, "I guess I will have to go myself," which he did, and brought the man out from the front firing line.

After leaving the Indian position, the column went on a few miles more and camped. The general received a despatch that General Middleton had just arrived at Fort Pitt with three hundred mounted men. An escort of one lieutenant, one sergeant and twelve men was ordered to escort General Middleton to our camp, and I was the sergeant. We left late in the evening and it soon got dark. When riding through some woods we heard shouting from quite a long way off; we shouted in return and kept it up until we heard them say, "We are escaped prisoners." We told them we were soldiers and four of them came staggering up to us. Two of them I knew personally, the Rev'd. Quinney[101] of the Church of England and W.B. Cameron. A very affecting scene took place, the four of them crying with joy. The Rev'd. Quinney, on recognizing me, placed his head on my stirrup and wept like a child. They were weak and very hungry stating they had escaped from the Indians during the fighting and had been wandering through the woods since then. They said all the other prisoners were well. We sent them on to General Strange and next morning we escorted General Middleton up to General Strange's camp at Frenchman's Butte.

I was present when the two generals met. General Strange told General Middleton what he had done, stating he had sent Major Steele and his scouts after the Indians to hold them in check, and that they were probably in action with them at that very time.[102] He requested General Middleton to send his three hundred mounted men on to help Steele. Well, do I remember the answer.

"Not a man! Not a man! Who is this Major Steele? It should not have been done."

They then went into the tent and nothing further was heard. It appears that just after we had left on escort duty, Steele's Scouts had gone to follow the Indians. On my return I begged the brigadier to allow me to follow after them, but he refused and said that General Strange wanted me to look after the few scouts left behind.

The next morning, May 30th, the Alberta column, minus Steele's Scouts, pulled out for Cold Lake as Big Bear and his Indians were supposed to be heading in that direction. We arrived there on the second day and found no signs of the Indians having been there. On the second night, about midnight, some firing was heard at one of our outposts and I was immediately called to investigate. I took Alec Rowland, the guide, with me and found Lieut. Starnes[103] of the 65th Battalion in charge of the outpost. He said they had a sentry watching a small path coming out of the woods and that when he arrived on the scene the sentry reported that an Indian on his pony had come out of the woods, dismounted, knelt down, and fired at him. The Indian then rode into the woods and disappeared.

This was the third or fourth time that I had been called out in the night under similar circumstances and decided to put a stop to it if possible. Rowland was sent to examine the small pathway and reported that although the ground was wet and soft, there were no signs of a horse having been there but that there were numerous boot marks in the grass at the edge of the wood. To my enquiry Mr. Starnes stated he had doubled his men up there to look for the Indian. The sentry was placed under arrest and pleaded guilty to the offense of perpetrating a false alarm. He was given three weeks' imprisonment and this put a stop to further incidents of this kind.

While at Cold Lake, Steele's Scouts rejoined us and reported they had caught up to the Indians at Loon Lake and had quite a fight with them.

Sergeant Fury, a Mountie who was also a sergeant-major in

Steele's Scouts, had been severely wounded.[104] The Indians had retreated and after a second smaller fight had dispersed into the woods for good. All the prisoners had been released.

A few days after this, the Alberta column returned to Fort Pitt to be disbanded. With the dispersal of Big Bear and his Indians, and the prisoners being released, the rebellion was virtually over, with the exception of the mopping up by the Mounties.

There were two or three steamers in the river at Fort Pitt waiting to take General Middleton and some of the troops east. While I was on the upper deck of the steamer *North West* chatting with Rev'd. George McKay and his brother Jimmy, General Strange was striding to and fro. Suddenly he stopped in front of me, called me by name, and stated he was pleased to tell me that he had mentioned me in his reports. A few years later when I was in Ottawa, I asked the comptroller if he knew anything about it. He said no, and presumed General Middleton had suppressed all the reports of General Strange.

Steele's Scouts were marched to Calgary via Edmonton to be disbanded. On going into camp one evening between Edmonton and Calgary, a prairie chicken lit in some long grass about seventy yards from me. There was an order against shooting in camp so I went to Major Steele and asked permission to shoot it with my revolver, as I wanted it for my supper.

He laughed and said, "I tell you what I will do, Parker. If you shoot it the first shot, I will give you a gallon of whiskey on arrival in Calgary." I said it was difficult to shoot a chicken with one shot with a revolver, and to allow me two shots, to which he agreed. A large number of the scouts were watching me as I threw myself down in the grass and started to crawl towards the chicken; just its head was showing above the grass. When within about thirty-five yards, I took careful aim and fired. It was a lucky shot, as the head of the chicken flew up in the air and the boys all cheered. The major came out of his tent to find what the cheering was about and was told that Parker was going to have chicken for supper!

On arrival in Calgary, Steele's Scouts were disbanded, so I reported to the NWMP barracks for duty. Supt. W. Herchmer was in command. That same evening I was ordered to take ten constables, late at night, and arrest a dozen or more hotel and saloon men in Calgary for selling liquor. I got the whole bunch by 1:00 A.M. and landed them in the guard room, followed to the fort gate by a crowd of their friends who demanded bail for the prisoners. I awakened Supt. Herchmer, who was very indignant at being disturbed at such an hour, but he consented to bail. I took in about $2,000 and the bunch were released to appear the next morning.

It appeared that a stranger had arrived in town that morning from Macleod and had purchased liquor from all the parties arrested. It was this man who laid the information before Colonel Herchmer. He was left in barracks that day and was allowed to sleep in the orderly room. By some means, the civilians and town police found out about this and early next morning, while our men were at the stables, two town policemen, dressed as civilians, tapped at the orderly room door. The man opened it and they nabbed him on a warrant issued by the mayor of Calgary.

I was sent down next morning to take notes at his trial before the mayor, where he was charged with selling liquor. The trial was held in a small one-roomed building which was packed with a crowd of cowboys and others peering in at the open door. The prisoner was standing up, when all of a sudden a lariat whizzed through the air and just missed going around his neck. If it had, he would have been dragged away by the cowboys. The man was convicted and heavily fined.

I did not hear of further results as I went to Regina. From there I was sent in charge of a large party of released Indians and half-breed prisoners, twenty-six in all, who were to be taken back to Battleford via Swift Current. On the second day out from Swift Current, we spelled at noon between two good drinking water lakes. Numerous ducks were flying to and fro very high and, as four mallards were coming past at about three hundred yards up, I grabbed my Winchester rifle. Giving them a five-foot lead, I fired, and one came tumbling down. The Indians and half-breeds were greatly surprised and said I was "Big Medicine."

Arriving in Battleford about the 1st of September, I found a battery of guns and some infantry still there, camped just outside the fort. For about two months I did several guards, watching over between sixty and seventy Indian and half-breed prisoners. Eight of these Indians were charged with murder,[105] with others getting long terms of imprisonment, and still others being released.

Top: Dufferin, Manitoba, 1874.
Dufferin was built as a depot for the
International Boundary Survey and was
located south of Winnipeg. It was here
that the Mounted Police congregated in
1874 for their march west.

Above: The feverish activity of the
Mounted Police in preparing for their
trip west was vividly captured by artist
Henri Julien at Dufferin in 1874. Julien
accompanied the Mounted Police for
most of their march.

A great thunder storm on the evening of June 20th
caused the Mounted Police horse herd to stampede.
They trampled over men and tents as they dashed on to
the prairies and away from Dufferin. In some cases, the
horses travelled far into the United States before they
were brought back.

Top: View of the Mounted Police at Roche Percée near the Souris River during their march west. It was here that the Police split into two groups, one continuing west and the other travelling northward to Fort Edmonton.

Above: The first police post on the western plains was at Fort Macleod, named in honour of Colonel James F. Macleod, the assistant commissioner. This sketch was made by Dr. R.B. Nevitt in 1875.

The Mounted Police were successful in
bringing law and order to the west. An
itinerant photographer, W.E. Hook,
photographed "C" Troop at Fort
Macleod in 1879.

Top left: Some of the men in this Mounted Police band at Battleford, Saskatchewan (1884), were involved in the Riel Rebellion a year later. Left to right are: Constables M.H. Meredith, W. Williams, W.H. Potter, and J.A. Symonds; Sergeants J.H. Storer and Fred Bagley; Constables J.C. de Gear, Lavoie, Fred Garton, and Gibson; Trumpeter P. Burke; Constables J. Davis and A. Grogan; and Trumpeter W.H. Hallhaus.

Top right: A handful of Mounted Police patrolled the vast prairies of western Canada. A patrol is seen here having lunch during a trip in 1875.

Above: An artist who was present at the signing of Treaty No. 6 at Fort Carlton showed the Indians going towards the commissioner's tent. A Mounted Police honour guard, with William Parker among them, is seen flanking each side of the government party.

Left: William Parker was stationed at Fort Saskatchewan when this photograph was taken in 1884.

Below: William Parker was a member of the police cricket team which played the civilians of Prince Albert in the early 1890s. Parker is identified by a cross over his head.

Right: View of a foot parade at the Mounted Police barracks, Prince Albert, in 1891.

Below: When the Barr colonists arrived at Saskatoon they had to buy horses and wagons and travel overland to their homesteads near Lloydminster. One of Captain Parker's duties was to assist these inexperienced English settlers in making the trip and becoming established.

This is a formal portrait of a number of
non-commissioned officers of the
Mounted Police. Staff Sergeant William
Parker and Corporal Kerr are reclining
in front. Others identified are: Sergeant
Shepherd, back row centre; Staff
Sergeant Wallet and Corporal Warden,
middle row centre.

The sergeants of "F" Division, Prince
Albert, were photographed in 1891.
William Parker is seated in front at the
extreme right.

William Parker; this photograph is undated.

William Parker, at left, is seen with two of his friends,
Constable St. Denis and Constable Weekes in Regina.
Both Parker and St. Denis were involved with the
Almighty Voice incident in 1897.

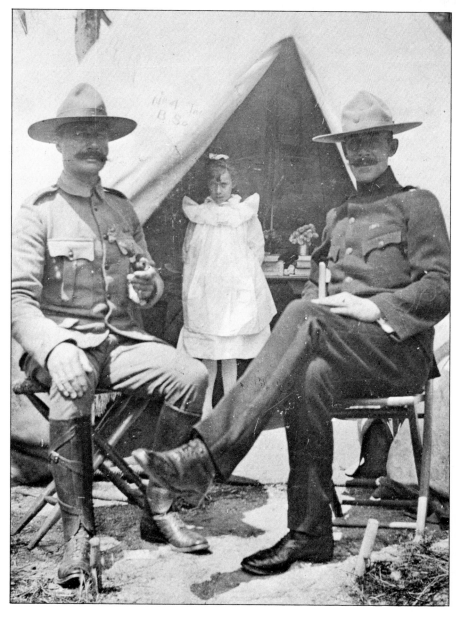

William Parker left, and his friend
Lieut. I.R. Snider are seen here in the
uniforms of the Lord Strathcona's Horse
regiment during the Boer War, in 1900.

Chapter Eight

1885-89. Transferred to Prince Albert—cold winter—new barracks—mail robbery—attacked by deer—loss of prisoner and successful pursuit.

At the end of October, 1885, I was transferred to Prince Albert, taking charge of seventeen recruits for that post. The winter had already set in with snow on the ground and the weather very cold. We left Battleford with three teams and three heavy wagons; three recruits and I were mounted; my wife and two infant children were in a lumber wagon, and balance of recruits were in the other two wagons. The roads were fearfully rough and slippery, and the horses were in poor condition after the rebellion. One of them died before we reached Fort Carlton and we ran out of rations, but luckily managed to shoot a number of rabbits. On receiving extra rations and oats from Prince Albert, we arrived there all right, but for six weeks my family and I had to live in a bell tent before we could obtain a house to rent.

There was no barracks so our "F" Division, about a hundred strong, had its headquarters at the east end of Prince Albert in an area called Goshen.

Soon after my arrival I was promoted to staff sergeant and quarter-master. That winter of 1885-86 was a bitterly cold one and for four or five weeks there was no sunshine and it was between forty and sixty below zero all the time. It was most depressing. A sure sign of the intense cold was the arrival of Arctic ptarmigan, which were quite plentiful. My brother Dyke Parker and I shot seven out of eight that came close to the house. They were pure white in winter and brown in summer. We found them very poor eating, the flesh being very dark, almost black.

During the winter we had a large number of horses and every forenoon the manure had to be carried away. On one particular forenoon, the fatigue party had a big load on the sleigh, when one of the team horses balked. They tried everything, even to lighting a fire underneath him, but it was no use. It was getting close to dinner time when Sergeant-Major Dann[106] appeared on the scene. On being told the trouble he said, "Hold on a minute, I'll make that horse pull." He rushed off to the main building where the troop kitchen was situated and came back carrying a large, hot potato, just taken out of the pot. He went up to the balky horse, raised his tail and slipped the potato under it; when the horse closed his tail down, he went off like a flash of lightning pulling the whole load and the other horse with him. The tighter the horse pressed his tail down, the more steam came out of the squashed potato. Needless to say, he never balked again.

In 1886, new barracks for a whole troop were erected on the brow of the hill, half a mile west of Prince Albert, and when occupied they were found well-built and most comfortable.

In July, the North-West Territories had their first mail robbery, when the royal mail stage between Qu'Appelle and Prince Albert was held up. The stage, with four or five passengers, had camped for the night in a tent near Humboldt. Next morning, at break of day, a bullet was fired through the top of the tent and a voice cried out, "Now, you sons of bitches, crawl out backwards one by one and hold your hands up. Bill, you lie over there, and Jim on the other side."

The driver and passengers crawled out as directed, after which the bandit armed with a rifle, lined them up, robbed them of their money, watches, rings, etc., then coolly stalked off amongst the numerous bluffs.

There was a single telegraph wire at Humboldt and the NWMP both north and south, were soon notified. Numerous parties patrolled the whole surrounding country for days but without success. A month later, in August, the bandit had the nerve to come to Prince Albert. There he was recognized by one of the passengers, was promptly arrested by the Mounties and received a sentence of fourteen years. It turned out that he was a homesteader from south of Prince Albert and committed the robbery all by himself.[107]

In the early spring of 1887, I was instructed to proceed to Fort Carlton with three constables to dig up the bodies of the three constables who were killed in the Duck Lake fight two years earlier. They were constables G.P. Arnold, J.M. Garrett, and W. Gibson. We found them buried in one deep grave, one on top of the other. The first two were fairly easy to get out, but the third, a very heavy man, was eight feet down and gave us a lot of trouble. It was getting dark when a French half-breed came along, driving a team and wagon. On seeing the two coffins and us working in the grave, he let out a piercing yell, lashed his horses into a gallop, and fairly flew over the rough prairies. We were very amused. We found the bodies in a wonderful state of preservation, especially the last heavy one, which was not decomposed at all. He was just as if he had only died. On our return they were buried in the cemetery of St. Mary's Anglican Church, Prince Albert.

During the winter of 1888–89, while stationed at Prince Albert, I went to a whist party at the home of John Betts. When the party broke up at 1:30 A.M. I started to walk about a half mile to my private house, just outside the barracks. It was a bright moonlight night and twenty below zero. As I approached a small open glade to a narrow path, a deer suddenly appeared coming towards me. At the time I was wearing a long, black police fur coat and fur cap, and had my crop whip on my right wrist. When the deer was within about ten or twelve yards from me, I noticed there was one of our helmet chains around his neck, and when he came within six or seven feet from me, I said, "Why it's Teddy, the tame deer from the barracks."

I raised my crop whip to hook it through the chain and I still do not know what happened next. I found myself down in a foot of snow, being prodded and pushed along by the deer with his two sharp pointed horns. They were twelve inches long and [the] same shape as a two-pronged pitchfork. I was pretty helpless in my long fur coat, but managed to grab one of his horns with my left hand. There was a poplar tree on my left, which I was tempted to climb, but [the] thought that he would stick my lower parts before I could get up the tree quickly enough made me choose a thick round bush on my right. I made a sudden jump to my feet and got behind it; the deer immediately backed up about twenty feet, and charged, but did not break through the bush. As he backed up again, I thought of my crop whip still hanging on my right wrist and as he charged I struck him a crushing blow across his long nose. He snorted, shook his head and left me, running away north. I had lost my fur cap in the struggle, but kicking around I found it in the snow, my ears being partly frozen.

It must have been 2:00 A.M. when I arrived home. I went up to the bedroom of my good wife, who had been in delicate health for some time. As I sat down on the edge of the bed she awakened with a start, sat up staring at me with eyes like saucers, and said, "Good gracious, what have you been doing?"

"I had a fight with a deer," I said.

"What did I tell you about going out and playing cards so often," she replied. "That was the old boy himself."

"What old boy."

"The devil," she replied, at the same time placing her two forefingers to her head making the sign of a pair of horns.

"The devil you say! For a devil, he had the longest horns and shortest tail I had ever seen."

Unknown to me, blood was running down the side of my face and I was covered with perspiration. Parts of my body, especially my ribs, were sore for days from the prodding I got; the fur coat probably saved me from being killed.

This deer was one of two confined in a small park at the barracks. About six weeks before this he had killed his mate by piercing her heart with his sharp horns. Afterwards I was informed the deer went north and a man living alone in a shack saw it standing with the chain on its neck. He pulled on his breeches and went outside to catch it and got the same treatment I did; but he managed to scramble back into the shack, minus his braces and breeches. The deer then went further north and was shot by an Indian.

In the summer of 1895, a widow woman of about fifty-five years of age and in delicate health, was criminally assaulted at Prince Albert by a young Norwegian half-breed named Nelson. He did it for revenge, because the widow had sent her good-looking young niece away so that Nelson could not court her. Nelson escaped into some woods west of town and two different parties which were sent out could not find him. Supt. Gagnon then requested me to go so, with six men. We entered the woods just at the break of day. As I surmised, in about half an hour we captured him sleeping in a settler's house. He was convicted and sentenced to five years in Stony Mountain Penitentiary.

Having some business to transact in Winnipeg, I volunteered to escort Nelson to the penitentiary. Foolishly, I did not shackle him, but instead, left on him a light chain fastened to one ankle and extending to his waist where it was held by a strap. We took the train and soon after leaving Dundurn[108] station, as my back was turned for a moment, the prisoner jumped through the door facing the freight cars. I was there in a second, but he had disappeared; on looking back through the passenger car, I saw him get up off the track and start off north over the prairies. The train was a mixed one, with only one passenger coach and about forty freight cars. There was no signal cord and no way of stopping the train, so at my request the brakeman ran over the top of the freight cars and in a few minutes the train started to slow down. I did not wait until it had stopped, but jumped and started on the run after him.

He had a good mile start on me and although I was a good runner I did not appear to be gaining on him. Finally I sat down, pulled off my top boots, opened my tunic and started again in my stocking feet, gaining to within a quarter of a mile of him. Unfortunately I had only a small Smith and Wesson revolver with me, which we used for train duty, but I tried a shot, thinking it might stop him. However, it only made him throw off his coat and go faster. Then I elevated the revolver, fired again and saw the bullet throw up the dirt fifty yards behind him. At that he threw off his vest. If I had had a heavy service revolver, which carries 1,000 yards, he could have been stopped.

I perceived that he was making for some heavy woods that jutted out on the prairies, ten miles from where we started from. I made up my mind that if he reached the woods four or five hundred yards ahead of me, it was no use my following him in there, as it would be impossible to tell which way he went. On reaching the woods, he stopped and faced me, so I shouted to him to think what he was doing, and to give himself up. As he turned and entered the woods I fired a parting shot, then ran back the ten miles to the railway line.

I had previously noticed a section gang working between

Dundurn and the place where I had jumped off so on reaching the railway I ran east along the ties. By this time my socks were worn out, the soles of my feet were raw and I suffered greatly from the hot ties. Besides, there was an excruciating heat of one hundred in the shade. By the time I reached the section gang of three men, I could not talk, as my tongue was swollen up in my mouth. I grabbed their kettle of cold tea, took a big drink and slumped to the ground. I felt as if molten lead had entered my lungs and a violent fit of coughing occurred. As I grabbed the rails of the track I thought a blood vessel would burst and the foreman said, "that Policeman is very sick, I think he is going to die." I then got the kettle of cold tea again, and after rinsing my mouth out several times, I was able to talk. I explained what had happened and told the foreman that he and his two men must help me to arrest the escaped convict, or I would have to arrest them. They agreed and pumped me on their hand-car to Dundurn station. The woman in charge there gave me a bottle of pain killer to drink, and a pair of socks and moccasins for my bleeding feet.

I then took their only pony and rode fifteen miles into the woods, to where I knew there was a large ranch, not far from the place where Nelson had entered the woods. I knew Mr. LaCourt,[109] the owner, and as he would be putting up winter hay, he would have about twenty men and horses. On the way, I noticed three or four houses in the area of the convict's escape route, one especially in the woods about two miles from LaCourt's. On arriving at the ranch, Mr. LaCourt saw that I was in an exhausted state and brought me some beer he had made for the hay-making crew. It picked me up wonderfully and after consuming about half a gallon, he had fifteen mounted men ready for me, and his buggy for me to ride in.

Just as we were about to start to comb the woods, I saw a young girl on the trail galloping madly towards us, so I halted the mounted men. The girl dashed up and said that the convict had called at her house only a short time before and had asked for water. He had drunk about two quarts and then asked for a rifle. He had been told they did not have one, but their neighbour, about a quarter of a mile away, did. The order was given to face, gallop, and surround the house. We were none too soon for we caught him in the stable filing off the end of the light chain attached to his ankle. Nelson turned as white as a sheet when he saw me. I think he thought it was my ghost for he never uttered a word, although I gave him a bit of my mind.

It was midnight when we got to Saskatoon. The following day I escorted him to Regina, and the next day brought him before Stipendiary Magistrate Richardson, the same judge who had tried him at Prince Albert. He had been on the same train that Nelson escaped from, and also had witnessed me pull off my boots on the prairie.

Nelson was charged with unlawful escape from a police officer. The judge opened court by saying, "Have you found your boots yet, Parker?" He then turned to the prisoner and said, "You blackguard, you blackguard! When I tried you at Prince Albert I meant to have added the lash to your sentence, but forgot it. Under this charge it cannot be done, but I will sentence you the full limit of two years, making seven in all for you to serve." I then had the satisfaction of putting him in the penitentiary. I was told afterwards that he refused to work; they tried bread and water punishment, but it was no use. Then they tried kindness by putting him in with the cook. There was a meat block in the kitchen and when the cook turned his back, Nelson grabbed the meat cleaver and chopped off one of his index fingers, saying, "Now you sons-of-guns, make me work."

Chapter Nine

1895-97. The Almighty Voice Affair.

In the autumn of 1895, Almighty Voice, a Cree Indian, having a sick child, applied to the Indian agent at Duck Lake for some beef to make broth for the child. His request was refused, so he went and killed one of the government beef animals, for which he was arrested by the Mounties and lodged in the Duck Lake detachment. The house there was a small one and not fitted up for prisoners, so Almighty Voice that night had to sleep on the floor of the front room. Sergeant Keenan,[110] being in charge of the detachment placed Constable Dickson,[111] a recent recruit, on guard. It appears that Const. Dickson, to pass the hours away, started to read a book and fell asleep; later, on awakening, he found that Almighty Voice had escaped.

Sergeant Colebrook[112] of the Batoche detachment was instructed to take a half-breed scout named [François] Dumont, and to scour the country for him. After several trips had been made, one morning when riding through the Birch Hills, Sergt. Colebrook and the scout suddenly saw Almighty Voice and his wife about a hundred yards ahead of them. At the same time, Almighty Voice pulled the gun off his back and loaded it as he ran. There was a big thicket on the left and Colebrook told Dumont to ride to the other side of it while he went in to get the Indian. Colebrook then went at the trot, with his revolver in his right hand and started after the fugitive. In the meantime Almighty Voice knelt down in the bushes as Colebrook came towards him, saying "Come here, I want you." The scout, at the other side of the thicket, shouted out to Colebrook that Almighty Voice was telling him in Cree to keep back or he was

84

going to shoot him. Colebrook kept right on and, when within about fifteen yards, Almighty Voice shot him dead. The scout then galloped into Prince Albert and gave the alarm. Sergt. Colebrook was a brave Mountie in wanting to take his man alive, but made a grave error in not keeping Dumont with him to hold a parley with the Indian. With a good explanation, Almighty Voice probably would have surrendered.

From then on, for about a year and a half, police patrols were kept going all the time, but they could find no trace of Almighty Voice and the Indians would not give any information about him.

On the 24th of May, 1897, the Mounties and civilians had a cricket match at the barracks at Prince Albert and during the evening we were holding a smoking concert when, at 10:30 P.M., Supt. Gagnon received a telegram from Duck Lake. It stated that Corporal Bowdridge[113] and scout Napoleon Venne had been out investigating a cattle killing case in the Minnichaneas Hills when Venne, in rounding a bluff, was fired upon at close quarters. He was badly wounded in the left shoulder and had nearly fallen off his horse, but managed to regain his seat. At the same time, Almighty Voice had jumped out of the bluff and gave chase, nearly catching the tail of Venne's horse. The scout had just strength enough to spur his horse and to elude the Indian who, in his rage in not catching Venne's horse, knelt down on one knee and fired again at Venne, putting a bullet through the brim of his stetson hat, just grazing his left temple. Venne got away and joined Corporal Bowdridge, the latter riding into Duck Lake and telegraphing the information to the O.C. at Prince Albert. Supt. Gagnon instructed Inspector Capt. John Allen to leave at once with two non-commissioned officers and eight men.[114] They left in less than a hour, travelling all night. Early next morning while scouting through the Minnichaneas Hills, one of the constables[115] reported that he had seen what looked like three deer jumping into a big bluff of trees and bushes, and that they might have been Indians. Capt. Allen said, "We will soon find out if they are deer or Indians," and ordered the bluff to be surrounded and searched. A few minutes after the search commenced, Sergt. Raven was shot through the thigh. On Capt. Allen riding his horse into the bushes he came right upon Almighty Voice. They fired at each other about the same time; Capt. Allen was badly wounded by a bullet in the right arm and fell off his horse. Almighty Voice raised his gun to shoot the captain again, but pulled it down, at the same time, pointing at the captain's cartridge belt and saying something in Cree. At the same instant, Sergt. Raven, who was badly wounded, appeared in the bushes. Almighty Voice suddenly jumped up, and threw himself backwards as Raven fired and missed him. Almighty Voice then got away in the brush again.

Corporal Hockin and a couple of constables arrived and they got Capt. Allen and Sergt. Raven out to a safe place. Capt. Allen then placed Corp. Hockin in charge, directing him to keep the Indians in the bluff until reinforcements arrived. At the same time he was to send a mounted man to Duck Lake with a telegram to Supt. Gagnon at Prince Albert, reporting what had taken place, requesting that a doctor and reinforcements be sent. Captain Allen was then removed by wagon to McKenzie's Crossing of the South Saskatchewan River while Sergt. Raven was made comfortable at the bluff.

Superintendent Gagnon received the telegram about 1:00 P.M. and, under his instructions, I collected eight more men, all that were available. With Supt. Gagnon in command, Doctor Bain, Staff-Sergeant West,[116] the eight constables and I all left for the scene of action. Arriving at McKenzie's Crossing we spelled to feed the horses and found Capt. Allen badly wounded. I held the captain's arm for nearly an hour while Dr. Bain took from it a heaped saucer-full of splintered bone. The doctor wanted him to take a drink of brandy but he refused; he just gritted his teeth and when the operation was over, he called for his pipe.

Our party then pushed on for the bluff. It was just about sundown when we arrived and observed a few men jumping about and swinging their arms near the edge of the bluff. On riding up to them, they told us they were out of ammunition and had just had another fight with three Indians, Almighty Voice and two others.[117] The Indians were in the centre of the bluff and had a concealed pit with narrow paths cut out of the thick bushes. Corp. Hockin, seeing the sun getting low and with no reinforcements in sight, had with his men rushed the bluff.

The result had been that Constable Kerr and E. Grundy, postmaster at Duck Lake, had been killed and were still in the bluff, while Corp. Hockin was severely wounded and was still lying a few yards inside the bluff. They pointed out the place and I called for a buckboard, which was not far away. We ran it into the edge of the bluff where we found Hockin still alive but unconscious. In placing him on the buckboard, a shot was fired from the bluff, the bullet hitting a spoke of one wheel, just missing the men and Hockin. I immediately returned the fire in the direction it came from, which stopped any more firing. We got Hockin out safely, but he died about five hours later.

After getting Hockin out, I posted sentries all around the bluff, about a hundred yards apart and two hundred yards from the bluff. At dusk they were drawn in quite close and at daybreak they were moved back again. Owing to a shortage of men, the same sentries had to stay on all night, being relieved after daylight by twos and threes for breakfast.

About 10:00 P.M. Supt. Gagnon returned to Prince Albert to send out the small seven-pounder gun. I had with me my famous shooting dog "Ike," an Irish setter, who hated Indians, and in going around the sentries that first night I found him most useful. In the stillness of the night we could hear the Indians chopping something with their knives. All the way around Ike kept growling and would bark once in a while, at the same time looking straight at the place where the Indians were. Next morning, Almighty Voice called out that we had brought dogs to help us. Odd shots were fired by both sides during the night; there was frost towards morning.

Early next morning, Friday the 26th, a crow lit on the top of a tall poplar tree in the centre of the bluff. A shot was heard and the bird fell, so we knew the Indians were still there. They wanted the blood of the bird to quench their thirst, as well as to have the meat to eat. It was just after this that Almighty Voice called out in Cree that he was a very brave man, that [he] had killed three men and that he was ready for another fight.

The small seven-pounder gun having arrived, it was served by Constable Joe Walton and, after a few rounds had been fired, it was found unserviceable and was not used again. Just before noon, Constable St. Denis[118] and I, being about a hundred and seventy-five yards from the bluff, saw part of a blanket the size of an apron, being waved in the bushes. We both fired at it together and the blanket dropped. Two days later, an Indian named "Dublin" was found dead at that very place, shot through the forehead.

During the day, quite a number of Prince Albert civilians arrived and helped as sentries around the bluff. About 10:00 P.M., Assistant Commissioner McIllree, with Inspector Macdonell, twenty non-commissioned officers and men, with one nine-pounder gun, arrived from Regina. Directly on arrival Inspector Macdonell requested me to show him around the sentries and, in spite of several having had no sleep for two nights, they were found on the alert. The nights were cold, especially the first night, and at daybreak the barrels of our rifles were white with frost.

The next day, the 28th, was bright and warm. About 9:00 A.M. the nine-pounder gun was used and shelled the bluff for half an hour. On ceasing fire, the Mounties and quite a large number of good Prince Albert citizens lined up and we charged into the bluff. The underbrush was dense and hard to push through. I was near the centre when, hearing two shots on my left hand, I went there and found the Indian pit. In it were two Indians, Almighty Voice and Little Saulteaux, the latter lying partly on top of Almighty Voice, his body quivering as if he had just been killed.

We got the bodies out, finding both dead, Almighty Voice evidently had been killed by a piece of shell going through his right cheek. The third Indian was found dead at the place previously mentioned. We recovered the bodies of Constable Kerr and Mr. Grundy. At the request of the Duck Lake Reserve, the three Indian bodies were handed over to them for burial.[119]

Chapter Ten

1900-12. Boer War—meet King Edward VII—to Canada then back to London for the coronation—promoted to inspector—try murder case in Snake Bay—aid to Barr colonists—transferred to Battleford and then to Medicine Hat—rustlers—trouble with "The Dreamers"—Lethbridge coal strike—Rudyard Kipling—retirement.

In February, 1900, after the outbreak of the Boer War, I was given a commission in Lord Strathcona's Horse as lieutenant and quarter-master, and then recruited twenty men for that corps. It was fifty-six below zero the night we entrained for the East. On arrival in Ottawa we were quartered in the exhibition grounds, and my department was kept busy equipping 560 of all ranks and providing for 600 horses.

One afternoon, a certain lieutenant with his troop was needed right away to be fitted out. The lieutenant could not be found and one of the staff said he was probably having tea with the ladies at the headquarter's building. So going there, I found about thirty officers and ladies having tea in a long narrow room, with the lieutenant at the far end. From the open door I beckoned to him to come out and when he returned to tell his lady friend that he had to go, she asked him, "Who was that hard-faced officer that called you out?"

From that time they christened me "Old Hardface."

Two or three weeks after this, on our arrival early one morning in Halifax, the officers had breakfast in a large hotel, with a great many civilians being present and a dozen or more pretty girls waiting on us. The tables were round and right when eight of us sat down together, one officer said, "Pass the mustard, Old Hardface."

I replied, "Who in the devil are you calling Old Hardface? You'd better look at your own mug first."

Then I turned to a pretty Irish waiting girl at my elbow and said, "Miss, do you think I have a hard face?" After hesitating a moment and blushing, she said, "Indade, Sir, I think you have a very handsome face." The civilians seemed to enjoy this part of the incident.

After a year's service in the Boer War in South Africa, the regiment went to England, arriving in London the night before King Edward VII was to open his first parliament. Next morning the regiment paraded on one side of Pall Mall for the event, with a swell Regiment of Guards being opposite to us.

The following day at the rear of Buckingham Palace, the regiment was inspected by His Majesty and afterwards he presented South African medals to all ranks. The officers were then in turn presented to him. We were told that when nearing the king we should transfer our sword to our left hand, and wait until our name was called. Then the equerry would present us to His Majesty, the king would shake hands saying, "I thank you for your services," and we were to reply "I thank your Majesty," and move on.

When I was presented to the king he looked me in the eye, smiling as we shook hands, but he said nothing. So we had a second shake, still smiling and then he said, "I thank you for your services," and as I was replying, we had a third hearty shake. As I joined the other officers, Colonel Steele said in a very loud voice, "Parker, what do you mean by shaking hands with the king three times, when you should only shake once?" For an instant I was nettled, but replied, "Sir, the king knew when he met a brother sport and was bound to have three shakes with me."

The regiment stayed in London for eight days, and John Bull gave us the treat of our lives. They would not allow us to pay for anything. Lord Strathcona gave the regiment two banquets, every man with a quart bottle of champagne at his elbow. During the last night of our stay in London, the Lord Mayor tendered a banquet to the officers of the regiment in the Savoy Hotel, many distinguished notables being present. The next day, at Liverpool, large cheering crowds met us and we were given another banquet. At the docks, the river front for half a mile was black with people to see us off for Canada.

It was a great relief and joy to get back to the West after the heat of South Africa, and on nearing Winnipeg I would stand outside on the observation car and draw into my lungs large drafts of that wonderful western air.

I had been back at Prince Albert for only a short time when I was elected as one of twenty-five to represent Lord Strathcona's Horse at King Edward's coronation. On my return from England I was promoted to sergeant-major and did both duties of sergeant-major and quarter-master.

In February, 1903, I was promoted to inspector and also made a justice of the peace. At the beginning of March, with one constable, a half-breed driver, two teams of dogs and an Indian guide, I left on a five-hundred-mile trip northeast of Prince Albert to arrest an Indian woman for the supposed murder of her stepson. It was a hard, cold trip, with the temperature at forty below zero most of the time and the snow two and a half to three feet deep. The Indian guide had to go ahead on snowshoes.

We crossed Montreal Lake and on the fifth day arrived at Lac La Ronge, a beautiful lake dotted with islands and full of fish. It took us all the next day to cross it on the ice and from there we went on to Pelican Narrows, finding the Indians there in a starving condition. The next two days brought us to Stanley Mission on the Churchill River, where a very fine English Church had been built, all the prayer and hymn books being printed in Cree. I called on a successful half-breed hunter and trapper, who showed me his catch of furs, worth ten thousand dollars. He made me a present of a magnificent black otter skin which subsequently I had made into a pair of gauntlets and cap, which lasted for over thirty years.

From Stanley Mission we travelled down the Churchill River on the ice for two days and arrived at our destination, a place called Snake Bay. It consisted of only four or five Indian huts and a half-breed family named Isbister. The woman was arrested and appeared before me, charged with the murder of her stepson, a boy of about eleven years old. From the evidence given, it appeared that in January the boy had run away to join his uncle about twenty miles distant, and shortly afterwards was found frozen to death. The two witnesses, who dressed the body for burial, swore there was not a mark or bruise on the body. No witness could be found that saw the woman beat the child, which she denied having done, so the case was dismissed.

Isbister informed me that the winter before, the caribou had passed there in thousands, taking all day to pass. They had killed close to three hundred in one day, the surplus meat being made into pemmican.

It being winter and everything frozen up, I could not describe the country very well, except to say that it was mostly wooded, with muskegs, creeks and beautiful lakes, the latter full of fish. There was quite a large stand of pine timber at Snake Bay. Gold and quicksilver were reported to have been found; regarding the latter, an old Indian at Snake Bay told an interesting story. Two of his Indians had chased and killed a moose and one went back to get a drink of water from a creek they had passed. On bending down to drink, he saw some silver bullets on the bottom of the creek, put his hand down under them and on drawing his hand up there was nothing to it. He could still see the bullets there and tried it several times to get them. Then he got scared and ran off, saying it was "mache-manito" (the Devil). The old Indian said they looked afterwards but could not find the place.

On our return journey we made much better time as we had a frozen trail to travel on, except for the last hundred miles when a big thaw set in. Then there was water everywhere and we had to walk for seventy-five miles through it up to our ankles and knees. We were completely played out when at last we met a team and sleigh about twenty-five miles from Prince Albert and the driver took us the rest of the way in for twenty dollars.

A few days after my long trip north, I was sent to Saskatoon to look after the Barr colonists who were then arriving from England.[120] There were two thousand or more of them, mostly married, and a refined class of settlers. Although quite a few had no experience with farming, a large number had, and they buckled down to their new surroundings in real earnest. The government had reserved a large stretch of virgin prairie land, a hundred miles west of Battleford, a journey of two hundred miles from Saskatoon. The colonists had to purchase their transport and some got good bargains, but others were badly taken in. One party had bought a partly broken team of bronchos, guaranteed quiet; on a complaint, I made the vendor take them back and refund the money. Another case was of a party who bought a yoke of oxen at a big figure, guaranteed as fairly young and sound. They were afterwards examined and found to be twenty years old; the vendor on being interviewed replaced them with a younger yoke. There were many other instances in which the Mounties gave their protection and advice. After about three weeks, the roads being dried up, they all successfully got away to their different locations, naming their new village "Lloydminster."

On the trek, one party consisted of a husband, wife and children, a pony drawing a single-seated buckboard, the back part of it being piled up with a folded tent, several boxes and trunks. The third day out, late in the evening, they arrived at Eagle Hills, not far from Battleford, and came down a steep hill. Then they observed a very long, steep hill facing them that they had to climb. The husband was walking alongside the played out pony, which he was whipping on the back when his wife said, "John, whip him on the stomach." John turned with a weary look in his eyes and said, "Maria, I am saving his bowels for that further rise."

In June, 1903, complaints were received that a young German count was issuing bogus cheques. Prince Albert and Battleford were notified by wire with the result that he was captured at Battleford. On being brought down to Saskatoon under police escort, they stopped at the half-way house for the night and while in bed with a guard lying beside him, the count quietly committed suicide by taking prussic acid from a small phial bandaged under his arm pit.

About this time Constable Beckwith, while patrolling north of Saskatoon, stopped at a settler's home for a night's lodging. In taking off his coat, his revolver fell out of the holster on to the floor and discharged, shooting him in the abdomen. He died shortly afterwards in great agony.[121]

A day or two later, Corporal Spalding and I were waiting at the ferry to go across the river, which was quite high. As the ferry approached our side and was within ten yards of the shore, the apron of the ferry was let down. At that moment we saw a child tossed upwards over the rail out into the river. Both of us ran down the stream and Spalding swam out into the river, but the child never came up again. He was the son of the ferryman and evidently had been standing on the long arm of the apron. When this was released, he was thrown into the river.

Some time in July it was reported that Doukhobor settlers, fifty miles north of us, were appearing naked. I sent a constable with orders to make them put their clothes on. Two days afterwards I was shown a photograph of six or seven Doukhobor women, all in the nude, standing in line with my constable on the right. I immediately raided the only photographer in town and seized the negatives he had. The constable was arrested, fined a month's pay, and dismissed from the Force.

Late in the autum I was transferred to Battleford, the Barr colonists having made a request for me to look after them for the winter. I was instructed to have a house built for myself at Lloydminster, but this could not be done as there was no lumber to be obtained, so I visited there once a month through the winter.

During my stay of nearly two years in Battleford, I did all the magistrate's work, and some very important cases were dealt with. Besides this, I did orderly officer's duty day about.

On the first of June, 1905, I was transferred to Medicine Hat, where I took charge of a large district consisting of three, and later, four detachments, which I inspected once a month. In July, I supervised the building of a large dipping vat for mangy cattle. It was situated south of Maple Creek, close to the U.S. boundary, a very bleak and dry part of the country. One afternoon we had a terrific hailstorm which killed numerous birds and jackrabbits, the hailstones being five inches deep on the level. It lasted for nearly an hour.

In the autumn of 1905, the Mounties, two hundred strong under command of Commissioner Perry,[122] were at Edmonton and Regina attending the inauguration ceremonies of the two provinces of Alberta and Saskatchewan. We gave a display of troop and squadron movements at the walk, trot, and gallop, which were well-received by the large crowds present. I was honoured by being placed in charge of Lieut. Governor Bulyea's first escort.

Soon after my arrival in Medicine Hat, I found that horse stealing and cattle rustling were prevalent in the district, so we got busy and met with success in the long run. One man had been stealing thirteen years. Sergeant Ash arrested him and he was convicted and given three years' imprisonment. The evening after his trial, when in his cell, he was like a raging lion. When told his wife and two children wanted to see him, he said, "No, I want to see that son-of-a-bitch lawyer of mine. I gave him five hundred dollars to get a couple of witnesses from across the line for me and he never got them." He then finished with another string of oaths. The lawyer was informed but only shrugged his shoulders and laughed.

In another case of horse-stealing, the man implicated had had two convictions against him. He gave my men a long chase, nearly to Saskatoon, being caught hiding in a haystack. He was convicted and sentenced to ten years. There were also several convictions for cattle-stealing.

The first two or three years at Medicine Hat, there being no city police magistrate, I did the work and, with our own Mounted Police cases, it gave me a busy time of it. Then again in all our criminal cases a separate crime report had to be made out and mailed to headquarters. Constant patrols were made regularly and all complaints attended to.

In 1908, a religious sect called the "Dreamers" gave us a lot of trouble. They were supposed to be Russian Germans who had come across the line from Dakota and settled on land twenty miles east of Medicine Hat. Anybody who did not belong to their sect, they called devils, and would not shake hands with them. It appears that if anyone of them had a dream that a certain devil should be punished or harmed, they would, at one of their meetings, appoint one of their number to carry out the punishment. Their leader, a very fine looking man, was called the "Son of God."

On the eleventh of April, at midnight, a farmer[123] living close to these people had his $1,500 house burned to the ground. His wife and four children were nearly burned alive, escaping through one of the windows in their night attire. They then observed that a large rock and some smaller ones had been pulled out from the foundation and a quantity of gasoline inserted right under the floor of the house. The building had burned fiercely and virtually nothing was saved. Warrants were issued and in a very short time Corporal Humby and Sergeant Ash had arrested nine men of the Dreamers, the last being the Son of God.[124] As the wagonload approached his place he was seen running from the stables towards the house. Sergt. Ash being mounted got to the house first and, on opening the door, found a loaded rifle standing just inside. The man denied he was going to use it.

The preliminary hearings before me then commenced and lasted for twenty-one days. I think every lawyer in Medicine Hat took a turn at it. Some of the letters produced as exhibits were most disgusting and too filthy to read. After days of sifting into the matter, I found there was no direct evidence as to who had set the fire, but that one young Dreamer had committed perjury. He was held and charged with that offense. The other eight were lined up in front of me and told if they gave their recognizance in five hundred dollars each to keep the peace for one year, I would let them go. The Son of God then asked what would happen if they refused. He was told that they would probably each be given one year's imprisonment. They agreed in a hurry, each acknowledging the recognizance and were allowed to go. The other Dreamer was convicted on the charge of perjury[125] and was sentenced to eighteen months imprisonment.

The real leader of the Dreamers, whom they called their "God," was living in Java, South Dakota, and had been writing threatening letters to different parties that did not belong to their sect. In one letter he said, "Show this to your Satan Judge," meaning me. We sent several of his letters to our Commissioner in Ottawa who took the matter up with the U.S. authorities. They arrested the "God" who was heavily fined.

After my warning to the Dreamers that they must obey our Canadian laws or we would have to put them out of the country, the sect seemed to have broken up, as they gave us no more trouble. Apart from this I must say they were splendid farmers, raising good crops, and were hard-working people.

About this time there was a coal strike at Lethbridge, and I was ordered with my detachment to go there by train. Arriving at midnight, we were rushed out to the mines where there were two railway coaches occupied by our officers and men. Just as I was about to step into the coach to report my arrival, an explosion of dynamite took place within about twenty feet from me. Evidently it had been thrown to blow up one of the two coaches, but had fallen short. There were other explosions during the night, one man having the front of his house blown in. Several arrests were made and it looked serious that night, but in two days the strike was over and the men returned to work.

Soon after returning from the coal strike, smallpox broke out at Carlstadt (now Alderson), a village thirty-five miles west of Medicine Hat. There were five cases, all men who were placed in a tent under strict quarantine with a constable in charge. The disease did not spread and they were all well again in six weeks.

In the early autumn of 1907, Rudyard Kipling paid a visit to Medicine Hat, spending a day looking over the city and vicinity. A committee of five of us showed him over the industries and manufacturing plants, including the three large flour mills, iron foundry, clay products, and others. He was most interested in our natural gas and on visiting the CPR shops, the gas in the large forge was turned on at full blast, making quite a roar. He jumped back in astonishment, saying, "Medicine Hat has all Hell for a basement."

We then drove him to a high point which commanded a splendid view of Medicine Hat, when he exclaimed it was a city that was born lucky! Just before taking his departure at dusk, the city gave him a farewell blast by lighting one of their several gas wells. It went off with a deafening roar with a flame fifty feet high. Mr. Kipling said, "That is Hell, all right."[126]

One day a report was received from Manyberries, a small place fifty miles south of Medicine Hat, that the night before, five or six horses belonging to a storekeeper had been shot dead for spite by a suspect named Herrington. I left immediately with Sergt. Ash, and found that Herrington had disappeared. We collected good evidence against him and Sergt. Ash was given the job of finding the fugitive. In about nine months time, Sergt.

Ash arrested him in a British Columbia lumber camp. He was brought before me and sent up to the Supreme Court for trial. Pleading guilty, he was sentenced to five years in the penitentiary.

A young woman made a complaint that a man named Nix, under promise of marriage, had kept company with her for three or four years and that two children had been born, but she could not get him to marry her. I had him summoned and locked up for the night. At the office in the morning he spoke to me through the cell door, saying, "Mr. Parker, if it will help matters, I will marry the girl."

The girl turned up in a short time, saying she wanted the wedding to go on, and that her parents had consented to it. I then told the sergeant to take the prisoner to a jeweller to obtain the ring and license, and I would find the minister. The Rev. Mr. Morrow consented to perform the ceremony and returned with me; the sergeant and Nix then came back with the license and ring. The couple stood up, and as there was no best man, I volunteered for the job, and was smilingly accepted. The Rev. Morrow then performed the ceremony. After tendering them his congratulations, I took the bride's right hand and bent over to salute her when, with her left hand, she gave me an awful wallop on my right ear which nearly floored me. "Nobody kisses me but my husband," she said, and the minister, sergeant and constables all had a great laugh at my expense.

After nearly eight years' duty in Medicine Hat and district, on the first of November, 1912, by Order-in-Council, I was retired to pension.

Letters
1874–1882

Sarnia
April 5th, 1874

My Dearest Mother
    ... And now I have got some news to tell you; your dear old son Willie
is a North-West Mounted Policeman. I joined the force, or rather was examined and selected with twelve others, out of about a hundred & fifty at
London, Ont., yesterday. Directly I got back from Woodstock I saw the
advertisement in the paper & I wrote for information and was told to meet
Col. French at London yesterday. I went down Good Friday afternoon and
stayed all night because there was not an early train Saturday morning. Well,
nine o'clock Saturday morning I presented myself before the colonel who
asked me a lot of questions. But I had forgotten to carry my character with
me & the colonel said I had no show without it, so I immediately telegraphed
to Alfred [Barber] for one, and I had to get an answer back in two hours. Well,
I waited anxiously for Alfred's answer but it did not come. At last I thought
of the Bishop [Hellmuth] so away I runs about a mile & a half up town to
find the Bishop and luckily he was in his office at the chapter house or else
I should have been scooped. His Lordship was very pleased to see me & gave
me a bully character. I immediately ran back like a beggar afraid of being
too late but could not get near the room that the colonel was in, there was
such a crowd trying for it. But after many a hard squeeze and many a good
stamp on my toes, [I managed] to send my character in. Then Col. French
had me in & sent me up to the doctor to be examined. It was great fun; I
took a cab & told the fellow to drive as if the Devil was after him, and so
he did. Arrived at the Doctor's; he told me to peel off and he examined me
thoroughly, measured my calves & chest, arms, and your dear old boy turned
out to be perfectly sound after knocking about in Canada for three years.
    I go to Toronto to join on the 9th of this month, that is next Thursday.
I am not sure when we shall go up to Manitoba. I rather think that we shall
remain in Toronto some little time first. Everybody around here thinks it is
a splendid thing for a young man to go into. The pay is very good, for constables a dollar a day & Sub-Constables seventy-five cents a day and everything
found, travelling expenses paid, a bully good horse to ride upon, and if I serve
three years I shall get a grant of a hundred & sixty acres of land. But this
is where the tug of war comes in.
    I thought to have been home this coming autumn and see all you dear
ones but Providence has willed it otherwise so we shall have to bear it the
best way we can. It is most probably that we shall not be wanted three years

and if we are not we shall get the grant all the same. I shall also be able to save a good pile of money and if you come to look over the thing, it is a very good opening for me. . . . There is only a hundred & fifty of us & they are all, you might say, the picked young men of Canada as the colonel is very strict. A hundred & fifty applied at Hamilton and he only took fifteen out of that large number. The colonel is a very nice man and if I behave myself properly I daresay he will push me on. . . .

Ever your most affectionate son,
Willie Parker, NWMP

North-West Mounted Police
New Fort
Toronto
April 15th, 1874

My Dear Father
. . . I arrived here last Friday evening and like the life very well so far. All the men & horses have not arrived yet, but will do so in a few days. There are about a hundred & twelve men and seventy horses here now. I was out for my first ride today and got on very well; the saddles have not all arrived yet so we had to ride bare back. Some of the fellows are sent spinning over the horses heads. They are a splendid lot of horses & very frisky; the stables are also very good. We have splendid rooms to sleep in, the size of rooms 40′ x 30′, twelve men in each. There are quite a lot of decent young fellows joined and a good many of them are from England, two are from Kent. I am very fond of drilling, in fact, I was told that I had got on capitally for one that had never been drilled before.

At half past six we have to fall in & are marched to the stables, clean & feed the horses & finish them up, fall in again, marched back in front of our rooms & dismissed for breakfast at eight o'clock. At nine there is a general parade to drill, dismissed at half past ten, parade again at eleven for riding exercise, dinner at one & fall in for drill at two & again at five for the stables, tea at six. We can go down town from six to ten so you see we have not bad times at all. It is very nice for I have some friends in Toronto. . . .

Ever your affectionate son,
W. Parker

New Fort
Toronto
April 21st, 1874

My Dear Father
. . . [This] is such a dreadful noisy place that a fellow has not much chance to write a good letter. There are bagpipes being played right under me & the NWMP's brass band is playing out side and four noisy fellows playing euchre close beside me, so am pretty well surrounded. . . . I am quite well and like my new life very much. Col. French arrived today & we get new uniforms tomorrow; some of them got theirs today. It is very stylish; the coat is scarlet

& a very pretty shape & made for riding. The pants are blue with white stripe down them, top boot & spurs, cap with white round it. . . .

Ever your affectionate son,
Willie Parker

New Fort
Toronto
June 3rd, 1874

My Dearest Father

. . . We start for Manitoba on Saturday morning, the sixth of June. . . . I rather expect we shall have pretty good times at Red River; we shall camp out in tents on the prairies all summer & back to Fort Garry in the winter. There is most splendid shooting up there and I am taking my gun with me, which I hope will do good execution amongst the prairie chickens. From what I hear there is magnificent fishing so we ought to live well. I still like the life very much; we live very well. I am very fat & strong; have played in two cricket matches since we have been here. . . . We are going to take up a lot of cricketing things with us so that we can still keep up the old game although we shall be a good way from our friends. The officers have bought two good footballs and we play some fiery old games of an evening. The horse that I have got now is an iron gray and he is a splendid fellow, can jump like a good bay. . . .

Ever your affectionate son,
Willie Parker

Dufferin
Manitoba
June 26th, 1874

My Dearest Mother

I expect by this time you will all be wondering where I have got to. Well, here I am at Dufferin, just three miles across the boundary line, quite sound in body & mind, after travelling for a whole week by rail and another week marching across the beautiful prairie of the great northwest. The country here is very pretty; on one side is Red River and all along its banks the trees grow. On the other is the boundless prairie which looks like one beautiful green field. It stretches away for miles with not a tree in sight and all around where we are encamped the wild roses grow very thick. . . .

In about ten days we shall start for the Rocky Mountains & Saskatchewan Valley which is about eight or nine hundred miles across the prairie from here, so you see we have a long march before us. I shall see some funny sights before I get back to that dear old home that I long to see.

. . . You must excuse bad writing as I have to write on my gun case put across my knees. This country is full of game, prairie chickens & ducks & plover by the dozens. There is also plenty of fish but they are hard to catch in the Red River as the current is very strong. I have had a good many baths; the stream is so strong that you can't swim against it at all. The mosquitoes are very bad up here. I am very nearly chewed up or rather swollen up with the brutes. . . .

Ever your affectionate son,
Willie Parker

Dufferin
August 4th, 1874

My Dearest Father
. . . I have had a very severe illness of typhoid fever, but I am getting quite well & strong again now. The first week in July we started from here on our long journey out west across the prairies. Two or three days before starting I did not feel at all well & the day we started I was quite sick, as the Canadians term an illness. When we camped that night I went to the doctor who gave me a dose of medicine which had not a very nice taste, I assure you. The next day I was a good deal worse and some of the men were told to make me up a place to lay down on in a spring covered waggon, which was better than sitting up or riding on horseback in the hot sun.

We travelled for five days & I still kept getting worse, till at last they had to help me in & out of the waggon. So the major of our troop & the doctor determined to send me back to Dufferin where there were quite a few sick left behind when we started. There was also another fellow from "E" Troop sent back with me. We made the journey back in two days. The other fellow who came with me did not seem very sick as he sat up the whole of the way back & was talking with the driver while I had to lay down all the way. He, poor fellow; while I got better here, he got worse & died.[1]

The first ten days I was here I knew nothing about being here but thought all the time that I was in that dear home which I left more than three years ago. Since then I have gradually pulled round till three or four days ago the doctor gave me leave to get up; but I did not care to stay up very long & soon found my bed again. Now I am able to get about quite nicely & I feel that I get stronger every day. I take iron and quinine four times a day.

There are three or four married ladies here whose husbands are on the boundary survey and while we were sick they used to come & visit us & send us all the good things in their power. There is one Mrs. Almon who has been a good deal kinder than the rest. She would send us breakfast every morning, after dinner, and always cocoa for tea. She still continues to send me my breakfast every morning of eggs, toast & tea. The other two fellows that were sick in the hospital when I arrived have got well; they have gone to Lower Fort Garry for a change. Capt. Clark, our paymaster, thought it would be better for them. He told me he would get me there if I liked after I get strong & well. One of the two fellows that was sick, named Fortesque,[2] sergt. major of "B" or "A" Troop, is nephew to the Archbishop of Canterbury, so you see we have some gentlemen in the Force as well as some cads.

This is a most beautiful country if it was not for the mosquitoes & grasshoppers. The former are a dreadful nuisance; you possibly can't go outside the door without getting bitten by them. We all wear mosquito nets which are fastened on to our helmets or caps and comes down over our shoulders. The latter are even worse than the former, as they pass over the country in millions & eat nearly all the crops that the farmer has got. In fact in some places they make a clean sweep of everything. Is it not a great drawback to such a great country? There is supposed to be a fly which is destroying the eggs of the grasshopper. They breed on the sandy plains of Dakota just across the line & they come from there in a regular army. I shall not invest any of my money in any land till I see how things work unless it is a town lot which is a good speculation most times. . . .

We heard of the Force some time ago, that they were going along capitally & were over three hundred miles from here & about sixty miles south of Fort Ellice. The men were in good spirits & the horses holding out good. This is a good country for sport, plenty of prairie chickens & pidgeons. There is also a beautiful little lake about a mile from here which is always covered with wild ducks, so when I get well I shall likely have some good sport as I have my faithful gun with me. . . .

Ever your most affectionate son,
Willie Parker

Dufferin
August 24th, 1874

My Dearest Mother

. . . You need not be alarmed at me being scalped by Indians or eaten up by alligators, as the former are very friendly and as for the latter the largest in the river is a beautiful fish which weigh nearly thirty pounds & are called catfish. There is [sic] no snakes either so do not be alarmed on my account. This will be a great country some day & I only wish I had about a thousand dollars I could speculate in land & I could make quite a big fortune. I have been out shooting twice, and shot two or three different kind of duck & snipe. I have commenced to cook today & like it very much. I am going to make bread this afternoon. . . .

Ever your most affectionate son,
Willie Parker

Dufferin
August 30th, 1874

My Dearest Father

. . . I am afraid I have missed all the fighting if there is to be any, as our forces must be pretty close to the enemy now and if they do not come to terms our men will have more trouble than they bargained for. I am quite well again now, thank goodness, and I think in all probability that we shall move from here very shortly in about two or three weeks time. Our headquarters are to be at Fort Pelly, about two hundred miles west of Winnipeg. There are fourteen buildings to go up before the winter & the contractor is working away with a hundred men as fast as he can. Capt. Clark, the paymaster of our Force, was down the other day to pay us & he says the buildings are to be very pretty . . .

Yesterday afternoon I went fishing for a hour in the river & had splendid sport. I caught eleven goldeyes; they are beautiful fish, nearly a foot long & covered with beautiful scales. After fishing for goldeye I put on a sinker & fished in the bottom of the river & caught two catfish; one weighed over twelve pounds. It was fine fun hauling him in; he pulled tremendously but I landed him after a little play. We had him for breakfast this morning with some of the goldeyes. My, but he was splendid; he was so large and fat that there is enough left for dinner yet.

We are living tip-top. In fact I never want better grub than we are getting now. We have fresh beef every day, good bacon, fish & birds and plenty of milk & splendid tea, which are two great things. There are only four of us here now. I expect the fellows out west would not mind if they were in our shoes. It is pretty rough living when in camp & travelling, such a lot of them together. The three of us have to take the cooking week about. I have just finished my week & I succeeded gloriously. I cooked so well that the boys have got fat & lazy and they want me to continue but I know a trick worth two of that. There is splendid shooting now and I would be a duffer if I do not enjoy a little, so likely this week will see a good many ducks, chickens & pidgeons slaughtered. . . .

From your affectionate son,
Willie Parker

Dufferin
September 18th, 1874

My Dear Father

. . . I am happy to inform you all that I am once more my old self again, as strong and healthy as I was when I first joined the Force. As a proof of it, when I first was able to get about I weighed about a hundred and twenty; at the present time it is close upon a hundred and seventy. . . .

We are expecting to leave here every day for Fort Pelly, our headquarters. The stores that are here are to be shipped by contract this week. . . . I am looking forward for the winter with no little concern. It is a steady cold from one end to the other; the Red River freezes over in November. The boundary survey is finished & quite a few have arrived here already; they are undergoing great hardships and most of their horses are played out. Hardly any sick, that is, the men.

Ever your affectionate son,
Willie Parker

Dufferin
October 2nd, 1874

My Dear Harry

. . . I want to see a Manitoba winter. They say it is pretty sharp, below zero nearly the whole winter. I am preparing for it all ready. I have bought a coat & trousers made of moose skin. I paid ten dollars for them to De Lane; he wishes to be remembered to you. . . . We have been very busy since Monday, moving the stores down on the river bank to be shipped to Fort Pelly via Winnipeg. The boat we expected on Tuesday night did not come till last night and we had to keep sentry go for two days & nights over the goods. The first night I was on for five hours with my revolver & fourteen rounds of ammunition and a jolly big knife by my side. The second night we pitched a tent & had a big fire burning & the three of us kept down there. We leave here tomorrow for Winnipeg and I expect from there to Fort Pelly on the River Assiniboine. I feel sorry at leaving Dufferin as I have had splendid good times since I got well & strong from my illness. . . . I had my last day at the chickens today & shot eight which makes a total of a hundred & nine that I have shot since here. . . .

Ever your affectionate brother,
Willie Parker

Winnipeg
October 12th, 1874

My Dearest Father

You see by the heading of my letter that I have arrived at Winnipeg, or as this side of the river is commonly called, Fort Garry. . . . I left [Dufferin] early on Sunday morning with two horses & got here about noon on Tuesday.[3] I enjoyed my ride very much across the prairie had to stop two nights at half-breeds' houses and got very nearly eaten up with bugs. They gave me very good meals, only two a day, morning and night. I made a very good shot with my revolver off horseback, shot a prairie chicken clean through the head. I put him in one of the saddle pockets and half-breeds cooked him for my breakfast in the morning.

We are camped out in tents between the barracks & the town and it goes pretty cold. Last night it was very nearly at zero and for the last three nights have had about half an inch of ice. There are only eleven of us here, waiting for a telegram from Ottawa, when we shall proceed to Fort Pelly. I am afraid we shall have some cold camps before we reach there as it is about four hundred miles from here and we shall have snow on the ground before we reach our destination.

Winnipeg is a wonderful place for the time it has been growing. Three years ago there were only about a dozen houses; now there is a population of about five or six thousand & some beautiful buildings going up. Everything very dear, meat eighteen cents a pound, bread, five cents, sugar, sixteen to twenty. I want to try & buy a lot or two, but they are too big a sum; some near the town [are] four & five hundred dollars. I am saving nearly all my pay & shall not be able to spend any if we get to Fort Pelly this winter. . . .

We Mounted Policemen take the shine out of the infantry & artillery stationed here. We turn out great swells with out helmets & silver spurs. I am writing in their recreation room; they have a splendid billiard table in it. The government are acting very well towards us, in fact spending an immense sum on the Force.

Ever your affectionate son,
Willie Parker

My Dear Harry

... You see by the heading of my letter that I have again arrived at the former scene of my late illness. I wrote to dear Father when at Winnipeg informing him that we were going to Fort Pelly.... We started for the West on the 22nd of October late in the afternoon and only made three miles, so we camped close against St. James Church. We unfortunately tied some of our horses round the church yard to a picquet [*sic*] fence; they were very restive all night [and] I had to turn out three times, they made such a rumpus. One got clean underneath one of the waggons; I had to get another fellow & haul him out by the tail. Another one that was tied to the cook waggon managed to push the lid off a big box & eat & spoiled about thirty lbs. of sugar, packages of baking powder, six pounds of tea & coffee. [He] broke the flour bags open and pulled the hams out on the ground. When we awoke in the morning one of our finest horses had tried to jump into the church yard. He got his forelegs over all right but the halter shank stopped him from going farther and he was horribly spiked right on top of the picquets. They were sticking right into his belly. [We] had to run for axes & saw to extricate him [as] he was dreadfully cut about. The vet came out & managed to take him to Garry where he has since kicked.

It all happened through not feeding them hay. There was plenty close by, but it was so late when we got there and [we] were completely tired out that we did not know where to go for it.

We stopped there all that day to get everything in proper shape for our long journey. The clergyman came over to see us, the Reverend Pinkham, quite a young man & very pleasant.[4] I had quite a chat with him. We started the next morning, fourteen of us altogether, including a Methodist minister,[5] two half-breed guides & a civilian, fifteen horses, six Red River carts, one light & heavy waggon & a buckboard. I drove a cart & I think I had the best horse of the whole fifteen. He had never been in a cart before & showed his disgust by trying to run away two or three times. The third day out it became very cold & three inches of snow fell which made things not very pleasant. We had to pitch our tents & make down our beds on the snow. We travelled at the rate of twenty-five or thirty miles a day.

On the sixth day, when we were crossing beautiful plains & nearing the Riding Mountains, I was getting on my cart & had jumped on the shaft upon my knees, when my fiery Charlie went off like the wind. I was so muffled up that I could not get command of the lines, so [I] had to jump off the best way I could. I must have had a very narrow shave for it; in fact the wheel knocked me down but did not run over me. The fellows behind were sure I was hurt, but I soon showed them I was all right by asking Sergt. Meloy[6] for his pony which I mounted & went after him like the wind. He had run about half a mile when I rode alongside & caught him. No harm came of it except things [were] strewed all along the road. The captain called me into his tent that evening & questioned me all about it. He was [sufficiently] satisfied with my statements as to give me a hooker of whiskey. I was on guard that night; there were so few of us that one had to do it the whole night long.

Capt. Clarke is a very nice man; he was very kind to us. Before we left he was going to give us a champagne dinner, but he said he did not know how to do it, as he was afraid we would all get tight. We told him we would rather he gave us a present of something to take up on the march, so he gave us forty dollars to buy things for the mess & if we wanted any more he would give it. A bully fellow that, eh?

The seventh day we reached the little Saskatchewan River; it is [a] pretty place. We forded it & camped the other side. It was a dreadful cold night, down to zero. The next day we met a large ox train & there was a despatch for Capt. Clarke, saying that the colonel, with "D" Troop, were coming into Winnipeg, on account of the barracks at Pelly not being finished. The next day we met them. Oh, were they not glad to see us! Such shaking of hands and how do you do old boy, how are you? What a sight they presented, their horses as thin as laths and themselves, clothes all torn & dirty. Some had not shaved since they left Dufferin & helmets [were] all dirtied & knocked to pieces. The greater number of them [were] driving oxen or walking.

The colonel[7] gave us orders to turn back with them. We were within a day's march of Ft. Ellice [and] about eighty miles from Pelly. We had gone about two hundred miles when we met them. They had great tales to tell us about the buffalo; they were nearly starving when they first met the buffalo. They were seen in herds of thousands. One day they had all they could do to keep them from running through their train; there were eighteen shot that day. They are immense creatures. Some of the old bulls are about three times the size of an ordinary ox. One when it was dressed weighed close on seventeen hundred of meat. The boys used to eat above five lbs. a day when they first fell in with them. They also shot lots of antelopes when at the Buttes.

It is a peculiar thing, when they were forty miles from the Buttes[8] they looked only about ten miles away. They could see them eighty miles away. The smugglers all cleared out before they arrived there. Indians & everything had a mortal dread of the M. Police. For weeks they were in the Blackfeet country but never saw one [Indian] although the Indians were watching them on all sides. They mounted twenty-seven for guard every night while in the Blackfeet country. They had dreadful rough times of it. For two hundred miles near the Bow River there was not a bite of grass for the horses, what with prairie fires & the buffaloes [and] the horses nearly starved.

We arrived back in Winnipeg on the seventh of November & were camped out for a week with the thermometer at zero. Then we were put into some beastly old quarters for another week, when we were all ordered to Dufferin in three detachments. I came in the first [and] expect second tomorrow. This is a dreadful cold country; it is twenty-five degrees below zero now. Two of our fellows got frozen pretty bad. With the exception of my ears getting pinched a little I am all right & am in good quarters but sick of the Police Force. If the management does not improve I shall skin out.

Your affectionate brother,
Willie Parker

Dufferin
December 27th, 1874

My Dearest Mother
. . . We have spent a very Merry Xmas here. I was to have taken my Xmas

dinner at Mr. Almon's but he is running for member of Parliament for Manitoba and in consequence had to go away on Xmas day. He invited me over to dinner on Xmas Eve, and a very nice dinner we had. Mrs. A.'s plum pudding was splendid . . . .I spent a very pleasant evening there & left about ten and found the boys keeping Xmas eve with a vengeance. We drank to absent friends & relatives so often that I am ashamed to say I got a little tender in my feet & in consequence was very sick all Xmas day. But I am quite well again now. . . .

Ever your affectionate son,
Willie Parker

Dufferin
January 17th, 1875

My Dearest Mother

. . . Four of us had to go to Winnipeg with three teams & sleighs to bring back the fourth detachment of our men. We drove through in a day & a half, sixty-five miles. It was intensely cold, between thirty & forty below zero all the time. But we all managed to get through without being frostbitten. While there I went to a dance. The dances were chiefly quadrilles, but they have such peculiar steps up here that I did not partake of any. I danced two round dances & then left. Winnipeg is a most dreadful place for drink, in fact everybody seems to drink. I bought two town lots there last November for seventy dollars & two weeks after I had bought them I was offered a hundred & fifty for them but I refused it, as I expect to make more than that out of them some day. My opinion is that Winnipeg will be a large city at no distant day as Bishop McLane[9] of the Saskatchewan termed it the other night in church at Winnipeg the Metropolitan of the North West. We expect him here to preach next Sunday or the one after. Two last Sundays the clergymen from Winnipeg preached to us they got me to pick out the hymns and lead the singing. We got on capitally. When we have no clergymen, we have a church parade and the captain reads a chapter of the Bible to us. He sent for me this morning & asked if we could not have two hymns, one before the chapter & one after. I chose two, the old Hundred (Thy will be done). . . .

While I was at Winnipeg I got my right ear frozen & it is very soar yet. I was hitching in four dogs for Capt. Clarke & I did not think to cover my ears & I never noticed it till I got in the warm when it began to thaw out & then I felt it. On our return journey the morning we left, it was forty-five below zero. We had to go fifteen miles before stopping, the cold was intense & yet the sun was shining brightly. One fellow got his cheek frozen & we all had our noses pinched a little; the poor horses would be all white from sweating & all round our faces from breathing would be all white with ice & frost. How would you like to live in this country, dear Mother? I like it very well for the last three weeks the sun has shone from morning to night without even a cloud in the sky & it has never been above zero; it is always dry under foot. We have double windows to our 100 men and the fire is never out. We are at present very busy branding & numbering a hundred & fifty oxes [sic] that we have taken over from the boundary survey what with them & eighty horses we have here we are kept pretty busy, but still we are having an easy time of it. Today being Sunday we had a splendid plum pudding in our room & we are living very well. I have been recommended for promotion but do not know if I shall get it as there are a lot of good men in the field against me.

My friend Mr. Almon here ran for member of Parliament for Manitoba & was beaten by twenty-nine votes by a Frenchman, the voters being chiefly French half-breeds. They are very kind to me and I often spend the evening there if Dufferin is very dull. Not much reading to be had; chief amusement of an evening is playing cards. There are two bagatelle tables, chess boards, drafts and dice in store sent up by the government for the men but they are not given out yet. . . .

Ever your affectionate son,
Willie Parker

Dufferin
March 2nd, 1875

Dear Father
 . . . We received very sad news to day from Fort Whoop-Up where three of our troops are now stationed. Two of the men have been frozen to death, both of them were young gentlemen of good family in Canada. I knew them well; how sad it must be for their relations & friends.[10] We have had some very cold weather here. I think there was only two days last month that the thermometer stood above zero & the coldest that it reached last month was forty-five below zero. The colonel has been down here now for nearly a week. We had a very nice service last Sunday. The colonel read the lessons & prayers very well & we sang two hymns. I think the singing surprised the colonel. It was a very nice church parade, the men were dressed very neat & nice. . . .

We are kept very busy now as we have to draw our own hay from fifteen miles out on the prairie; it is rather a tough job on a very cold day, but then my turn only comes about twice a week.[11] I went out shooting to day, but the snow was so deep in the bush, that I soon got tired out with only one chicken. . . . [12]

Ever your affectionate son,
Willie Parker

Dufferin
March 15th, 1875

My dear Father
 . . . I have received my first promotion which no doubt you will all be glad to hear of. Yesterday I was promoted to act as a constable (acting constable). There is no increase in pay but it is much better than being a sub-constable. To day I entered on my new duties and had charge of a fatigue party with three teams drawing wood up from the banks of the river. [I] had to leave off at 11:00 A.M. & have not done anything for the rest of the day except go to evening stables. It was a terror of a day, could hardly see twenty yds. in front of myself. It is what they call a blizzard up in this country. . . .

There has been some talk I believe about disbanding the Force but nothing is certain. [Hon. Télesphore] Fournier, the minister of Justice, is passing a Bill to punish deserters from the Force with seven years' imprisonment & fined. I believe there is an order for us to be under canvas on the 15th of May. . . .

We have to draw our own hay from fifteen miles across the prairie. The other day [I] had to drive a four-in-hand & coming down the steep river hill lost control of my leaders through not taking off my big buffalo mitts, but managed to get through the difficulty.

Ever your affectionate son,
W. Parker

Dufferin
April 5th, 1875

My Dearest Mother

. . . I think I wrote & told you that I have received my first promotion to acting constable, and I am quite swellish now, with two very pretty gold stripes on each arm. You must excuse me if this letter is hurried as I am orderly sergeant for the troop this week which keeps me pretty busy calling the roll five or six times a day; this is my first day and I have done very well so far. Yesterday the Regiment Sergt. Major Griesbach, an old soldier & a son of an English clergyman, talked to me like a father & told me how to conduct myself in my duties, and said he hoped to see me a full sergt. by & by. He & Sergt. Meloy were the two with my good character that got me promoted. . . .

Ever your affectionate son,
Act. Const. Parker

Dufferin
April 20th, 1875

My ever Dearest Mother

. . . We have not had a south mail for over a week on account of the rivers overflowing and the ice breaking up, so that the stage from Moorhead, N.P.R., cannot cross. We have been having some lovely weather, the winter has quite gone. The Red River has risen thirty feet & if it goes on much more will soon be over the banks; in some places the ice is five feet of solid ice & is starting down to Lake Winnipeg. It is very pretty to see it; it jams & mounts a tremendous height. Ducks are very plentiful.

We are kept very busy drilling now & have been for the last fortnight; we get nearly nine hours a day of it, both riding & foot drill. I have got a very nice horse & he is beautiful & clean. All our horses look well now. Our oxen, which number 128, are out on the prairie at some large hay packs with four of our men & a sergeant. Sergt. Meloy has not left for England yet. I like the Force much better since I have been promoted. It is much better than being a sub-constable. . . .

Ever your affectionate son,
Will Parker

Dufferin
April 29th, 1875

My Dear Annie

... I have been out all the week about ten miles from here with another man, on the lookout for a deserter from Winnipeg. We stayed at a farm house & had very good times, had to search the stage every time it passed, but we were unsuccessful and returned yesterday. One day we saw a man walking at a great pace across the prairie and avoiding the stage station. So I shouted boots & saddle & we turned out in three minutes. We had to swim a river on horseback before we could get to the fellow, who turned out to be a large specimen of half-breed. He was a kind a skeared [sic] when we charged down on him. My horse swam the river bully. I put my legs up on his neck & held on to the saddle, and never got wet at all.

We have been having some very nice weather, the snow has been gone for some time and the river has risen a tremendous height—can water our horses right at the stable doors so you can fancy how dirty the water must be. We have to drink it because there are no wells sunk here. It was very pretty watching the ice go down the river. It used to get blocked & it was the amusement of an evening to get on it with poles & start it off. One night four of us went on a piece & it started off with us. I got right out in the middle of the stream & we had a longer ride than we expected as it went down the river nearly a mile before we could get [to] shore. ... We expect to be leaving here about the fifteenth of May for Winnipeg, where I believe we shall be stationed three weeks. My kind friend Mrs. Almon was confined of a son the day before yesterday. It is their first child; she is doing well. The first steamer of the season went down to Garry today.

Ever your loving brother,
W. Parker

Winnipeg
May 19th, 1875

My Dear Father

You will see by the heading of my letter that your dear son, the Mounted bobby, has arrived in Winnipeg. I left Dufferin last Thursday evening & arrived here Friday noon. I came on the new steamer *Manitoba*; she is a first class new boat built by an opposition line last winter. The fare now is more than one-half cheaper than last it was last year; she was very crowded, with three hundred passengers & 375 tons of freight. I enjoyed the trip down immensely. There was a Mr. & Mrs. Bray on board who I got an introduction to through Mrs. Bray being the owner of Spot, the dog I had shooting last summer. They were very nice & kind to me & Mrs. Bray gave me Spot which I am very glad of as she will be very useful out on the plains. They are both English & very well off. Mrs. Bray is a Kentish lady.

Now, dear Father, I must inform you of our movements & doings. You see we have been recruiting here, that is Sergt. Major Griesbach has, & he has got hold of some fine men. There are about thirty of them. The sergeant-major has been drilling them for the last ten days & they do him credit for I think they beat the old hands at it. In fact there is always a number of spectators looking on. Griesbach is a through [*sic*] Englishman, son of an old Yorkshire clergyman. It was him that sent for me to come up & help him with the recruits & for him to push me on a bit, for Dufferin was getting pretty warm for me since the colonel & Griesbach left. I was put under arrest twice & came being nearly reduced. Sergt. Meloy was the first to place me under arrest for not putting another man under arrest who was slightly inebriated. I got a great telling off from the captain who is not educated enough for the position he holds. I was admonished on that crime. The other was for joining in athletic sports when on the sick list & off duty. I had bruised my leg two or three days previous when out riding which made me a little lame, so the doctor put me off duty. The evening in question my leg was all right & I was passing where they were throwing a sledge hammer & I picked it up and threw it back to the parties that threw it. The hospt. sergt. saw me & placed me under arrest for that simple thing; up in the morning & fined three dollars.

We expect the rest of these men up from Dufferin at the end of this week. We shall likely remain here two or three weeks when we leave for Fort Pelly, so after you receive this, direct [your] letters to Pelly. . . . They are strengthening the Force. Our new uniform has arrived; will get photo taken & send home. . . .

Believe me your affectionate son,
W. Parker

St. James Camp
June 10th, 1875
Dearest Mother

Here I am sitting down in a bell tent, just after having my breakfast of bread & tea, and as I have a spare half-hour I take the opportunity of writing you a few lines. The troop arrived from Dufferin about two weeks ago & we were all camped close to Winnipeg for about a week when we were obliged to leave our tents for three days on account of so much rain; we were flooded out & very cold weather. We moved from Winnipeg last Saturday to St. James about two miles from Winnipeg where we are at present. It is a very nice camp ground, high & dry, any amount of grass for the horses which are looking very well. There is also any amount of grasshoppers, in fact there are millions of them. They are very small yet, but the farmers say they are eating all the crops off close to the ground. In fact [they] have done so [to] wheat that was six inches high. . . .

I am kept very busy this week as I am troop sergt., have to see & know about everything that transpires in camp. We are all in good spirits & I believe we start for the West in about four or five days. If nothing interrupts, shall be in Fort Pelly before you receive this. . . .

The colonel was going to make me a constable the other day but the captain spoke against me, so am still your loving son Act. Const. Parker.

Ever your affectionate son,
W. Parker

Swan River Barracks
North-West Territories
July 8th, 1875

My Dearest Father

I now have a little spare time, after our very tedious march from Winnipeg. We arrived here on the evening of the sixth, the evening before last making nineteen days since we left Winnipeg. We did not travel on Sunday. A Methodist minister[13] was along with us and we always had service. He is here with us now and I believe is to remain with us, sent by the government. I would rather he had been an English Church clergyman, but he is a very good man, and we sing our own church hymns.

Now I will tell you something about the march & our new home & headquarters of the NWMP Force. We left Winnipeg on the 16th June. All [were] in good spirits & health, with the exception of some of the boys who, knowing it would be their last chance for tippling, went into it pretty heavy & caused us a little trouble. There were very few mounted men as nearly all the horses had to go into waggons of which we had about thirty, & two of them, the Right & Left Division baggage waggons, were four-in-hands. There was also a very large bull train of fifty waggons which started four days ahead of us & we caught them up at the Little Saskatchewan River in the mountains a hundred & fifty miles from Winnipeg. We came along bully with the exception of a few waggons getting mired when passing through soft places.
. . .

Ever your affectionate son,
W. Parker

Swan River Barracks
July 22nd, 1875

My Dear Annie

. . . We have been here nearly two weeks and begin to find it rather dull. Some of the fellows gave a concert the other night & I believe it was very good. I was not able to attend, was in hospital at the time with a very sore throat and I was pretty poorly for a week but I feel alright again now. We are expecting a General Smyth who will stop here for a few days on his way to British Columbia. There is to be twenty of us to go as an escort with him. I do not think I am to be one of the escort although I would have liked it very well. To day they had a great turn out of both troops mounted; they were served out with blank ammunition with which they went through a great deal of skirmishes all round the barracks.

This is a dreadful country for mosquitoes in fact they are biting me so now I can hardly write. We have to keep smudges burning night & day so that the horses can go to the smoke when ever they like for sometimes they are nearly driven crazy by the flies & mosquitoes. . . .

There are no end of wildflowers around here; they look very pretty but a fellow cannot enjoy a walk very well on account of the mosquitoes which are a terror. And now I hear that the grasshoppers are coming quite close here by thousands. They have never been known to come here before. I am afraid if they come they will destroy everything in the garden & on the farm. . . .

Your affectionate brother,
Bill

My ever dear Mother

I have just arrived back from Winnipeg after being away five weeks. . . .
I have just answered Harry's letter; he wishes to join the Force & so I have
given him a full description of the Force & all its drawbacks. I do not recom-
mend him to join. We are working like niggers now, chopping & drawing out
logs to build a fence round the barracks a mile square. The fire has run
through the bark & the wood is all black, so we are a pretty looking sight
at evening. We are a small party here now, most of the fellows away on escort
at treaty-making with the Indians. . . .

I had a spiffin time coming up from Winnipeg, just one man with me.
We lived high all the way on fried chickens & ducks; we were two weeks
coming up, had pretty good loads on.

Ever your affectionate son,
Act. Const. Parker

Swan River Barracks
October 12th, 1875

My Dearest Mother

. . . You must excuse the writing as I am on guard. It is in a large tent
so I am sitting on the ground and writing this on my bed, as there is no table
in the guard tent. The last time I was in charge of the guard I was very
unlucky. There is a large flock of sheep here which are penned up every night,
and the guards have particular orders not to allow any dogs to molest them
but as it happened, about three o'clock in the morning, my sentry reported
to me that all the sheep were out of the pen and being chased by dogs. It was
very dark and [we] had great trouble to keep the dogs away & keep the sheep
together. When morning came there was one killed and four very badly
wounded, which have since died, and strange to say out of a hundred sheep,
the five that were killed belonged to the colonel, so you can fancy how mad
he was, especially after losing two beautiful horses, his own private ones. He
ordered an investigation to be held about the sheep and we have all been
examined & our evidence written down. I do not know how it will turn out,
but I hope all right. It is thought that the guard will have to pay for the sheep
killed, and that I shall be reduced.

I was out shooting today, you might say for the first time since I have been
here. I had pretty good sport with rabbits, shot fourteen of them, and one
partridge which is a very pretty bird & beautiful eating. I had such a load
that I could hardly get home with them. I gave the colonel a brace of rabbits
and the partridge hoping to get round him in the sheep business.

Capt. Walker brought from Winnipeg about three weeks ago, one of our
men who deserted from us in Dufferin a year ago last spring. The colonel tried
him and sentenced him to two months' hard labour. He has to work with a
sentry over him all the time. The fellow is a pretty hard case. I remember
him quite well in Toronto, so when I am on guard keep a pretty sharp eye
on him.

The colonel leaves tomorrow for two weeks shooting. I think officers &
men are glad to get rid of him for that length of time, as he is a terror for
making us work. We are hourly expecting the mail which was due yesterday
& has not arrived yet. Our men at Cypress Hills have taken three prisoners
down to Winnipeg to be tried for murder committed in the northwest.[14] A
few days ago a half-breed shot a white man at Fort Ellice and our detachment
at Shoal Lake nabbed him and have also taken him to Winnipeg.[15] This is
a miserable place to be in, and I only wish I was out farther west with our
men, who I believe are having a good time of it. I shall try all I can to go
out next spring.

Ever your affectionate son,
W. Parker

Swan River Barracks
North-West Territory
October 27th, 1875

My Dearest Mother
 . . . The winter has quite set in here; it has been freezing pretty sharp
lately, and today it is snowing quite fast; the ground is perfectly white. I have
been shooting two or three times lately. The first day I shot fourteen rabbits
& one partridge; second time shot eighteen rabbits & three partridges; third
time eleven rabbits, nine prairie chickens & two partridges; the last day I was
out shot eleven prairie chickens, two partridges and two rabbits. There are
a great lot of rabbits around here; they are just like the old country rabbit
only they do not burrow. They are turning perfectly white as the winter comes
on.
 We have moved from upstairs [to] downstairs, and the plasterers are hard
at work slapping the plaster on as fast as they can. Small detachments that
have been out all summer keep coming in. Capt. Clark arrived from Winnipeg
on Sunday last with another deserter;[16] he is lodged in the guard tent & will
likely be tried today. That makes two of them here now and they come in
very handy cutting up wood for the fires. I have not heard anything more
about the sheep business, but think it is all right. . . .
 I am orderly sergeant this week, which keeps me pretty busy. This is a very
poor place for news, and we are always glad to get hold of all the newspapers
we can. I do not see much chance for me being made a sergeant as there are
no vacancies and have all the bother of being the senior act. const. of my troop
and in charge of the barrack room, responsible for everything that goes wrong
with it. There are nearly forty men and it is no small trouble to keep order
amongst them, but still I manage to get along pretty well.

Ever your affectionate son,
W. Parker

My Dearest Father

... I have read the book written by Capt. Butler[17] on his travels through the N.W. Territory and I should say it is a very true picture of the country. We are now undergoing most severe weather tonight; it is forty-four degrees below zero; it cuts like a knife. I was on guard last night over two prisoners, two deserters of this Force who are in custody of the NWMP Force, one for two months & the other, four months, both with hard labour. They are very handy cutting wood for us. Well, it was a dreadfully cold night close on fifty below zero. I had to relieve the sentries every half hour and then they would get a little frostbitten. It was pretty tough on me, did nothing but keep relieving sentries but still did not have to remain out very long, just long enough to say "Sentries port arms, give over your orders, sentries pass, shoulder arms, front, sentry right about turn, quick march, half. Front. Port arms. Right turn. Large Arms." It is the form we go through posting & relieving a sentry.

We have splendid comfortable quarters; they are very warm. It was a good thing that we got them plastered. We shall have Xmas about our ears before we know where we are. So I wish you all a Merry Merry Xmas and a Happy New Year. ...

Ever your affectionate son,
W. Parker

Swan River Barracks
December 9th, 1875
My ever dearest Mother

... We are going to try and be as merry as we possibly can [for Christmas] under the circumstances. Have formed a mess and there is to be a large meeting of us tonight to settle what we are going to eat, and how large the plum pudding is to be. We intend decorating the rooms with pine branches; it is very much like your fir trees at home. We are all very merry as Xmas approaches; tonight I can hardly write for the merriment going on, most of them are together singing some very nice songs with jolly good choruses. The favourite is "We are Tenting Tonight on the Old Camp Ground." Another is "Tis Growing very dark, Mother" and "My heart still bends to those good old friends, to those good old friends of yore." These three are principally the favourites as they have a good chorus and remind us of old times.

We have been very well off for ministers this fall, or rather autumn. There were three of them, a Roman Catholic, Methodist & Presbyterian; the priest left three weeks ago, and the Methodist, Mr. Morrison, has been ordered by the government to leave and goes down by the mail tomorrow.[18] But "D" Troop are a generous lot of fellows and at a meeting of our mess last night, the motion was put to the meeting that we present him with an address and open a subscription list. I rose and had much pleasure in seconding the motion. It was carried by a large majority; the subscription was started immediately. I headed the list with three dollars; it was directly followed by five, and so on till within an hour, it rose to a hundred & one dollars and it has not been round more than half the men.

This is not the only thing our mess has done since it was formed. The man Mooney, who deserted our Force last spring and is imprisoned here for a period of four months, has a wife and large family in Winnipeg, who I believe are nearly starving. We immediately started a subscription list & with officers & men it amounts to a hundred & fifty dollars. The *Free Press* in Winnipeg, has accused one of our officers as being a tyrant & not fit to be over men & the said officer is likely to lose his commission over it as there is an investigation pending. We drew up an address to Capt. French flatly denying the accusation, expressing our feelings that he was anything but a tyrant. . . . [19]

I think you would like to take a peep at our room at the present moment. It looks very clean & nice, the beds are arranged on each side, the bed tick neatly rolled up & the blankets folded on top, & over each of the beds a buffalo robe is spread. In the centre is the table; it is so clean & white that it is like the snow. I see that the table is laid out, the plates, cups & saucers are enameled blue on the outside & white inside. The knives & forks are clean & there are four plates of bread all ready cut in the centre of the table. Our fare is very simple: bread & coffee for breakfast, generally roast beef & potatoes for dinner, bread & tea for tea, but we often have extras, as we subscribe a dollar & a half each month towards buying them. . . .

Your affectionate son,
William Parker

Swan River Barracks
North-West Territory
January 4th, 1876

My Dearest Mother
The last mail arrived here at a most appropriate time, just three days before Xmas. Directly the mail was seen coming through the gate, there was a general rush made for it, the dogs were caressed, and called most affectionate names for coming through in such good time, a hundred and forty miles in two days. Being Xmas there was a large mail. I was one of the most lucky ones; received seven letters. Perhaps you can imagine how lively I dived into their contents. Yours were the first, there were three, one enclosed by Harry, and two swell ones straight from yourself, one from dear Father which was very interesting, one from Harry who did not injure himself by writing too much, one from old Tadpole,[20] telling me of the splendid times he enjoyed at St. Mary & he thinks he would like to become a "buck policeman." The last was from my kind friend, Mrs. Almon, at Dufferin; she says the weather there is most disgraceful, forty below zero when she was writing. . . .

We have been having a very Merry Xmas. In the first place we decorated the room, which I assure you looks really beautiful and would do credit to any civilized country. In one end facing the door is an evergreen arch, with a Merry Xmas on it in large red letters, underneath is a crown with two small Union Jacks on each side, under that again are two carbines crossed and two Royal Standards on each side, with a star of ramrods between, and at the bottom of all, our best friends in need, the Babcock fire engine polished up very bright. At the opposite end, another arch with a Happy New Year on it, and underneath, God Save the Queen, in evergreen letters made by myself in the old St. Mary's style. I must say, though I shouldn't, they were much admired by the fair sex. The three pillars in the centre were covered with evergreens, and all along the centre of the ceiling there were wreaths all round the room, and on the walls between each window a ring of evergreen with two carbines crossed over them and two revolvers crossed inside the ring. In each window hung a sort of birdcage made of evergreens with a candle burning in the centre. There were three evergreen chandaliers [sic] hanging up the centre of the room.

But the dinner was the main thing, three tables struggling under the weight of good things of every description. It would take up too much time & room to name them all, nevertheless I can give you a little insight into the matter. There were four hundred & fifty pounds of roast beef, the choicest joints, rabbits cooked in about sixteen different ways, prairie chickens & partridges, mutton hot, mutton cold, seven cold hams. The pastry composed of sixty pounds of plum pudding, fifty-four pies of every kind of canned fruit, such as gooseberries, peaches & stawberries. After all this came soothing jellies of different varieties, almond & raisins & plates piled high with candies or rather, sweets. But there was something we missed greatly and that was a wee glass of wine. Coffee & tea were poor substitutes at Xmas time.

After dinner was over and we had had an hour's breathing, the pleasures of the evening commenced. Amongst the visitors were Col. & Mrs. French, Col. Griffiths[21] and his two fair daughters, two sub-constables' wives and all the officers; we all enjoyed ourselves thoroughly. One of our sub-constables, who has been an old lawyer in his time, took the chair and he fulfilled his position bully.[22] I was called upon to open the proceedings with a song which I did by singing the "Roast Beef of Old England"; it took immensely. Then the speeches & toasting commenced. Some of the speeches were bully & there was great laughter. The toasts were given by three lusty cheers. The dear ones at home seemed to get the loudest cheer. We were complimented greatly on our decorations; there were some splendid songs sung & some very good singers amongst us, although I cannot sing worth a cent. The proceedings broke up about twelve o'clock, after thoroughly enjoying ourselves. There was also a shooting match between the officers; the Canadian officers came out victorious.

We are now very busy preparing to meet the New Year. There is to be a dance and grand shooting match between English, Scotch, Irish, and Canadians; it is looked forward to with great interest and will be hotly contested, five men to represent each nation. We were practising today. I did pretty good, came out second best.

I am afraid you will think your son Bill a course 'un when he comes home; never mind, I will try my best to please you. I wish you would be so kind as to send me three or four songs & glees such as the "Roast Beef of Old England," "All amongst the Barley," "See our oars with feathered spray," & "Maggie May." I think those four are the ones I would like to have the most.

Ever your affectionate son,
W. Parker

Dear Annie

... I am having at this present time the honour of doing the first guard in our new guardhouse. It is a splendid, snug little house & very warm; there are two rooms with a stove in each, also three strong cells for prisoners. ... Everything is new in the place; they only plastered it last week and they had quite a time getting it dried, but now that it is dry it is almost too warm and yet it is about forty below zero outside. I see the sentry passing the windows to & fro, his muffler that is round his neck & face is all ice & frost; in fact you would wonder how he stands it without getting frozen. Being the first guard in the new house, it had to be celebrated by what the boys call a tuck-in, which means get all the good things that can possibly be bought at Jones' Store, at a fabulous price, such as preserves & canned fruit of different kinds. But a most extraordinary thing happened; the tea that we made proved to be old stingo. It was very strong & as we thought & said, "went spyffin." But I had my suspicions and on examining the kettle I found no less than twenty rounds of carbine & revolver ammunition had been boiled with it. The tea & sugar had been emptied into a small box in which we keep some of our ammunition and the man that made the tea did not know of this so he put the whole thing into the kettle. We are none the worse for our cartridge tea but feel bully after the tuck-in, or rather supper. My turn for guard comes just once a week and it is a pretty soft thing, that is for me being in charge. All I have to do is relieve the sentry every two hours so am in the warm all the time. One of the boys, while at stables this morning, got a bad kick for a horse; I saw them carrying him over to the hospital.

Ever your affectionate brother,
W. Parker

Swan River
North-West Territory
March 29th, 1876

Dear Father

... After being cleared out by the grasshoppers five succeeding years, some of the farmers [of Manitoba] are in a destitute condition. It is a great pity as Manitoba is a splendid farming country if it was not for the hoppers. They laid their eggs very thick around here last fall so they are sure to be as bad as ever this year. We commenced our spring drill two days ago and it comes pretty tough on us at first, five hours a day steady at it, chiefly extension motions to begin with, and I feel stiff all over. But it is good for a fellow, makes a different man of him after loafing all winter. We fortunately have a very good drill instructor and I shall make the most of him and try and learn all I possibly can, shall find it very useful some day. The weather has been and is now splendid, beautiful sunshiny days; the snow is disappearing fast, although it is two feet deep on the level yet.

The seal of government is not going to be here as supposed, but at Battle River a hundred & fifty miles west from here & eighty from Fort Carlton on the north branch of the Saskatchewan. ...

Your affectionate son,
W. Parker

Fort Pitt
North-West Territory
September 10th, 1876

My dear Father

I have travelled five hundred miles since I last wrote home and will most probably travel seven or eight hundred more before you will receive another letter from me. We leave here tomorrow for Battle River then south to Cypress Hills and from there west to Fort Macleod for the winter. The Canadian government are putting nearly the whole Force along the boundary line in case the Sioux Indians try to cross the line while the Yankees are pitching into them. . . .

I have not had a chance to post this letter yet, so will write you a few more lines. We left Fort Pitt on the 12th after tough work getting across Saskatchewan and arrived here on the 16th inst. So you see that we have been here nearly a week. I was afraid we might leave before I could write, as I have had a dreadful bad hand. The night we crossed the river at Pitt some poisonous insect or animal bit me on the wrist & it swelled up to an enormous size; it has been very painful. The doctor lanced it the day before yesterday & now the swelling is commencing to go down so I am now able to use my fingers.

Your affectionate son,
W. Parker

Fort Macleod
October 31st, 1876

My dear Father

I have at last found a little spare time, so take the opportunity of writing to you, just to let you know that your son Bill is all hunky, that is, he is taking good care of himself. . . .

We arrived here on the 23rd inst. after performing a march of over 1200 miles. Sometimes in crossing the plains, where nothing grows but cactus & sage bush, we would have no water & of course, no supper. What we call a dry camp. In crossing the big plain we did not see a stick of wood for weeks, had to burn buffalo chips which made a very good fire when dry, but if it rains we are gone up, no warm cup of tea to cheer a fellow after his long days march. . . .

This is the worst fort I have been into yet for comfort. The buildings are miserable, mud floors & mud roofs, so when it rains there is a devil of a mess. I am now in charge of the guard, one corporal, six men & five prisoners. Three of the prisoners are in for horse-stealing & the other two for murder, so I have to be on the alert all the time.

Ever your affectionate son,
W. Parker

Fort Macleod[23]
January 6th, 1877

My dear Father

. . . You ask me if I intend giving up the Force. I shall certainly not let the Force stand between me & all the dear ones I love better than gold. I have been thinking of taking on again if they will give me six months' furlough. The conditions of taking on are three months' furlough, forty dollars and a hundred & sixty acres. The last does not amount to much as there are millions of acres in the northwest open for settlement. Of course, it is not a very good country for farming as the winter is so severe and yet I believe the winter here is milder than in Canada. There is hardly ever any sleighing here. The land is not very good around Ft. Macleod, but I am wandering away from my subject. Under the circumstances, I think I cannot do better than take on again, as I hear times are pretty tough all over, but it is only on condition that they give me the six months' leave. You see, my pay will be going on all the same & [I] shall get the forty dollars. If I do not take on, the government would have to pay my way from here to Canada, which amounts to quite a sum from this out of the way place. In the new engagement we have to pay our own way at the end of our three years. I have fully made up my mind to see you all some time this year if God in his mercy will spare us. . . .

Ever your affectionate son,
W. Parker

P.S. Please excuse this Yankee paper. I dislike it very much myself & anything that is Yankee. Old England & her good old style for ever. W.P.

Fort Macleod
January 16th, 1877

My dear Annie
. . . We were all turned out the other day in a great hurry, had to mount our horses bareback as we had no time to put the saddles on, and were galloped away ten miles to put out a prairie fire which was raging with great force & threatened to burn up the only grass left around the Fort. When we arrived [we] were divided into two parties each under an inspector. We threw off our coats & pitched in; it was terrible hot work as we only had empty bags to beat it out with. Sometimes, where the grass was thick, the flames would rise fifteen feet high. We commenced work at 10:00 A.M. & managed to put out the side next to the fort just as the sun was setting. Several of us got burnt & my whiskers that I had blocked out to come home in are singed off, also my eyebrows & eyelashes. It was a plain we were working on so there was no water to be had. The only way we could get a drink was by going to the buffalo wallows where we would sometimes find a handful of snow. The weather we are having is delightful & has been so for the last month. It freezes middling sharp at night & then comes out a beautiful, bright warm day. I now & then have a skate on the river.

Your affectionate brother,
W. Parker

Fort Macleod
January 18th, 1877

My dearest Mother

... I was told by my teamsters who come out from the fort every day that there were four letters for me & that they had forgotten to bring them, so I determined to walk in for them the next day. The day came & with it a terrible storm of wind & snow; it was also very cold. Although I had to face it, it did not daunt me with such treasures as your dear letters waiting for me. It took me nearly four hours to reach the fort, having lost myself once on the prairie, but after circling round in the storm twice I managed to discover the river again & you bet I did not leave it till the fort hove in view. When fine we can walk to the fort in an hour and a quarter, but how well I was repaid. I made a beeline for the letters then for the sergeant's mess with a good warm coal fire, then into a solid rocking chair, and then the best of all, a jolly good read....

I suppose you are anxiously looking forward to my return. It is not much more than two months when my three years' service will expire and I cannot say for certain if I shall be able to come home then or three or four months later on in the summer. But you may depend on me seeing Old England & all you dear ones sometimes this year, God willing....

Your affectionate son,
W. Parker

Fort Macleod
February 15th, 1877

My dear sister Alice

... Times are very dull here. I am still with my party of men cutting wood; since I last wrote we have moved six miles from Fort Macleod. On our arrival here we set to work and built ourselves another house; it is a famous structure & does credit to us. It's a long way ahead of our first. Luckily the last three weeks we have been having lovely weather, quite warm; we slept out in the open air three or four nights till the roof was on the house. The wolves & owls made a queer old noise around us every night. We could hardly sleep for them, but now we are in our house & nice & comfortable we are. I wish you could take a peep at us, you would think I was leading rather a strange life, but it is honest & that is the main thing....

We shot a buffalo cow the other day; it was very fat & makes famous eating. We also shoot a good many prairie chickens. I have not been smart enough to get another deer; they are too wary for me. Our herd of horses are kept close by here so I shall catch one tomorrow and ride into the fort to see if the mail is in. I shall enjoy the ride across the prairie as there is no snow & we are having splendid weather, so different from Swan River....

Your affectionate brother,
W. Parker

Fort Macleod
March 14th, 1877

My darling old Mother

. . . Colonel Macleod, our Commissioner, is on his way from Canada with a hundred & forty recruits. You will see by my letter to Annie that I have re-engaged in the Force again, on a promise that I have five months' leave to see all you dear ones again, but I do not know when they will let me go. I do not think it is possible to get away this summer; perhaps I shall be able to in the autumn. The country around here looks beautiful; the grass is so green & the prairie is covered with different flowers. I only wish I could present you with the nosegay I have just picked, but suppose wishing will not do any good, so will enclose a few of them.

I am still with my wood party & have a boss old time. We find it rather warm cutting wood [in] this weather & the mosquitoe begins to find out where the best blood circulates. I have been having some glorious fishing. Yesterday I was out & caught twelve, the largest three feet long. I sent them as a present to my friends at the fort. The shooting also is pretty good. I see hanging up before me now six ducks, two curlews, two plover, one moorhen, seven real English snipe, and two hares, also two chicken. You must not think I bagged the whole of them as it is between three of us. Directly the spring opened I set to work & made a garden. I found it hard digging for ground that never saw a spade before. My green peas are coming up good, also radishes & onions; the garden is more of an experiment than anything just to see how things will turn out in this part of country.

Your affectionate Son,
W. Parker

Fort Macleod
March 31st, 1877

My dear Father

. . . Your idea of Ted joining this Force, that is if he returns home, I think is a very good plan if they would take him on. They are very strict in taking on recruits who have to know a little about riding & undergo a very strict examination by a doctor, as this is a pretty rough life after civilization. He must not mind having only dry bread & tea sometimes twice a day out of the three meals. If I can get home sometime this year I shall be able to judge if he would suit. . . .

Your affectionate son,
W. Parker

Fort Macleod
April 27th, 1877

My dear Annie

. . . I must give you a little insight into what I am about. The first thing is that I am a Mounted bobby for three more years. Two weeks ago I did it by taking the oath of allegiance to our Great White Mother, as the Indians call the Queen, and also the oath of office, but before doing so I was promised five months' leave to come & see you all. I cannot say for certain when I shall be able to get away as they will not let me away this spring. I shall try the fall with them if I see any show of getting away. I am still with my wood party & we have a very good time of it. We are busy now building a canoe to cross the river with. I have been enjoying some good fishing & duck shooting, in fact we partly live by the rod & gun. . . .

[Whist] is about the only game of cards I play at. Gambling is carried on to a great extent in the town at the fort, but this rooster steers clear of such work. There are a great number of hard cases knocking about who have very extraordinary names, such as Slim Jim, Spanish Joe, Dutch Fred & Buffalo Bill; some squaws the same, such as "The double-barrelled-pair-of-scrissors" and "The-good-stealer."

Your affectionate brother,
W. Parker

Fort Macleod
June 6th, 1877

Dear Father

. . . I wish you could see my garden that I have made here in the bush; the peas are just taking hold of the stocks, onions, radishes, & lettuce nearly fit for the table. I put in a small patch of wheat & it looks splendid. There is also scarlet runners, turnips, tomatoes & Indian corn. I put up a good substantial fence around it, in case I am called into the fort as I am just through cutting the dry wood. The assistant commissioner wants me to cut green wood for next winter. I do not know if I shall take it or not.

The country is looking beautiful, in fact it is a second Emerald Island, it is so green. The prairies are one mass of flowers which smell delicious when I take my evening walk. The bush here is full of wild gooseberries & strawberries; the former are at present rather nasty to work amongst on account of the thorns, but when the gooseberries are ripe we will not mind them so much.

We have been having large quantities of rain which is very beneficial for the garden. The feed for horses & cattle is glorious; they are all rolling fat. I think stock-raising would pay well here although a fellow is liable to have them stolen, more especially horses. Two nights ago about thirty of the best horses were run off by an expert horse thief & he has only just got out from our guard house after putting in a year for the same offence. There are several parties out after him. He is a desperate character & will not allow himself to be taken alive so if they come up with him there will be warm work as he has two or three accomplices & they are all armed with sixteen shooters.

The Indians here are all preparing for the treaty this fall. It commences on the 1st of September and I expect it will be quite a sight. The Blackfeet seem favourable for a treaty, the Peigans & Bloods and Ponderays are against it, and may cause some trouble.

Last Sunday my lads went for a hunt and one of them shot a lynx just as it was in the act of springing on him. It is a large beast measuring over five feet in length & something like a cat. We celebrated the Queen's birthday in great style at the fort, at 12:00 a Royal salute of twenty-one guns was fired from the nine-pounders; in the afternoon a rifle match took place. The ground being too wet on the 24th the athletic sports were put off till the 26th when every lad seemed to enjoy themselves [*sic*] thoroughly. I managed to take away four prizes, two firsts & two seconds; everything was well-contested, especially the "tug of war." I was captain of one side. Both sides were doing their level best when the rope broke & both sides lay pretty level; there was great laughter by the onlookers. The day's amusement finished up by two very good horse races. I think there is to be more sports on Dominion Day, the 1st of July, so I am training a little so as to stay with the boys and not let them quite run away from me; a good many are training.

We expect the recruits up shortly to replace the 1874 men that have left the Force. We have a visitor this afternoon, a Coutenay [Kootenay] Indian from the mountains. He is sitting before me & staring with all his might at me slinging ink at you. He is a very red warrior & smells as strong as those tame rats that I used to keep at home. Some of them are great for hanging around if there is any chance for some grub; the poor beggars are nearly always half-starved, especially when the buffalo go south.

Your affectionate son,
W. Parker

Fort Macleod
June 22nd, 1877

My dearest Mother

. . . I have finished my wood contract to satisfaction and am now in the fort at duty again. It is an agreeable change as it commenced to get very hot & the mosquitoes very bad working in the bush. We are very early risers, reveille at 5:30 A.M., drill from 6:30 to 7:30 before breakfast. . . . We have been having splendid weather lately and the gardens look beautiful, especially the regimental one which is very large, supplies the whole Force with vegetables. [A] good many of the men have private gardens of their own.

We expect every day to hear that England has gone to war with Russia. I see that the Canadians are offering ten thousand men to the English government if they do go to war. It is very good on the part of Canada; she is a colony that England and Englishmen ought to be proud of.

Your affectionate son,
W. Parker

Fort Macleod
July 8th, 1877

My dear Annie

. . . We are very busy here & drilling hard. I get two drills with the sword daily & the chief constable says that I am going to make a good swordsman as I make some vicious old cuts & points when going through the exercise. There are sixty recruits expected here sometime next week; they are on the road between Fort Benton & here. Forty more went to Cypress Hills. I hear there are quite a lot of swells amongst them; one is the nephew of a lord &

two others have held commissions in Her Majesty's service, but this is the place to take the swell out of them. I am to have a squad of them to drill.
. . .

I had a letter from Cartwright this morning; he seems happy & getting along alright. He says our baggage has arrived there & will be forwarded shortly. He saw my old gun case amongst it. How well do I remember when the same old gun case was laying open in Father's dear old study with Harry's beside it for inspection by our friends. . . .

Today is Sunday & we had a very nice service this morning. The singing was delightful & we still keep to the old tunes & chants. How I long to see the dear old church again & listen to the dear old governor preaching. . . .

I had a very nice ride this afternoon down the river to a dairy farm where I was given any quantity of cream & milk to drink. The prairies look lovely. We have been having terrible heavy rains & might just as well have been outside as in the barracks as all the roof is composed of is dirt. We had to move into the Q.M. [quarter-master] stores as they have shingle roofs.

Your affectionate brother.

Fort Macleod
August 6th, 1877

My dear Father

I was delighted yesterday by receiving a very kind letter from you dated June 13th and more so to know that you think I did right by engaging with the Force again, the only drawback is my not being able to come home this summer. I have seen Colonel Macleod about my leave. He said that I could go to England next spring on my three months' furlough, that it was not in his power to give me more but he will write to Ottawa for two months' leave and thinks there will be no difficulty in me procuring it. I might possibly be able to come this fall if a good chance offers for me to get down to Winnipeg, but the spring is best as I shall be able to travel cheaper & quicker, which will make a great difference both as regards pocket and pleasure. . . .

I only wish you could see our regimental garden; it looks better than any garden I have seen since I left the old sod. We have as many as six or seven different kinds of vegetables for dinner every day, also some very good salads; the new potatoes are very large, in fact everything looks splendid. I got a rise [sic] in my pay of ten cents a day from the 1st of July, which makes it a dollar a day, but of that I have to pay fifteen cents a day to sergeants' mess and the washing is very dear here, $1.50 a dozen, but still I am able to put a little for a rainy day.

Fifty recruits have arrived here & the place is quite lively again. They are a fine lot of young fellows & a good many of them young gentlemen. We are putting them through their drills—three rides a day besides three hours of foot drill that they get at the hands of we sergeants. I have a squad & I have been complimented once or twice on the way in which they drill. They do very well seeing they have never been drilled before. We old hands get an hour's squadron drill before breakfast at six in the morning when it is nice & cool. They give us a great deal of skirmishing as that is the way we are supposed to fight the Indians on the plains, if we ever do come to the scratch, which is not likely.

The Blackfoot nation have presented a wonderful bear skin robe to the Force in token of their thanks for suppressing the liquor traffic, by which they are all becoming well-off again. The robe is painted all over in brilliant colours showing where all the different tribes with their names are situated. There are also paintings of [Mounted Policemen] on horse back riding up & capturing the whiskey traders while in the act of trading it to the Indians who are drunk & murdering each other. The Great White Mother is represented standing by a [Mounted Police] officer looking approvingly on & giving orders to the officer for his men to capture the traders. There is also a big medicine pipe presented with it & the sides are trimmed with war eagle's feathers. . . .

About two weeks ago we received our baggage which was left behind at Swan River last summer. I was very glad to get mine although quite a few things have been stolen by those black half-breeds. On the whole I must think myself lucky as I did not lose half as much as some of them who had watches, money & jewellery stolen. You see, when we left Swan River we all thought we should return there & were only allowed to take a field kit. My album arrived safe & I have been devouring the photos ever since. My bible that you gave me when I went to Redland Knoll is safe & sound. We have church every Sunday in the recreation room, the Commissioner reads the prayers & the singing is very good. I have not procured my land warrant yet; the Canadian government are so slow in doing business.

Your affectionate son,
W. Parker

Fort Macleod
August, 1877

My very dear Annie
. . . We have been having & are having dreadful hot weather. It is often ninety in the shade at eight o'clock in the morning & rises from that up to a 106, once to a 109½, and we have to drill to have the recruits ready for the treaty. Three of them have been sunstruck but not very badly. The other day one got his leg broken by being thrown from his horse.

There is great preparation going forward for the treaty with the Blackfeet nation. We have to march about one hundred miles which is thought a very short distance in this country to the Blackfoot Crossing on the Bow River, where we expect to meet about 10,000 Indians of different tribes. This is the last treaty to be made on this side of the Rockies and will be a grand affair. The band will accompany us, also our two nine-pounder guns, with six horses on each gun. We shall fire a few rounds just to show the Indians what they will do. Our force will number about 130, including officers, not a very large body amongst so many, but still the Indians have a great respect for Queen Vic redcoats, who are not a bad lot of fellows and determined to do their duty.

You ask me if I have met with a young lady yet. This is the last place in the world to find one, but still I have my eye on a very pretty squaw. Come now, wouldn't you like her for a sister? I am afraid she would make you all feel squeamish if I was to fetch her home, which there is no chance of my doing. . . .

If I go to the treaty I am going to get some Indian curiosities to bring home with me next spring. I have already had made a small teepee or lodge to bring with me, but it wants painting yet. . . . There is a great stir this evening in barracks preparing for a mounted field day for us all tomorrow. There is generally lots of fun, fellows being thrown & a few runaways. We have just taken over fifty splendid young horses, some of them are buckers from away back & will give some fun breaking them in.

Your affectionate brother,
W. Parker

Fort Macleod
September 8th, 1877

Dearest Mother

. . . Last Tuesday the lieutenant-governor of the North-West [Territories][24] arrived here. Col. Macleod took the two troops & the artillery out to meet him & escort him into the fort. We met him about two miles out. He was agreeably surprised to see such a large turnout of redcoats, all mounted. The artillery fired a salute of thirteen guns & as we came through the town the citizens presented him with an address very appropriately worded; he replied from his carriage & was cheered several times.

Yesterday was field day for us all; we were put through a whole lot of manoeuvres & great deal of skirmishing drill to finish with a march past in review order. The governor was greatly pleased & flattered us very much. We are all under canvas now, camped just outside the fort, getting into shape for our march to the treaty. I think we leave on the 12th or 13th. I shall take my gun along as I hear there is good shooting along the road. . . .

Your affectionate son,
W. Parker

Fort Macleod
October 29th, 1877

My dearest Mother

It is quite a long time since I last wrote home & I hope you have not been uneasy about me as I am perfectly safe and sound. The treaty with the Indians went off very satisfactorily. . . .

Old Crowfoot, the chief of the Blackfeet, is a fiery looking chap & has killed many a white man in his time. He said he only wished he could read and write but hopes his son will be able to do so before he dies. The government paid every man, woman & child $12.00 each when they took the treaty, so some had a large amount of money, as most of the chiefs & bucks have as many as five wives each. They would always come over to us & get us to go and count their money for them, as they would not trust the traders. When they wanted to buy a horse they would get the first Mounted Policeman they could see to go and pick a good one out for them & count out the money for it. The poor things were cheated greatly by the traders who had things there to sell, as they did not understand what the money was worth & could not tell the difference between a five dollar bill & a one.

We had splendid weather while at the treaty, till we started for home when it turned very cold and [we] had snow all the way back, but since we arrived [we] have had the Indian summer which is splendid weather. The sun rose & set for two weeks without a cloud in the sky & the country [was] enveloped in a blue haze. Directly after our arrival here from the treaty I had a chance of going with a party of our officers up into the Rocky Mts., so took advantage of it. We were away just a week & a bully time I had of it; the scenery was glorious & the trout fishing surpassed anything I ever saw before in the way of angling. On our way we stopped for half a day at the canyon, which is a dangerous place to get into. The rocks on either side went straight up to a height of 200 feet & the water rushed through at a great rate. In some places there were some very deep holes with salmon in them. I managed to catch one which weighted ten pounds. We left soon after my capture on account of the place being so dangerous; half the time you would have to crawl & hang on by your teeth. When we got up in the mountains we camped at a very pretty spot on the South Fork of Old Man's River. The first time I threw in my flies, I had four on the line; I had a trout on each fly all at the same time. There was a great commotion in the water & before I could land them, lost two with the flies also. While there we caught between us about 200 fish, a good many of them weighing two & three pounds each. There were a great number of buffalo around us, so the second day I had a great run & shot a nice young cow. It was very dangerous country to run in on account of the hills being so steep. I thought I was going to be thrown once. Going down the side of a very steep hill I found myself riding for quite a distance on a horse's neck but managed to regain the saddle again. One day we took a long ride without guns & visited some very pretty lakes; one had a beautiful round island in the centre of it. From the lakes we rode over to the falls on the middle fork of Old Man's River.[25] The water fell about forty feet into a large basin of solid rock; when looking over the ledge we could see the trout swimming around in large numbers. The whole thing was very picturesque. During our ride we shot several ducks & prairie chickens and saw numbers of buffalo. The grass there is very long, being as high as a man in different places; the pine timber too is very fine. I saw a few partridge and two grouse but did not get a chance to shoot any. Coming home we met the Coutenay [Kootenay] Indians returning to the other side of the mountains where they live. It took us a long time to get by them all; they had about six hundred horses all packed with dried buffalo meat, which they come over for every summer. . . .

We have all just been put through a course of musketry instruction and fired fifteen rounds each. I made very poor, shooting twenty-five points out of a possible sixty at three ranges, two, three & four hundred yds. The best that was made was 42.

Your affectionate son,
W. Parker

My dear Annie

... Today is Sunday & seeing how far we are from civilization is kept in a proper manner, no work doing except guards & pickets. At 11:00 A.M. there is a general parade in full dress uniform when we are inspected & marched into the library for church. The colonel reads the service which is just like your morning service at home; we chant & sing the hymns just the same. At 12:00 the men have dinner & we lunch as we dine at five, and on Sundays always have a splendid plum pudding.

But we were a little disturbed today. Just after lunch the assembly sounded and we all had to fall in on parade the quickest way possible and then doubled down below the fort about a mile to the Sarcee Indian camp where they had set fire to the bush & prairie. We soon had it put out by running and beating the fire out with empty bags. It was amusing to see the squaws pulling down their lodges packing up & moving away in a great hurry. They kept their tongues going the whole time & what with the dogs howling, the horses neighing & the shouting of the police, [it] made quite a little din.

Last Friday the Dramatic Club gave their first entertainment & it went off very well. The acting was splendid, also the scenery & dresses; the house was crowded & I believe we have another next Saturday. The weather is very mild, going in our shirt sleeves; the coldest we have had was about two weeks ago when it only got down four degrees below zero & four inches of snow on the ground which has all disappeared again. I have had a little shooting & bagged seven or eight hares & a few prairie chickens. As soon as the snow falls again I am going over to the Belly River for four or five days to try & shoot a deer & other game for Xmas.

There are large camps of Indians around us and the buffalo are quite close. All the night through we hear the tom-toms going & the Indians dancing & singing; in fact they make night hideous with their yells. They brew large quantities of tea and put tobacco in it which makes them drunk.

I spoke to the colonel the other day about my leave and he told me it would be all right, so if everything goes well you are pretty sure to see me in the spring.

Your affectionate brother,
W. Parker

My dearest Mother

I am ashamed to say it is nearly a month since I last wrote home. We have been having a great old time, one continued round of festivities from Xmas Eve till New Years. . . . The Thursday before Xmas I took a team & two men up to the mountains to procure some evergreens for decorating our rooms. We were away four days & stayed at a trader's post & were treated very kindly by the trader. He was doing a great business with the Indians, taking in great numbers of buffalo robes. The Indians recognized us & told the trader that they wanted to give us a dance so that night just after tea they commenced to arrive until the trading room was quite crowded with squaws & bucks got up regardless of paint & feathers. The tom-toms commenced to beat & the dance started; they all stand round in a circle & sing & keep time with their feet to the tom-toms. They also gave us their war dance, which was capital. They would get so excited over it that you could hear their yells a mile off & see the paint running off their faces with the perspiration. After the war dance two of the prettiest of their squaws came over to us & we had to stand up in front of them & dance. After dancing a few minutes they surprised us greatly by throwing their arms around our necks and giving us a great old kiss. We then gave them all the tea they could drink & then they dispersed.

On Xmas day we gave a splendid dinner & invited lots of our town friends. Our mess room was very nicely decorated & the dinner is said to have been the best ever seen in the North-West Territories. I can vouch that it made our pockets considerably lighter, but then we enjoyed ourselves thoroughly. The Commissioner gave us permission to have a little liquor & managed to get five gallons which we found hardly enough. It was pretty expensive—$12.00 a gallon.

The day following Xmas we spent in horse racing; there were some capital races. The hurdle race was the most exciting, several spills; the worst was Corporal Ward[26] who was coming in in splendid style when his horse fell & nearly killed him. He is in hospital yet but getting around alright. On New Year's day we made up a party & went skating on the river. In the evening we gave an oyster supper and after that was over, went to a dance at Sergt. Major Bray's[27] house, where we "hoed it down" till a quarter to twelve. And then went over to the Commissioner's house and with the help of the band sang "Auld Lang Syne," gave three cheers for the colonel & three for his wife, besides several tigers given afterwards. The colonel then invited us all in and made us partake of all the good things in spite of ourselves. They made me sing them the "Roast Beef of Old England" which seemed to amuse them greatly. After several songs we retired & went back to the dance & kept it up until daylight did appear. So you see, dear Mother, we were bound to enjoy ourselves & I think we succeeded pretty well. . . .

I fully expect to get away sometime in April & then we will have a good old time.

Your affectionate son,
W. Parker

Fort Macleod
March 16th, 1878

Dearest of dear Mothers

. . . Tomorrow is Sunday & I hear them practising the hymns & chants in the recreation room. I cannot attend as I am on guard. I come off at ten in the morning so shall be in time for the service which is at eleven; the colonel reads the prayers very nicely. Our late Commissioner G.A. French, I see, is at Woolrich. He is a major in the Royal Artillery there. I think I shall call & see him when I come home. That is the question, when I come home. Things are turning up which look very bad at present for me obtaining my leave. The darned dirty half-breeds, who are about three thousand strong on the plains, are bucking against the laws passed by the North-West Council last year. They and all the Cree Indians meet on the 5th of April, but what they intend doing it is hard to say. Then again there is Sitting Bull who has to be carefully watched. The Commissioner has already refused leave to several parties. I spoke to him about mine the other day & he said if it was possible he would let me go. It will be hard lines if I cannot come, as I have been looking forward to the great pleasure so long. Still we will trust for the best. There may be no disturbance & then I shall surely come along.

I had a bully long ride the other day. I was sent with a message up to the Rocky Mountains where a party of men are getting out logs for our new fort. They are seventy miles from here; it took me two days to go there. The second day I was chased by a band of wild cattle; I suppose the redcoat made them mad. I had a good horse so was not scared of them although they bellowed & roared plenty. The day after I arrived at the camp I spent in the mountains. I rode about twenty miles till I came to a beautiful lake which was partly frozen over & full of fish. It was surrounded by immense mountains of rock with their tops full of snow. I had my field glasses along with me & spotted two grizzly bears out sunning themselves on the side of one of the mountains. They were too far up to get a shot at; coming home saw several wolves & deer.

I reached Lee's, a trader's post, about four o'clock; it is about thirty miles from the fort.[28] Just as I got there he was turning out with his squaws and the rest of his family to try & save his place from a great prairie fire which was raging at the time & threatened to burn up everything before it. As soon as I got my horse in the stable & got something to eat, I threw off my coat, rolled up my sleeves & went to the rescue. When I arrived on top of the hill the sight was so grand I never saw anything like it. [I] could see all around the country for miles, which was burning in all directions in the heavy grass. The crackling & roaring was tremendous, almost makes a fellow's hair stand on end. The fire was running in all directions. In one place I saw a herd of antelope & deer running before the fire for their lives. We worked from 4:00 P.M. till past midnight & then we had the place secure. I laid [sic] in bed pretty late the next morning as I was terrible stiff & tired. This has been the mildest winter I ever saw anywhere, no snow yet & hardly any frost, beautiful bright warm days; the ground & grass is terribly dry. The buffalo are dying out on the plains for the want of water.

Your affectionate son,
W. Parker

Fort Macleod
May 5th, 1878

My dear Father

If that letter of mine dated 3rd of May arrives before this, tear it up, rip it, and utterly destroy it so that a vestige of it does not remain. Hurray! Gov'nor the Commissioner has given me my furlough. There is no mistake about it, the fatted calf is out of luck this time. I leave here on the 7th inst. for Winnipeg, shall be on duty as far as there taking down Slim Jim, the great horse thief whom we captured a short time ago. He gave us a chase of five miles & several shots were fired. He was sentenced to five years in the Manitoba Penitentiary. Tell you all about it when I get home. Will write from Winnipeg & Ontario so that you will know about when I said.

Your affectionate son,
W. Parker

Bowles Temperance Hotel
Liverpool
September 25th, 1878

My dearest Mother

I have arrived here quite safely . . . .It was dreadful hard tearing myself away from you and all the dear ones. I thought I should break down several times today especially leaving the dear old Rectory. . . .

Your affectionate son,
W. Parker

The Polynesian
September 27th, 1878

My dear Father

. . . We did not leave Liverpool until 7:00 P.M. The wind blew very hard last night but I have not been ill yet. . . . We expect to arrive in Quebec tomorrow week. . . .

Your affectionate son,
W. Parker

Winnipeg
October 22nd, 1878

My Dear Father

I arrived here late last night and am quite well. . . . I went to Ottawa to see if there was anything mentioned about my extra leave or if there was a chance of me getting on duty back to the northwest but there was none. If I had been back a week sooner [I] could have gone on duty right to Macleod in charge of ammunition. I asked Mr. White, who is at the head of our office in Ottawa, about Ted joining in the spring. The first question he asked me, if he was married. Of course I had to say yes; he immediately said "no, that the government would not take any more married men in the Force. . . . "

There are two new fellows here sent up by the government to join the Force. The three of us leave for Shoal Lake tomorrow. I am told that they have been building very comfortable quarters up there so I shall be all right for the winter. . . .

Your affectionate son,
W. Parker

Shoal Lake
October 30th, 1878

My dear Father
... I am so glad to have arrived here. They have built splendid barracks
& are the best in the northwest. There are very few men and I think I shall
have very easy times. There is only one officer here, Inspector Herchmer. A
party of our men leave here tomorrow morning with a prisoner for Winnipeg;
we only get a mail every three weeks which is rather hard lines.

Your affectionate son,
W. Parker

Shoal Lake
November 29th, 1878

My dearest Mother
... Fancy, it is just a month today since I arrived here. We have been
having glorious weather, hardly any snow. Since the captain & sergt. major
came back from Winnipeg [we] have had lots of leisure time. Yesterday &
the day before, hitched up our train of dogs and drove across the lake. I tell
you we went at a great pace, seemed to fly; also have had a little skating,
fishing & shooting, and have set a few traps for foxes. I think I shall try and
stay here next summer and intend buying as much land as I have money for
because I know for certain that all the land around here & all for twenty miles
west of here will be taken up next summer.

I wrote to the colonel about Ted & explained the case but am afraid it
will be some time before I hear from him as he is in Canada and I addressed
it to Ft. Walsh.

Your affectionate son,
W. Parker

Shoal Lake
December 18th, 1878

My dearest Annie
... I just arrived from off a long trip with dogs; was away eight days &
in that time travelled two hundred & fifty miles. Every night when I was
making my bed down in the snow, thought of you all. ...

I will tell you something about my dog trip. Just after I got here Act.
Const. Dobbs,[29] a young friend of mine in the Force, was sent with one man
& horses to arrest an Indian horse thief. When away about a hundred miles
the horse he was riding fell on him & broke his leg in two places. I believe
he is getting along pretty well. Then they sent the sergt. major but he could
not get through on account of the country being too swampy, so the Captain
waited till there was plenty of snow & sent me with two half-breeds and
Indian guide and three trains of dogs, that is four dogs in each cariole or sled.
We went north over Riding Mts. to Dauphin Lake; the snow was three feet
deep on the Mts. and the woods were very thick. One of the breeds used to
go ahead on snow shoes to make a track for the dogs. It is so pretty to see

136

them in harness & hear their bells ringing. After travelling four days [we] came to an Indian camp, so we stopped & went in and had a smoke, first telling my interpreter to obtain all information possible without causing suspicion. What I was after, I must tell you, was big medicine because I travelled under the name of Lord Parker just out from England going moose hunting. After about half an hour my interpreter found out my very man was there but out hunting. In about two hours he came in. I ran to my cariole, put on my revolver and had him captured before he knew what was up. The squaws & other Indians were awfully surprised. He came along quietly & I enjoyed the trip very much; it certainly was a little cold, fourteen below zero the coldest. I ran nearly the whole distance there because the snow was so deep & no track & I wanted to give my dogs a chance. Coming home, I rode plenty; one day we travelled sixty miles. We were travelling two hours before daylight but it was beautiful moonlight and I shall never forget how beautiful the scenery was when I was sitting wrapped up in my buffalo robe in the cariole gliding along under the pine trees. While away the only thing we lived on was biscuit, pemmican & tea. . . .

Ever your loving brother,
W. Parker

Qu'Appelle
January 2nd, 1880

My sweet sister Annie
. . . Yesterday being New Year's Day we had to entertain the Indians. It is a great day with them; they go from house to house to shake hands & the squaws to kiss. I am sure you would never kiss me again if you could only see some of the old beauties that kissed me yesterday. I had everything prepared to receive them. I got Mrs. Griesbach, the officer's wife, & Mrs. [John] McDougall, one of our constable's wives, to make a lot of small currant buns & then I got a very large kettle which we made full of tea. About 9:00 A.M. they commenced to flock in thick, not only Indians but whole gangs of half-breeds. I tell you we had to fly around & crack our heels together to wait on them all. Some of the chiefs made big speeches, which all finished up by begging for grub.

At noon we locked up the station & hitched up our four-in-hand to our double sleigh & we all went for a drive down to the mission. The horses were fresh & spanked along at a great rate. The road too was splendid right across the lake over the ice. We stopped at a half-breed's house & went in. The fiddle was going & they were hoeing down the Red River jig to further orders. The missus of the house took me by the hand & pulled me out into the middle of the room & I had to dance a jig with her. We have been having tremendous cold weather for nearly a week. It was forty below zero and one night it was fifty one and a half below; everything froze up solid.

Your affectionate brother,
W. Parker

Qu'Appelle
February 1st, 1880

My dear Father

... One of our constables, a married man, has been dreadfully ill; we thought he would die. I prayed for him & I think the Lord, who is always gracious, heard my prayer & spared him, as he is coming round alright. When he was so very bad, I rustled around & got a half-breed to take a train of dogs & travel night & day to Shoal Lake (a distance of 150 miles) for a doctor; he went there in three days & the doctor arrived here on the 7th day after the half-breed left here.

The day before yesterday I arrested a man for bringing liquor into the Territories without a permit.[30] He was fined $50.00 & $11.00 costs, or six months' imprisonment; he paid the fine & I received half of it and one dollar & a half of the costs. Paying business for me, eh? The prosecutor in such cases always get half of the fine.

One of our men at Ft. Walsh has been shot dead by Indians;[31] they also took his horse tied it to a tree & shot it dead. They tracked the Indians to the camp of the Blood Indians but [at] last account they had not discovered the murderer. Our Indians here are keeping very quiet & so they ought, as the government is feeding the most of them. Since the agent arrived he has got a good many of them to work chopping & hauling firewood. Never having worked before in their lives they call it cruel of the government to ask them to do so.

Your affectionate son,
W. Parker

Qu'Appelle
February 20th, 1880

My sweet sister Annie

... At present I am busy reading up my drill, ready for the spring because we generally have to drill for about two months steady every spring & most probably I shall have to instruct. I have done so before so will not find it difficult. There is a nasty disease going amongst the horses here, all their hair comes off & the poor beggars freeze stiff. I am afraid my horse will take it & kick the bucket; he is worth one hundred dollars so I shall be quite a loser if he does. We are living very well here. Today we had white fish for breakfast washed down by about as good a cup of coffee as I want to drink; for dinner a brace of prairie chickens served with bread sauce & potatoes & coffee to drink; then for tea, roast beef followed by a grand looking plum pudding with a good cup of tea. The secret of our coffee being so good [is] we have a cow & not making butter, put all the cream into the coffee, so you see we bachelors know how to live. There are only three men here living in the barracks & they take week about at the cooking.

Your affectionate brother,
W. Parker

Qu'Appelle
March 9th, 1880

My very dear Mother
    ... We have been having & are still having a frightful winter. The mail
that has just come in had to turn back twice to Ft. Ellice before it could get
through & then was obliged to leave one of the largest & heaviest bags on
the road. ...
    Old Veterans in the Force have the choice of re-engaging for three, four,
or five years, so I shall only go in for three years. About promotion I am not
sure, might possibly get a lift in the spring. Anyways I am very contented with
my present lot & have commenced to save the spon-du-licks [money] again;
there is nothing like having a few for a rainy day. ...
                                                    Your affectionate son,
                                                            W. Parker

                                                        Qu'Appelle
                                                       April 4th, 1880

My dear Jue
    ... This is going to be a great country at no distant day, and there are
some of the best openings for a fellow to make a fortune in a very short while,
if he only had a little capital to start on. Farming is surest but slowest; stock-
raising can't be beaten, no expense & sure profits. But the best chance of all
is a saw mill or grist mill, but it takes quite a little pile of money to start ahead
of civilization. I am pretty sure to go into one of the above-mentioned busi-
nesses at the expiration of my present three years, that is if I do not get a
commission in that time & the chances are two to one against me. No influence at Ottawa.
    It is just six years ago today that I first joined in London, Ont. You must
try, old fellow, and not get into debt as it is a very bad practice. Do you know
that I have never been belly-up since I first left the dear old home & hope
I never shall be. Our winter is toughing it out yet, much to our disgust; the
ducks have not arrived yet, have seen a few geese but could not get a shot
at them. There are going to be some great changes in the Force this summer.
I believe the headquarters are to be transferred to this part of the country.[32]
The Indians here are starving & are getting very cheeky.
                                                    Your affectionate brother,
                                                            W. Parker

                                                        Qu'Appelle
                                                       April 8th, 1880

My dear Mother
    ... We have spring at last; it has been such a lovely day today, not a cloud
to be seen and the sun giving the snow goss. I have been busy all afternoon
making drains around the house & stable to run the water off or else we
should be flooded out it comes down off the hills so very quick.
    This valley is in a very bad state at the present time, Indians and half-

breeds starving and the horses dying of a disease called the scab. But now [that] spring is close at hand there will soon be plenty of ducks & they will be able to catch any quantity of fish, and I think the green grass & warm weather will cure the horses. It has been a dreadful winter, the hardest I have seen since I have been in the country. . . .

Your affectionate son,
W. Parker

Qu'Appelle
May 6th, 1880

My dearest Father
. . . I have been very unfortunate lately having lost or had stolen from me my pocket book that Harry gave me with two hundred dollars in it. I cannot get any trace of it. I suspect a certain half-breed and am going to get a search warrant to search him & his house in a day or two. Then again the men here under me are pulling against me and I think are trying all they can to get me reduced. I have one of them under arrest now & think I shall be able to clear myself of anything they bring against me. Yesterday a new officer arrived with a corporal and three more men. I am awfully sorry to be parted from Insp. Griesbach; he is a splendid officer & has been very kind to me. He proceeds to Swan River barracks & Inspector Antrobus relieves him. Ever since the latter came, I have hardly had time to look around. . . . He has taken stock of all my stores & is very well pleased with them. . . .

Your affectionate son,
W. Parker

Qu'Appelle
May 14th, 1880

My very dear Annie
. . . My troubles commenced about five weeks ago, when I happened to have a few words with one of the men under me. He reported me to the officer in command on a frivolous charge, for which he has since been put under arrest. He is also bringing some more false charges against me, but I think I shall be able to get justice done me. The fellow is an Irishman & I believe hates me from the bottom of his heart because I am an Englishman. Just as all this row was going on somebody stole my pocket book with two hundred dollars in it and I cannot get any trace of it. In the middle of the worry a lot of new men & new officers arrived here, and I had a great deal of extra work to do. Then again I have lost a good officer & friend in Mr. Griesbach who has gone to Swan River barracks with his family. I think the worry of the whole business kind of floored me. . . .

We have got out spring at last; the grass is growing fast & the leaves coming out on the trees. The river is thick with fish, I see the Indians & half-breeds killing them with clubs. I had a little fishing just before I was taken sick & caught several weighed twelve pounds. . . .

Your affectionate brother,
W. Parker

Qu'Appelle
June 15th, 1880

My dear Alice
... I am afraid I have lost my two hundred dollars for good as I have not been able to discover anything about it. I obtained a search warrant to search certain parties but could not find anything. My suspicions are now strongly against one of our own men, but I cannot prove anything against him. It is very unlucky for me, as the money was really worth twice its own value to me to speculate on. It serves me right for being so careless & has taught me a lesson. ...

Your affectionate brother,
W. Parker

Qu'Appelle
June 26th, 1880

My dearest Mother
... The annual payment of the Indians by the government takes place in two weeks time, when there will be any amount of cash throwing around. Mr. Antrobus, our officer, is away north to Ft. Carlton, so I am at present in charge here, and am very busy getting the officer's house plastered & white-washed inside & out. On Dominion Day, that is 1st July, we are going to have quite a little time, all kind of sports, horse racing, big dance in the evening. ...

Your affectionate son,
W. Parker

Battleford
September 2nd, 1880

My dearest and best of Mothers
... We are still under canvas and expect to be so until the snow commences to fly, as our quarters will not be ready until about the end of October. The barracks are very fine buildings but were never properly finished, nor kept in repair, so there is a great deal of work to be done. The captain's going to have them plastered so we shall be nice & comfortable for the winter.

This place is very far north, nearly 300 miles north of Fort Walsh & 350 northwest of Qu'Appelle and situated between the North Saskatchewan & Battle rivers; the former river is from a quarter to half a mile wide & full of beautiful islands, the latter is about eighty yards wide. I am still acting sergt. major & am kept very busy, telling off the different duties, and keeping the troop orderly sergeant to his work. He has to see that every man is working & at his proper post.

I will just tell you the doings for today & it will give you a little insight [into] what we do in the great lone land. Reveille at 6:00 A.M., we all rise, fold blankets & make up beds, tidy tents; 6:30 to stables, see horses groomed & fed; 7:30 breakfast, consisting of coffee, cold beef & bread; 8:30 fatigue commences & lasts until 11:30. Two constables who are working on the buildings at $2.50 extra per day refused to go to work because they had to attend stables. I was ordered to place them under arrest for disobedience of orders; after I made the charges out, the troop orderly marched them to the orderly room. Superintendent Herchmer tried them & told them he had a good mind to give them each a month's imprisonment; as it was they were both good characters & he reprimanded them. Morning fatigue as follows: one man at plaster, one carpenter, two hauling sand, two blacksmithing, one saddler, three cleaning out & straightening big store, one troop book, one officers, one hauling water, one baker, one trumpeter, two officers servants, one officer groom. 11:45 A.M., dinner consisting of roast beef, potatoes, bread & tea. 1:00 P.M., fatigue commences & lasts till 4:30.

At 1:30 Capt. Herchmer, Surgeon [Robert] Miller, Corporal [Harry] Nash and two constables left with nine horses & two waggons for Fort Saskatchewan. Fatigue same as morning with the exception of two men driving teams on the horse power for sawing wood. Tea at 4:45 P.M. consisting of dry bread & tea. The ration of meat only lasts enough for two meals. I was more fortunate than the rest in having a fine duck for my tea. 5:30 P.M., stables again, the horses all driven in by the herder, groomed, fed & turned out again for the night. Directly after evening stables are over, I rush to my tent, throw off my uniform & put on my oldest duds, shoulder my breech loader & start for the swamp. When I arrived it was just full of beautiful young ducks & the first shot as they got up I knocked down five. With the help of the rascal Sneak and Wizzen Face, I managed to get the five. The mosquitoes & sand flies were so bad that I could not wait for another shot. Retreat sounds at sunset when Mr. Union Jack is lowered down for the night. Some of the men stroll off to the village of Battleford, which consists of about twenty houses, three stores or rather shops, & a telegraph office. Above the village on the hill is situated Government House where the lieut. governor of the Territories resides & the North-West Council is held every autumn. There are also three other very fine houses for this country, a stipendiary magistrate's, the registrar's & sheriff's. Most of the men, however, stay in, either play cards or get up a stag dance with the fiddle; a stag dance means no ladies.

First post sounds at 9:30 P.M. when I betake myself over to see the orderly officer & get the detail of work to be done the following day. I then tell off the different duties to the troop orderly sergeant & when he goes around to call the roll, warns the men for their different fatigues. Second post goes at 10:00 P.M. when the orderly reports if any man is about or if they are all present. At 10:15, lights sound out, but sergeants are allowed to have them on to 11:00 P.M.

I hope I have not tired you with this long rigmarole of our duty at the present time. I started to write this after lights out so it must be nearly 11 o'clock now. I am sitting in my bell tent; I have one all to myself and have it very nicely fixed up.

I have a chance of earning a little extra pay by working in the harvest field & start tomorrow to bind oats at two dollars a day & my other pay goes on the same, so I am in hopes to soon make up for the $200 I had stolen from me at Qu'Appelle. I have also applied for all the government ploughing which I expect to get. I sold my horse to the government & made $35 on him & he is still my trooper.

Your loving son,
William Parker

Battleford
October 28th, 1880

My very dear Mother
... We only got in from under canvas the night before last & many a cold night we had of it before we did get in, snow on the ground three inches deep & about 20 degrees of frost. ...

I forget whether I told you about poor Bill Hooley's death; he used to be in my old troop at Macleod & was son of a clergyman in either Norfolk or Suffolk. He was Colonel Macleod's four-in-hand driver & while swimming his horses & waggon across Belly River, was drowned with all four of his horses. I feel greatly for his parents at home. He was a splendid fellow & greatly beloved by all his comrades. And now we have just received more sad news from Ft. Walsh. Captain Clark, my old commanding officer, died very suddenly from heart disease. He was talking to Dr. Kennedy when he threw up his hands & dropped dead. The news has cast quite a gloom over us all. He has been in the Force ever since it was first raised & did many a good turn for his men; he was an Englishman & always gloried in anything English. ...

I have a very nice room to myself but at present everything is hung up on the floor. I had to mud the walls myself, whitewash it & paid a squaw fifty cents to scrub the floor. This afternoon I made myself a very good bedstead. For the last two weeks we have been having riding drill & foot drill. I have to attend the former & instruct in the latter. I am no longer acting sergt. major. When Captain Herchmer went up to Ft. Saskatchewan he brought down Sergt. Major Belcher[33] who is just married & has a very pretty bride. He is English to the backbone & we get along first rate.

Ever your affectionate son,
Willie

Battleford
November 15th, 1880

My dear sister Annie
... Now that they are pushing the Canada [sic] Pacific Railroad on west of Winnipeg we might possibly obtain a mail next spring every two weeks. I am informed that the above-named road will pass quite close if not through my four hundred and eighty acres of land at Shoal Lake, which is very lucky for me, as it will be worth about ten times as much as it is now. ...

At present we are all hard at work putting up a stockade around our fort so that if the Indians get too cheeky we can stand them off. On the ninth of this month we had holiday horseraces in the afternoon and in the evening we gave a ball. I was president of the Ball Committee & in consequence had my hands full. There were only two single young ladies present, one a half-breed but very pretty & the other a Canadian but her feet are so big that she can't keep herself warm when she walks. Everything passed off well, with the exception of a couple of civilians who had got hold of some liquor somewhere & commenced to be very noisy so we landed them in the guard room.

We have a very nice clergyman here by the name of Clarke;[34] he comes from Brighton. Last night I crossed over the river on the ice; it was not very safe as I went in with one leg up to the knee, and went to church. Mr. Clarke plays the harmonica himself & I help with my singing. There was quite a large congregation for Battleford, about forty being present. The lieut. governor was there; he stands about six feet four in his stocking feet. The Indians call him the walking crane.

Your affectionate brother,
W. Parker

Battleford
December 6th, 1880

My dear Ju

... I think that I have made a pretty lucky spec in locating 480 acres of land near Shoal Lake as the Canadian Pacific Railway will pass close by it. If so the land will be worth about ten times more than what I paid for it. My two town lots in Winnipeg too are getting valuable; the city is growing very fast, a second Chicago. Ever since our arrival here [we] have been worked like niggers. It is one continual grind; the men are getting very discontented. We hardly ever get five minutes to ourselves. We thought when the winter set in that there would be an end to the fatigues, but ... they are just as thick as ever. The weather for the last three weeks has been very severe, from ten to thirty-six below zero every night & below zero all day.

I am troop orderly sergeant this week & a sweet-scented job it is, on the go from morning to night & about a thousand different orders to see carried out. The worst job is going to see all the horses watered twice a day; have to ride about a mile & this morning got my left ear frozen stiff and if I had hit it against anything it would surely have broken off. Now it is very sore & as big as my fist. At present we & the civilians in the town are getting up a concert for Christmas to be held in the council hall at Government House where the lieut. governor lives. I am going to sing "It's funny when you feel that way"; the other night I sang it at one of our rehearsals & the whole crowd went into roars of laughter & declared it was amusing. ...

Your affectionate brother,
W. Parker

Battleford
December 29th, 1880

My dear Father

... Our Xmas has been rather dull and I being orderly sergeant on Xmas day could not get to church much as I wanted to. I lent a hand in decorating the church and it looks very nice. I cut out & made the letters for "Glory to God in the highest" & got great praise for the manner in which it was done. The Tuesday before Xmas we had a shooting match for a supper. Two captains were chosen, then they picked up sides and the side who got the least game had to pay for the supper for the whole. I took a horse and sleigh and left for the shooting grounds about an hour and a half before daylight. It was a dreadful cold drive, being thirty below zero. After going seven miles I arrived at a place called the sand hills, where the prairie chickens used to be very thick. It was not quite daylight, so tied up my horse, fed him and then lit a big fire. When daylight arrived I was thoroughly warmed and ready for the warpath, so throwing off my buffalo coat & grasping my breech loader, I started out but had very bad luck [and] could not find many chickens. It came on to snow and I think they kept in the middle of the woods; after hunting all day and getting lost twice, I had to return with only six chickens and one partridge. But it was a very poor day, as when we met in the evening, out of twenty-two shooting my bag was second, the largest being ten chickens. I was also on the losing side. . . .

Your affectionate son,
W. Parker

The Fort
Battleford
January 12th, 1881

My ever precious Mother
  . . . The last week we have been kept very busy threshing our oats. They turned out very well, about fifty bushels to the acre. Our fellows grumble a good deal for having to do such work, as it is a long way from what a police-man ought to do, but I always think the same as the officers that they are better doing that than idling. . . .
  Battleford is a dull place. The only thing of interest is the bulletin that comes out every evening from the telegraph office and gives an idea of what is transpiring at Ottawa where Parliament is assembled. A syndicate is formed for building the C.P. Railway through this country and the present government is agreeable to giving them twenty-five million acres of land, and twenty-five million dollars. The Canadians are bucking strongly against the terms & I think they are right.

Ever your loving son,
Willie Parker

The Fort
Battleford
February 10th, 1881

My dear Annie
  . . . The Indians all over the country are getting very cheeky. A few days ago a young warrior tried to stab one of the farm instructors. Three of our fellows were sent to arrest him. They had quite a lively time after making the arrest & [when] going to put the prisoner into the sleigh they were surrounded by about forty Indians with knives and axes. After a scuffle the prisoner was put in the sleigh when he was jerked out again by his friends. After another scuffle our fellows again got him in & this time sat on him. Other Indians had the horses by the head and one was going to cut the reins with a knife when Const. Carruthers, the driver, gave him a terrible cut with the whip right across his eyes. The team then started out, as an Indian had his

axe raised to split the corporal's head open. They all started on the jump after the sleigh brandishing their knives and axes. It was then that Sergt. Major Belcher drew his revolver and leveled at them & it immediately stopped the cowards. The prisoner was tried the same day and sentenced to two months' imprisonment with hard labour. We are the gainers,[35] as we have him cutting wood for us, with a ball & chain on his leg & a sentry over him. We have still to arrest two or three of the ring leaders who tried to rescue the prisoner so I expect we shall have some more fun.

We have also just got news of an Indian at Ft. Pitt who has stabbed his wife. Inspector Antrobus & four men leave on Saturday to arrest him; it is a hundred miles from here.[36] I asked to go but cannot on account of having to act as sergt. major as the sergt. major is going on leave to Fort Saskatchewan.

I get tired of being cooped up in the fort all the time. Yesterday afternoon I took my gun & went for a long walk across the Saskatchewan River which is a mile wide here. It was very hard walking, the snow laying up on the tall prairie grass. I managed to shoot two chickens and one rabbit, the latter as white as the snow; they always turn white in winter & grey in summer. . . .

Your loving brother,
W. Parker

The Fort
Battleford
March 17th, 1881

My dear sister Annie

. . . Some big Canadian capitalists are starting a large stock farm in the Bow River country near Fort Macleod. Mr. McEachran, who I stayed a week with in Montreal on my return from England, is one of the head men.[37] He wants me to accept a position on it. I have telegraphed him if he can get me out of the Force I will do so. I have not heard from him yet. I am getting about tired of the Force as they do not give a fellow fair play and the Force, instead of improving, is just the opposite.

Your loving brother,
W. Parker

The Fort
Battleford
June 8th, 1881

My dear Annie

. . . By the last mail I wrote to Mother and told her the news of my engagement. I suppose it would rather surprise you all. I have come to the conclusion that I have roughed it, made up my own bed, swept out the room, mended old clothes, sewed on buttons, darned old socks and been single long enough. My betrothed has gone on a fortnight's visit to Fort Pitt, about one hundred miles west of here. I believe her relations & friends are going to make the wedding a swell affair. There is to be a breakfast and a swell ball in the evening. From what I can hear the bride will also be the recipient of a large number of presents.

Mrs. Calder has a private income of her own, but I believe it is not very large, just about enough to keep herself. She is very kind & is getting a great number of things for Mary. When I remonstrated with her she said, "She is my only daughter," & that she must give her a good send off. I am busy at present looking after timber to build myself a house. . . .

Ever your affectionate brother,
W. Parker

The Fort
Battleford
July 8th, 1881

My very dear Mother,

. . . Since I last wrote home I have been on a short trip. I was out with one man, four horses and a waggon to meet Captain Herchmer who was on his return from Ontario where he had been on leave of absence. After going one hundred & twenty miles in two days we met the captain. He was very pleased to see us & get our four fresh horses, as his own horses' shoulders were very sore. He had five with him, all new ones from Canada; they are very fine horses. On our way down & back we lived on mushrooms. The prairies are covered with them, & many was the queer old feed we put away. We did the return journey in two days & a half, making two hundred & forty miles in four days & a half. It rained nearly the whole time we were away & in consequence the roads were heavy & my teeth ached very much. . . .

Ever your affectionate son,
W. Parker

Battleford
July 27th, 1881

My dear Father

. . . It would be very doubtful if [Ted] could get a job on the stock farms unless I am there, as they only want men that have been in the country & had some experience with wild cattle. It is most probable that I shall have nothing to do with the concern [if] they do not offer anything better than my present position. But I expect to hear again from the director, McEachran, who is now in the country. I have just seen a couple of men who have been working for them. They give the outfit a hard name, low pay & plenty of labour. . . .

You know before this that I am engaged to be married & most probably will be before the winter sets in. I have often thought of taking a partner, but have never until now run across the right kind of girl. A man cannot very well start farming in this country without a wife, & if all goes well & I find by selling some of my land I still have enough capital, I shall go into farming when my present term of service is up a year from next 1st of May. I believe that the young lady will be the owner of 480 acres of land in Manitoba &

will come in for some money on the death of her mother, how much I cannot say but I think it will not be very much. . . .

Your affectionate son,
W. Parker

Battleford
September 7th, 1881

My very dear Mother,

Many thanks for your very kind and welcome letter of July 13th in answer to mine informing you of my intention of getting married. There is no doubt about it that you are the best and kindest of Mothers, for I know when I wrote that letter that the news it contained you would not like, but like a dear soul that you are, you swallow your chagrin to please your unworthy son Bill. Many, many thanks my sweet Mother for your congratulations and blessing.

Now, I must tell you something that will please perhaps as much as the last disappointed. The engagement is broken off and I am a free man again. It all came about by our not being able to agree. The young lady has not a very amiable temper and my own [is] not of the very best, so we both came to the conclusion it was best not to get married if we could not agree. Another cause on my side was because I knew you would not be pleased at home & if I was married I would stand a very poor chance of coming home to see you dear ones again. An end to this blessed love affair; let us discuss something more sensible.

I am very tired this evening, having just returned from a fifty-mile ride since daylight this morning. Our men that were herding our wild cattle (that we kill for beef) lost them, & I with another sergt. & a corporal were sent to find them, which we did. They are very dangerous brutes, having horns two or three feet long & wilder than the buffalo. They cannot be approached on foot, always have to be herded on horseback. In coming home with them I had a very narrow escape. I was crowding them rather close when one turned & made a charge for me and, instead of my horse answering the bit to turn around, he passaged towards the animal. It gave a vicious toss with its head, the horn striking between my leg & the saddle. Just at the same instant I drove the spurs into the horse's side & he took a great bound which probably saved my own life & that of the horse. . . .

You remember me speaking about a splendid dog I used to have named Spot, the same in the photograph that you have of me as a corporal? I lost her five years ago when marching from Swan River for Fort Macleod. The other day I was down in the town & recognized my old dog with a farmer that was going up to Edmonton. I claimed my dog & offered to pay expenses, but the fellow said he was the owner of the dog & he was going to keep her. That got my Parker blood up & I seized the dog, when the fellow drew a revolver. When he found I would not let go of the dog, he said, "I will let you see it is loaded," & fired it off down the street. Finding that did not scare me, he tried to get the dog from me & in the scuffle I managed to get hold of the revolver, intending to arrest the man. When he found I had the bulge on him he very readily gave up the dog & I returned him his revolver. I gave him a chance to fight me, but he was not taking any, so the business dropped.

Since I have my old dog back I am able to play old Harry amongst the ducks & prairie chickens. Have shot about a hundred since the season opened.

Ever your affectionate son,
W.P.

Battleford
December 11th, 1881

My dear Julie,

... You will have heard before this that my engagement has been broken off for some time. Directly after the break, the young lady & her mother went on a visit to Fort Edmonton, three hundred miles west from here, & they only returned the other day. She looks very nice & I think has a weakness for this child yet; it is very hard to say what might happen. ...

We have had a great shotgun shooting match for a supper. I was elected one of the captains. There were thirteen on a side; the shooting was only to last the one day & every man's bag counted in the evening. I left here an hour before daybreak on horseback for the sand hills, about seven or eight miles distant. I passed several on the road bound for the same locality as the prairie chicken are very numerous there. You could not see rightly when the bombardment commenced (chickens flying in every direction). I never saw so many before; the trees were literally covered with them.

I found myself beside the captain & three men of the opposite side. Well, my dear fellow, if you ever saw such fun it was there! Here was I just spoiling the shooting for them & at the same time making a good bag for myself. For every bird that would fall there would be such shouting. Then we would see chickens on the trees ahead of us, and there would be a grand race to get there first. I shot altogether twenty-six chickens, one raven & one whisky Jack, making altogether 270 points. On counting up the game in the evening my side came out victorious by eighty points, so we got a free supper.

Since then there has been rifle match after rifle match, mostly between ourselves. The volunteer Infantry Company challenged us & we beat them by five points. Then the civilians went at us for a supper & beat us badly. They had the advantage for we had to shoot with our short carbines against their long rifles. To wind up the whole thing we gave a ball which passed off capitally; everybody enjoyed themselves first rate. The civilians are talking of returning the compliment and giving us one. ...

Your affectionate brother,
W. Parker

Battleford
December 20th, 1881

My dear Father

... Our horses are giving us a great deal of bother this winter [as] a great number of them [have] fallen sick. I was ordered this morning to shoot one that had the "glanders," and it was only the other day I shot another. Several have died without being shot, mostly horses that have been used up by the governor-general's trip.

149

We expect Colonel Herchmer back tomorrow from Edmonton & I expect about New Years he will be leaving for Qu'Appelle. He told me that I would have to go with him. I do not care much for the trip, about 350 miles [for we] will have to sleep out in the snow about ten nights going & the same coming back, & a good deal of open plain to cross. I have just got a splendid buffalo head from a half-breed. I gave him five dollars for it. I intend to get [it] stuffed & try & get it home some day. . . .

Your loving son,
W. Parker

Battleford
January 12th, 1882

My dear sister Annie

. . . I have hardly any news to tell you with the exception that we gave a grand ball last week, which was one great success. I had charge of the decorating committee and though I say it myself, the ballroom looked splendid. The music was good and the supper everything that could be desired; our guests were delighted & all went home happy. On Boxing Day I was invited to dine with Mr. McKay[38] of the Hudson's Bay Company and after dinner we danced to six in the morning; in fact, this has been the merriest Xmas & New Year's that I have spent in this country.

You ask me if I ever see Mary. Why, yes I do, and you must not be surprised to hear of my being wed after all. I try to fight the passion but it always gets the best of me. There is talk of great changes taking place in the Force and the strength may be increased 200 stronger. If all goes well I shall probably have the working of the farm here and possibly get the hay contract of one hundred & fifty tons. So if I do, will have my hands pretty full & will have to work hard.

Ever your affectionate brother,
W. Parker

Battleford
January 31st, 1882

My dear Mother

. . . Potatoes are fetching a big price on account of so many being frozen last autumn. Sergt. Price & I sold thirty bushels of ours yesterday for five shillings a bushel. If we keep them till spring we will get eight & nine shillings a bushel. We are not going to sell any more just yet. I expect to be kept very busy this coming summer as I shall most probably have the running of the police farm again. It is the intention at present to break thirty acres more of sod for oats and summer fallow & manure the other fifty that was in crop last year. I may also have the contract to furnish 150 tons of hay for the police; if so, I shall have my hands full.

Ever your loving son,
W. Parker

The Fort
Battleford
February 21st, 1882

My dear Father

... I, in company with a friend of mine by the name of Corporal Wardin,[39] have been down to Prince Albert's Mission on pass. It is about one hundred & fifty miles east from here & is in a very fine country. There is quite a large town springing up, some very fine houses, both brick & frame, three saw mills, two grist mills, the latter running night & day grinding the wheat into flour; also a splendid college built by the Bishop of Saskatchewan belonging to our church. It was quite civilized-like to see the farmers coming in from the surrounding country with their loads of wheat. If Prince Albert only gets a railroad running into it, it will become quite a place. While there I invested in two town lots, but have only paid half down, the other half in eighteen months [with agreement to] build a house on one of the two. If I do not build within eighteen months I lose the lots. Most probably I will sell before then if there is a rise in value.

It was glorious fine weather going, but coming home we caught it. [We] had to sleep out two nights. The first night [we] camped in a clump of willows [at] twenty-five below zero & a strong wind blowing; the following day was dreadfully stormy for travelling over a bare plain. The second night [we] camped in a bluff of poplars; the wind went down & so did the thermometer to forty-five below zero. It was so cold that we could not sleep, so we got up at 2:00 A.M., put on a big fire & made a cup of tea. [We] fed the horses oats and at 3:00 A.M we once more started out. For three hours it was very dark and we lost the road several times. The cold was something dreadful. I have been out when the thermometer has been lower but never felt the cold so much. It was on account of a breeze blowing in our faces & travelling over a bare plain. It was just all we could do to keep from being frozen very badly; in fact, we worked hard, that is, rubbing the places touched with frost & keeping up the circulation of the blood. [We] could not ride in the cariole more than ten minutes at a time.

Before we could make any dry wood [we] had to travel till 10:00 A.M., making seven hours of agony that we travelled. The icicles on my moustache stuck out beyond the tip of my nose and to prove how intensely cold it was, I happened to put out my tongue & on it coming in contact with one of the icicles it froze to it & before I could get it in again it pulled the skin off. At present the skin is peeling off my nose & cheeks where it was [sic] frostbitten.

Wardin is a good deal [more] worn than me. You never saw two men more pleased than we were when we struck Battleford. We do not intend going on any more outings in winter unless it is a case of duty. ...

We have a great deal of sickness amongst our horses this winter & have lost about fourteen so far with "glanders." Now a new disease has just appeared amongst them by the name of "pinkeye." It keeps us all our time looking after them.

Our Force, I believe, is to be increased two hundred stronger and they are going to build new headquarters of brick, but where it will be is not decided. Several new officers have been appointed, [but] only one taken from the Force; he is a Sergt. Norman & joined the same time as I did. He is very clever. They have overlooked several of our old sergt. majors. It takes a good deal of influence at Ottawa for a fellow to obtain a commission in this outfit.

If all goes well I expect to have the running of the police farm this summer. Of course I will have to work like a nigger but will earn extra pay. ... My time will be up in the Force a year from next April and I often think of starting farming and making a home for myself. To do so I would have to sell my land in Manitoba. There are a great many discomforts in this life. A fellow is not his own master. You get ordered around so much & constantly ordering other fellows around yourself.

Your affectionate son,
W. Parker

Notes

Introduction

1. "William Parker—'74 Original," *RCMP Quarterly*, vol. 2, no. 1, July 1945, p. 43.
2. Letter, Parker to his father, November 8, 1873. Parker Papers.
3. *Statutes of Canada*, 1873, 36 Vic. Chap. 35.
4. Letter, Parker to his mother, April 5, 1874.
5. Letter, Parker to brother Harry, November 28, 1874.
6. Letter, Parker to his mother, April 5, 1875.
7. Letter, Parker to his mother, April 20, 1875.
8. Letter, Parker to his father, May 19, 1875.
9. Longstreth, p. 55.
10. Ibid.
11. Idem, p. 83.
12. Letter, Parker to his mother, August 3, 1876.
13. Letter, Parker to his father, September 10, 1876.
14. Letter, Parker to his father, October 31, 1876.
15. Letter, Parker to his father, January 6, 1877.
16. "William Parker—'74 Original," p. 56.
17. Introduction to original manuscript. Parker Papers.
18. Letter, Parker to his mother, December 9, 1875.
19. Introduction to original manuscript. Parker Papers.

Reminiscence

1. Isaac Helmuth was a Polish Jew who joined the Anglican Church and was Bishop of Huron from 1871 to 1883.
2. George Arthur French (1841–1921) was the first Commissioner of the North-West Mounted Police and served in that capacity from 1873 to 1876.
3. Parker had apparently told his enlistment story so often that he had forgotten the facts as related to his mother at that time. A reference of good behaviour from his bishop, not a telegram about his drinking and fighting from his cousin, had resulted in his appointment. His cousin Alfred never replied.
4. James Farquarson Macleod (1836–94) was assistant commissioner of the North-West Mounted Police, 1873–76, and Commissioner 1876–80. During his term he gained the trust of Indian tribes through his honesty and understanding and was well-liked by his men. He served as stipendiary magistrate, 1880–87, and puisne judge of the N.W.T. supreme court 1887–94.
5. William Latimer, Reg. No. 190, was a member of "D" Division.
6. James Morrow Walsh joined the police in 1873 and was promoted to inspector in the following year. He built Fort Walsh in the Cypress Hills in 1875 and was actively involved with the refugee Sioux that fled to the area after the Custer battle. He retired from the force in 1883 and later re-engaged for service in the Yukon, 1897–98.
7. John French was a brother of Commissioner G.A. French. He joined the Force in 1874 and remained until the early 1880s. At the outbreak of the Riel Rebellion in 1885 he organized French's Scouts and was killed at the Battle of Batoche.
8. James Walker joined the police in 1874 and served most of his term in charge of Battleford. In 1880 he resigned to become manager of the Cochrane Ranche Co., and later started a ranch and a lumber business in Calgary.
9. However, according to Turner (1:128), "Close to the hour of departure, there had been thirty-one constables, acting constables, and sub-constables absent without leave—deserters in the true sense of the word. . . ."
10. This was Inspector Theodore Richer. His dismissal was linked, according to D'Artigue (p. 3), with the Commissioner's unpopular orders forcing the men to act as teamsters. "Inspector Richer of 'F' Division, being well-aware that if these commands were obeyed the men would soon be on foot, was not in a hurry to produce the number of horses required, and an altercation ensued between him and Colonel French."
11. She was the wife of Cotton M. Almon, who had been brought west in 1872 by the Boundary Commission to raise coarse grains for the horses. He later farmed on

his own and went into the real estate and dry goods business in Emerson, Manitoba.

12. Edmund Dalrymple Clark was a nephew of Prime Minister John A. Macdonald's wife. He joined the Force in 1873 as paymaster and was popular with all ranks. As Parker states later, Clark died of a heart attack at Fort Walsh in 1880.

13. Swan River barracks, or Fort Livingstone, was a contentious site from the time of its selection in 1874. Planned as the first capital of the North-West Territories, its isolated, rock-strewn location proved to be inappropriate. When government contractors failed to complete construction in time, the site came into so much disfavour that the headquarters of the Force was moved to Fort Macleod and the Territorial capital to Battleford.

14. Mike Slevin, Reg. No. 220, was a former policeman who joined the Force in 1874 and was attached to "D" Division, while Pat Wheeler, Reg. No. 388, was in for only a few months before deserting.

15. Arthur Henry Griesbach was a professional soldier who joined the police in 1873. He was promoted to sub-inspector in 1876 and later to inspector, serving much of his term at Fort Saskatchewan. Parker later served under him at Forts Qu'Appelle and Saskatchewan.

16. Francis J. Dickens (1845–86) was the third son of the novelist Charles Dickens. He joined the Force in 1874 as sub-inspector and later was promoted to inspector. In 1885 he was obliged to retreat from Fort Pitt when it was surrounded by Big Bear's forces. He resigned from the Force in the following year and died a short time later in Moline, Ill.

17. This was Sergt. Robert Wyld, Reg. No. 231, who was attached to "E" Division.

18. These were Const. Douglas Alison, Reg. No. 6, and Const. W. Long, Reg. No. 29, both of "D" Division.

19. According to building superintendent Hugh Sutherland, the fort was much more extensive than Parker's description. In 1875, he said it included the Commissioner's residence; officers' quarters; men's quarters, consisting of two one-storey buildings each 156 by 26 feet, and one two-storey building 156 by 26 feet; married men's quarters 250 by 26 feet; hospital; bakery; three store houses; guard house; and two stables. (see Klaus, 102-103.)

20. Commissioner French was outspoken in condemning the condition of the barracks. In a letter to the minister of Justice, July 27, 1875 (see Klaus, 100-101), he stated: "The buildings are constructed of green timber, felled, cut up and erected within a few days, therefore already warped and open at the joints. The planks are mostly unplaned and the floors difficult to keep clean, the barrack rooms too large and so difficult to keep warm. . . . "

21. Mrs. Albert Shurtliff.

22. Likely Sergt. Robert Wyld, a member of "E" Division whose parents lived in Hamilton.

23. Among the six constables were W.S. Grant, Const. Daly, George Boswell and Roderick Cook. (Data from Parker's diary entries.)

24. It is significant to note Parker does not claim that this was the first Mounted Police band, as does Turner (1:262.) In a letter from New Fort barracks in Toronto two years earlier (April 21, 1874) Parker mentioned that "the NWMP's brass band is playing out side."

25. Frank Norman (1847–1906) joined the police in 1874 as staff sergeant, Reg. No. 342, and acted as secretary to Col. Macleod. He was appointed inspector in 1880 and retired to Toronto in 1897.

26. Considerable controversy accompanied Col. French's career with the Mounted Police. He was disliked by some of the men for his rigid discipline and before the great march, D'Artigue (p.30) said he was a leader whose ability "was already being questioned among the men." A civilian correspondent to the *Manitoba Free Press*, November 12, 1875, accused him of being "a sour despot who is not only hated by his own force, but by others also, with whose personal freedom he constantly interfered." D'Artigue (p. 102) said his resignation was greeted with "great joy of almost every member of the Mounted Police" and came "just in time to save the government the trouble of dismissing him." Parker obviously did not

share these views.

27. William Macaulay Herchmer had been appointed a sub-inspector two days before arriving at Swan River. He was a brother of L.W. Herchmer who, in 1886, was appointed Commissioner of the Force.

28. The confrontation did not occur for, as Lieut. Gov. A. Morris explained (Morris, 181), " . . . a few wandering Saulteaux or Chippewa, from Quill Lake, in Treaty No. Four, had come to the Crees and proposed to them to unite with them and prevent me from crossing the river and entering the Indian country. The Crees promptly refused to entertain the proposal."

29. William Drummer Jarvis, a former surveyor, joined the police in 1873 as an inspector and took the first contingent of men to Fort Edmonton in the following year. In the spring of 1875 he constructed Fort Saskatchewan, where he remained in charge until a year before his retirement in 1881.

30. Const. C. Chassi, Reg. No. 64, was a new recruit who had enlisted a month earlier. He died of typhoid fever at Lethbridge in 1886.

31. Corp. B. Welstead, Reg. No. 221, was a member of "E" Division. When Commissioner James F. Macleod arrived at Touchwood Hills on August 28, he noted it was the site "where Inspector Walker had fixed to establish a Post. The situation chosen is a very pretty one, but there is no good water to be had. . . . Not seeing the utility of establishing a Post at that particular point for the present, I determined not to build until a more suitable location was decided upon, and ordered the detachment, consisting of one acting constable [corporal] and three men to rejoin their Division at Battle River." (Letter, Commr. James F. Macleod to Secretary of State, October, 1876. RCMP Museum, Regina.)

32. This was John Alexander MacKay, who was ordained in 1863 and was at Stanley Mission from 1865 to 1876. After the signing of Treaty No. Six he remained in the Battleford and Prince Albert areas (see Boon, 61-62).

33. The chief in question could not have been Sweet Grass; he did not attend the session at Fort Carlton but was present for the negotiations at Fort Pitt a week later.

34. "Kangaroo" was a well-known police horse. In February, 1875, when the horse was at Dufferin, Insp. Walker learned that a man had deserted. He ordered a sergeant "to put my saddle on Kangaroo, a race horse we had, and I would go after him." (Walker, 9.) He succeeded fighting his way through a snow-blocked trail and captured the fugitive.

35. Edmond Frechette joined the police in 1875 and was in charge of building the post at Battleford in 1876. He was being transferred to Fort Macleod when he was with Parker's party.

36. Insp. E.D. Clark.

37. Parker failed to mention that the troops became lost en route and took the wrong trail. On September 14 Parker noted in his diary: "Left camp at 6:00 A.M. Found out that we are on the wrong road. Struck telegraph line thirty minutes after we left camp so left road to follow the line along till we come to the road we missed." On the following day they "struck our old road at 10:00 A.M."

38. Joseph Kenny, Reg. No. 142, was a member of "D" Division.

39. Francis Carruthers, Reg. No. 56, was in "D" Division.

40. According to Parker's diary for October 1, the doctor "dished out a horn of sherry last night and one of port tonight to every man," for medicinal purposes.

41. Commissioner Macleod outlined some of the problems in crossing. They reached the South Saskatchewan on Sept. 29th and "after spending some hours in looking for a place to cross, the guide reported that he had found the ford, but that on account of the depth of the water, the swiftness of the current and the boulders at the bottom it was impracticable. We were about a mile from the forks of Elk [Red Deer] River, where I had been given to understand that a Post was being built by the 'North West Fur Company,' and that they had a boat which would enable us to cross. We found no traces of either the Post or the boat so the rover had to be crossed with the means at our own disposal. The river at the point we struck it is about 200 yards wide with a current of about two miles an hour and very deep. By covering two waggon boxes with sheets and lashing them together with waggon

reaches at each end, a very serviceable boat was constructed with which we proceeded to cross over our waggons, camp equipment, rations, forage, &c. and early on the 1st October we had everything across.

"The ox train arrived just as we had finished and next evening it, also was safely on the south bank of the river, notwithstanding the cold weather and heavy gale which had set in. We had a great deal of difficulty in crossing the horses and oxen which refused over and over again to take the water. I cannot speak in too high terms of the manner in which the men worked during the three days it took to cross the river. The water was excessively cold and it was absolutely necessary for a number of them to be continually in the water sometimes up to their armpits, but so far from their complaining they all went into it with the utmost good humour and appeared to consider the matter rather enjoyable than otherwise. I have much pleasure in bringing to your notice the excellent example shown to their men by Sub. Insptrs. Clark and McIllree, who worked during the whole three days with the men detailed to work the boat and never left the self-imposed task till everything was across. I beg also to mention Sergeant-Major Mitchell and Sub. Const. Daly who, seeing the difficulty there was in getting the horses to take the water, stripped and after one ineffectual attempt swam their horses to the other side." (Letter, Commr. James F. Macleod to Secretary of State, October 1876. RCMP Museum, Regina.)

42. The Force almost got lost again, for Parker wrote in his diary, Oct. 6th, that it was "Very smoky, cannot see very far, the guides very doubtful about us being on the right course." The next day, however, they "Met some Indians and half-breeds, hired an Indian to guide us to the Fort."

43. Joseph Francis (1838–81) had been with the British army at Balaclava and in the charge of the Light Brigade. He joined the police in 1874 as sergeant-major, Reg. No. 250, and retired to Toronto in 1879, where he was killed two years later when trying to rescue some people from a burning house.

44. Parker is a year out on this date. This incident occurred on June 19th, 1877, not in 1876. See Turner, I, 332-33. In his correspondence, Parker blamed Marchand for not saving the constable.

45. "In consequence of the Indians in the adjoining Territory of Montana being engaged during the past summer in conflict with the United States troops," stated Comptroller Frederick White, "it was considered necessary, as a precautionary measure, to increase the force at Forts Macleod and Walsh (Cypress Hills); one hundred men were accordingly ordered there from the northern posts." (NWMP Report, Sessional Papers, Vol. 10, No. 7, appendix D, 1877, p.21). Another reason for Parker's troop being moved to Fort Macleod was the transfer of the headquarters from Swan River to that point.

46. Jerry Potts (1840–96) was a famous scout for the police. Of Scottish-Blood ancestry, he had an uncanny sense of direction and was invaluable to the Force during its early years. See *Jerry Potts, Plainsman*, by Hugh A. Dempsey. Glenbow-Alberta Institute, Calgary, 1966.

47. Sweetgrass Hills, just east of Coutts, Alberta.

48. James H. Christie, Reg. No. 59 had joined the Force on Sept. 1, 1876, and was a member of "E" Division.

49. One of the tribes of the Blackfoot nation.

50. Constables John Carruthers, Reg. No. 51, J.A. Prongua, Reg. No. 221, and W. Johnston, Reg. No. 137.

51. Here Parker fails to mention a diary entry that earlier in the day he had appeared before his commanding officer "for neglect of duty" but was released.

52. Parker undoubtedly refers to Eagle Tail, not Eagle Head. Literally, his name was "Sitting-on-an-Eagle's-Tail."

53. James Brooks, alias Slim Jim, was born in Lanesville, Ohio, in 1849 and learned the trade of printer. He apparently had the reputation of being a horse thief in Montana before coming to Alberta, where in 1878 he ran off with horses belonging to J. Hughes, J. Bastion and J. Smith of Fort Macleod. He was released from prison on April 13, 1882, and all that is known of his later career is that mentioned by Parker.

54. William Winder joined the police in 1873 as an inspector and spent his entire period at Fort Macleod. He retired in 1880 to begin the Winder Ranche Cattle Co. and to open the mercantile business of Winder & Co. at Fort Macleod.

55. Thomas T. Lake, Reg. No. 153, was a professional soldier who joined the police in 1874 and was promoted to sergeant later in the year and to staff sergeant in 1877. He was best known as the bandmaster for the Force. Lake committed suicide at Golden, B.C., in 1887.

56. Three of these men, identified in Parker's diary, were Const. C.F. Boyle, Richard Pentland and T. McLeod. Parker also indicated that Insp. Francis Dickens and Insp. W.D. Antrobus accompanied the party as far as Fort Walsh.

57. After going about a mile, Parker's party, according to his diary, "had to go back and hunt up the guide who was not on hand when we started. His name is Kiou Moro [Baptise Moreau], the best guide between here and Qu'Appelle. He is a French half-breed, short and as black as the ace of spades, but he is a first rate fellow and full of fun. He has got his wife along in a Red River cart and three horses. The government is paying him $4.00 a day as guide."

58. George Borradaile, Reg. No. 46, was a member of "D" Division.

59. The next night Parker wrote in his diary, "Had a devil of a time in the evening. Borradaile and I went off about eight o'clock and hunted up a lot of half-breed girls, eleven in all, and brought them up to the house, also brought along old McKay, who played the fiddle for us. We had a splendid time of it and tripped the light fantastic till about two in the morning. The girls were most of them English half-breed, which made it so much nicer as a fellow could talk to them."

60. Shown in the police records as Ka-we-ti-osh. He was charged with a felony on March 7, 1879 and sentenced to three months' hard labour.

61. This was Mattew Ryan, former Montreal lawyer, who had been appointed stipendiary magistrate for the North-West Territories in 1878. He also was a member of the North-West Council, which was governing body of the Territories.

62. Sub. Const. J. Farrell, Reg. No. 310, and Sub. Const. Burgess.

63. Touchwood Hills post was located near the present town of Punnichy, Saskatchewan.

64. Actually, this was the second contact with Ko-wee-ta-ass since his escape, for Parker noted in his diary for June 6 that "Donaldson brings news . . . that [Const.] Sutherland tried to retake the prisoner that escaped from S.L. [Shoal Lake]. They fired several shots at each other and the Indian got away."

65. Angus McBeath.

66. Probably William Daniels, who had worked for the Indian Department.

67. Yellow Quill, or Oo-za-wask-oo-quin-ape, was an Ojibwa leader who signed an adhesion to Treaty No. 4 on August 24, 1876. His band settled on two reserves at Nut Lake and Fishing Lake where they lived by hunting and trapping.

68. Samuel J. Donaldson, Reg. No. 79, was in "D" Division.

69. Ambroise Lepine had been Louis Riel's adjutant general in the rebellion of 1869-70. In 1874 he was tried and served two years in prison for the murder of Thomas Scott during the uprising.

70. This was the same Matthew Ryan whom the Mounted Police had arrested a year earlier.

71. William D. Antrobus, Reg. No. 285, joined the Mounted Police in 1874, as a member of "F" Division.

72. Owen E. Hughes, manager of Stobart, Eden & Co.

73. Cut Nose.

74. Other accounts make no mention of the toll gate problem. The report in the *Saskatchewan Herald* (August 16, 1880) was as follows: " . . . When the cattle intended for rations for the Indians during the recent payments at Duck Lake had been driven there, Beardy demanded possession of them; and this being refused he and some of his followers shot three of them and caused three others to stampede. . . . He next endeavoured to help himself to goods from the store of Stobart, Eden & Co., whereupon a warrant was sworn out against Beardy and one of his councillors, and against Chiefs Cut Nose and One Arrow. . . .

Shortly after the offence was committed Superintendent Herchmer arrived at the scene of the disturbance, with twenty-five men on the way from Shoal Lake to Battleford. Taking Captain Antrobus and six men with him he went to the camp to make the arrests. On entering it he was confronted by a large number of Indians armed with knives, which they brandished and threatened to use; and another portion of the band had guns, with which they tried to frighten the police by firing a volley over their heads. But they were not in the frightening mood just then. The Beardy and his two associate chiefs were quickly assigned places between files of police and marched to a place of safe-keeping preparatory to their removal to Prince Albert...."

75. Beardy, One Arrow and Cut Nose were acquitted by jury in Prince Albert on a charge of killing government cattle. Omenakaw, who was later arrested, was found guilty of the charge and ordered to pay for the cost of the cattle.

76. Const. C.S. Hooley, Reg. No. 181, was trying to take a balky team across the river at Slideout when the accident occurred.

77. Sixty miles north of Battleford.

78. Robert Wyld.

79. An account of this incident, entitled "Fire at the Barracks," is contained in *Saskatchewan Herald*, Battleford, April 11, 1881.

80. Poundmaker was a prominent Cree chief who was adopted by Crowfoot, head chief of the Blackfoot. His followers were attacked by troops at the Battle of Cutknife Hill at the beginning of the Riel Rebellion in 1885 and Poundmaker is credited with preventing his people from inflicting heavy casualties on the attackers. However, he was sentenced to prison and died shortly after he was released in 1886.

81. Corp. J. MacNeil, Reg. No. 143.

82. Pierre Levallier, a prominent Métis, who established a farm at the Forks early in 1880.

83. Const. J.D. Hanafin, Reg. No. 152, was a member of "D" Division.

84. Although Parker identifies two of the Indians as Little Buffalo and Thunder Horse's son, the official police records show them as The-Bull-Painted-Red-Who-Walks, The Ghost, Cloud Old Man and Esktope. According to the *Saskatchewan Herald* (October 31, 1881), "Sergeant Parker left here on the 15th with warrants for the arrest of four Indians who had stolen horses and gone to the plains. He reached the Red Deer River on the fifth day out, and found two of his men on this side of the river and two on the other. He first crossed over and made sure of the latter, and then recrossed and secured their partners. The Indians were inclined to resist arrest and had to be put in irons to make them at all manageable. This was worse than the arrest, for they have a strong aversion to being 'hoppled like horses,' as they describe being ironed. Finding resistance useless they soon quieted down, and were rewarded by being freed from their irons during the daytime. The stolen horses were recovered, but one of them had to be left behind in consequence of a severe flesh wound that one of the Indians had inflicted on it to make it easy to catch..."
When the Indians appeared before Judge Richardson on October 31, Bull-Painted-Red, Ghost and Cloud Old Man were acquitted of horse stealing, while Esktope also was acquitted of shooting a horse. Like his experience with Beardy, Parker fails to mention that his "adventures" in capturing Indians ended with the natives being cleared of charges against them.

85. During August, his brother Harry, who had come to Canada with him in 1871, joined Parker in Battleford and announced that he would settle in the district. Prior to this time he was living in Sarnia, Ontario (*Saskatchewan Herald*, August 5, 1882).

86. The only mention of the wedding in the *Saskatchewan Herald* was a formal announcement on September 2, 1882; "Parker-Calder. At Battleford, on the 22nd of August, by the Rev. Thos. Clarke, assisted by the Rev. S. Trivett, Sergeant Wm. Parker, of the North-West Mounted Police, to Miss Mary Margaret Calder, of this place."

87. These two men, Dancing Bull and Mustoos, were tried and convicted at Fort Pitt of killing a government cow. Dancing Bull was sentenced to two months and his

companion to four months.

88. Sévère Gagnon joined the police in 1874 as a sub-inspector and served under Insp. W.D. Jarvis when he established Fort Saskatchewan.

89. The McKays were friends of Mrs. Parker. William McKay had taken charge of Fort Pitt in 1872 for Hudson's Bay Co. and remained there until his death in 1884.

90. John Delaney.

91. Vital J. Grandin, O.M.I., was Bishop of Saskatchewan.

92. Const. P.J. Curran, Reg. No. 38, was a member of "A" Division.

93. Harrison S. Young came west to Fort Edmonton as a Hudson's Bay Co. employee in 1870 and was at Lesser Slave Lake, 1873–83, Lac La Biche 1883–88, and then moved to Edmonton where he died in 1909.

94. The nine men killed at Frog Lake were Father Leon A. Farard, Father Felix Marchand, Thomas Quinn, John Delaney, John A. Gowanlock, William C. Gilchrist, George Dill, Charles Gouin, and John Williscroft.

95. Const. D.L. Cowan, Reg. No. 635, and Const. C. Loasby, Reg. No. 925.

96. Thomas G. McLellan, Reg. No. 308, was a member of "E" Division.

97. This was Meeminook, a prominent Cree hunter from Saddle Lake. For a detailed account of his death see Cameron, 178-81.

98. Alex Rowland was a prominent Métis from Edmonton.

99. This was the Battle of Frenchman's Butte.

100. The three injured were Privates E. Lemay and J. Marcotte, of the 65th Battalion and Const. J. McRae of the police.

101. Rev. Charles Quinney was the Anglican missionary at Onion Lake. William Bleasdale Cameron later became a free lance writer.

102. They were engaged in the Battle of Loon Lake.

103. Lieut. C. Starnes was a member of No. 3 Company, 65th Montreal Regiment.

104. Sergt. Major William Fury, Reg. No. 333, was shot in the chest but recovered.

105. Of these eight, Wandering Spirit, Round the Sky, Miserable Man, Bad Arrow, Man Without Blood and Ikta were hung, while Louison Mongrain and Charles Ducharme received life sentences.

106. Sergt. Major Frederick G. Dann, Reg. No. 649.

107. When the holdup occurred, the Mounted Police suspected that a gang had come up from the United States, so a number of detachments were sent out to search. On August 18th, G.L. Garnett came into Prince Albert and was recognized by the stage driver as the holdup man. He was arrested in the general store and sent to Regina for trial, where he was given a fourteen-year sentence. The money, estimated to be $1,300, was never recovered. (See Turner, II: 296-300, and *Prince Albert Times*, August 20, 1886).

108. Dundurn is the first station south of Saskatoon on the Regina line.

109. Probably the Hon. W.A.H. A'Court, who started a large ranch along Beaver Creek in 1886. (See *The Saskatoon Story*, by M.A. East, 1952, 33.)

110. Sgt. Henry Keenan, Reg. No. 301.

111. This was Const. R.C. Dickson. According to Almighty Voice's father, Const. Dickson jokingly told the prisoner he was to be hung for killing the steer. This caused him to take the reckless actions of escape and murder. Const. Dickson was convicted of negligence for permitting the escape and was sentenced to two months at hard labour.

112. Sergt. C.C. Colebrook, Reg. No. 605.

113. Corp. W.J. Bowdridge, Reg. No. 2357.

114. Included in this group were Insp. John Beresford Allen, Sergt. C.C. Raven, Reg. No. 1128; Corp. C.S. Hockin (No. 3106); Const. J.R. Kerr (No. 3040); A.N. O'Kelly (No. 3052); W. Hume (No. 2259); W.W. Ferris (No. 3119); D. Williams (No. 2959); C.M. McNair (No. 3135); D.L. McClean (No. 2865) and Const. Ascott.

115. Const. Ascott.

116. Staff Sergt. C.H. West, Reg. No. 2141.

117. The other two were a brother-in-law, Topean, whom Parker calls "Dublin," and a fifteen-year-old cousin, Going-Up-to-the-Sky, whom Parker identifies as Little Saulteaux.

118. Odilon St. Denis, Reg. No. 568.

119. This incident was to reflect

unfavourably upon the Mounted Police in later years and was used as an example of unnecessary brutality. "The Brave they Fought with Cannons" was the title used by *Maclean's* magazine in recounting the event (July 1, 1951, 16-36) and "One Brave Against the North-West Mounted Police" was the title used by *Canadian Cattlemen* (March, p. 38, and May, p. 23, 1956).
120. These were a group of English settlers, many of whom had no farming experience, but who responded to a call from Isaac M. Barr to establish a large agricultural colony in western Canada. When Barr left the party, Rev. G.E. Lloyd assumed control and the town of Lloydminster was named in his honour.
121. This was Const. C.W. Beckwith, who was killed at Gillis, Saskatchewan, on August 18, 1904.
122. Aylesworth Bowen Perry (1860–1956) joined the Mounted Police in 1882 as inspector and was promoted to superintendent after the Riel Rebellion. He was appointed Commissioner of the Force in 1900, serving in that capacity until 1922.
123. John Lehr.
124. These men were Jacob Merkel, Jr., Jacob Reib, John Reib, Fred Neiman, Christian Gill, Emanuel Gill, Daniel Gill, August Neiman and Karl Otta. Of these, Jacob Merkel Jr. was known as the "Son of God" while his father, in South Dakota, was the leader of the sect and was called "God Jacob." (Medicine Hat *News*, April 16, 23 and 30, and May 7, 1908.
125. August Neiman. He was sentenced to two years in Edmonton Penitentiary.
126. For Kipling's own account of the visit see "The Town that was Born Lucky," in *Alberta Historical Review*, Winter 1961, 5-7.

Letters

1. Likely sub-constable A. McIntosh, Reg. No. 309, who died at Dufferin on July 20, 1874.
2. A.L. Fortesque, Reg. No. 9, joined the Force in 1873.
3. According to Parker's diary, he and Const. M. Hennigan, Reg. No. 243, were supposed to have taken the S.S. *Selkirk* to Winnipeg after loading the supplies on the S.S. *Cheyenne*. However the boat was

too crowded, so Parker took the horses overland.
4. Rev. W. Cyprian Pinkham, later Bishop of Calgary.
5. Rev. W.R. Morrison.
6. George Horace Meloy, Reg. No. 157, was a member of "D" Division.
7. Commissioner G.A. French.
8. Sweetgrass Hills, on the Alberta-Montana boundary.
9. John Maclean, Anglican Bishop of Saskatchewan.
10. These were Const. T.D. Wilson, Reg. No. 228, and Const. Frank Baxter, Reg. No. 247. Details of their deaths were published in the Ottawa *Free Press*, Feb. 26, 1875: "Baxter and Wilson left Fort Kipp on the 13th December, for Fort Macleod, to see some friends there, and when on their way back on the 31st, they stopped at a fort a short distance from Macleod, till dark. When leaving for home the people tried to persuade them to stop all night, but they thought they were all right and knew the way. They started for home and nothing was known till the next day till about 3:30 P.M. when their horses came home saddled and riderless. Capt. [E.A.] Brisebois immediately started to see what was wrong and while on his way he met an Indian boy who said he had seen one of the men lying in the snow dead. The captain sent the boy to the fort for a waggon, and while proceeding in the direction shown him by the lad, found Wilson not quite dead. On arriving with him at the fort he sent for a doctor from Fort Macleod, but before the courier had gone ten minutes poor Wilson expired. Baxter was found next night lying in a snow heap quite dead. Both men [were] buried with military honours."
11. Apparently the men did not relish this task, for on January 31, Parker noted in his diary that he "Signed a petition to Capt. Walker for us not to draw our own hay." Two days later, "Every man had to be on parade at 2:00 P.M. and Capt. Walker made us a speech about the petition. He said it was mutiny and tore the petition up before our faces."
12. Another interesting incident was recorded in Parker's diary for this period: Feb. 6th—"Big excitement in the evening. One of our fellows, Const. Helliwell,

deserted with a horse. Half a dozen men and Capt. Walker chased him and the captain caught him, brought him back, mounted a guard and handcuffed him."
Feb. 8th—"The prisoner was brought up before Capt. Walker but remanded for further evidence. The guards have their revolvers loaded all the time. The picket also at night armed with loaded revolvers."
Feb. 11th—"Team arrived from Garry with the sergt. major, Sergt. [Percy R.] Neale and Meloy. Helliwell was taken to Winnipeg, by Capt. Walker, Sergt. [C.] Knight and two sub cons., to be tried by a jury."
Feb. 12th—"Our revolvers called in to stores. . . . "
Feb. 18th—"Team arrived from Winnipeg with the guard that went down with Helliwell, the prisoner. Jury found true bill against him for horse stealing; sentence, three months. . . . "
13. The Rev. George Young.
14. These three men, Philander Vogel, James Hughes and George Bell, were accused of killing a number of Assiniboine Indians in the Cypress Hills massacre of 1873. The Canadian government tried to extradite others in the party from Montana but were unsuccessful. The three went on trial in 1876 and were acquitted.
15. Angus McIvor, a freighter, shot another freighter named George Atkinson and wounded a man named Baptiste Charette. He was executed on January 7, 1876.
16. Sub. Const. Thomas Mooney, Reg. No. 305, was a member of "E" Division.
17. The Great Lone Land, by William F. Butler. Sampson Low, Marston, Low, & Searle, London, 1874.
18. Rev. W.R. Morrison, the Methodist, who was first on the scene, objected when Rev. Alex Stewart, the Presbyterian, arrived. Morrison immediately took action to have him removed but was obliged to leave instead.
19. The officer in question was John French, the Commissioner's brother, who was the subject of a letter to the editor of Manitoba Free Press, November 6, 1875. Entitled "The Mounted Police Outrage" and signed "A Sufferer" from Swan River, it stated: "The thanks of the men

of the Mounted Police Force are due to you for your public mention of the outrage perpetrated by Capt. John French on a man named Daley, on the road from Winnipeg to here, by strapping him to a sergeant's stirrup, whereby his collarbone was broken; but it does not appear that it has, as yet, led to justice being done. I have known of an officer being severely rebuked for speaking too sharp and using some oath to a sub-constable, but sharp words break no bones, and that man was not the Commissioner's brother. If it was not for the public press, we might very likely be worse treated than we are, not by men who have served Canada, and know the people, but by blusterers like this Captain French. I think if the present government had been in power when Colonel French got the command of this body, we should have been spared two tyrants."
On the day that Parker wrote to his mother, he also was the second man to sign a petition supporting French. This was published in the Manitoba Free Press, December 18, 1875, with a covering letter from Edward Maunsell, secretary of the mess. The petition stated: "Sir, we are the sub-constables of your troop having read the letter in the Free Press newspaper dated 13th of November, 1875, published at Winnipeg, wherein your character as an officer is asserted to be tyrannical, and yourself designated as a tyrant and purporting to be the expression of the general opinion of the troop; we beg to state that the sentiments expressed in that anonymous communication are not the sentiments entertained by the men of this troop, and we gladly avail ourselves of this opportunity, not only to give this infamous accusation an unqualified denial, but to assure you, sir, that the care and attention you have always shown for the comfort and well-being of the men, under the exceptional hardships of a service in the North-West, have been sincerely appreciated, and that no feelings exist amongst us toward yourself, but those of kindness and respect. James Brooks, William Parker, Alfred Beaudoin, Thos. T.A. Boys, R.P. Pentland, John McDougall, F. McLeod, G.H. Herchmer, J. Mulqueen, Jos. McDermot, John J. Miller, Robt. Hayward, W. Latimer, W.

Chisholm, A. Goyer, W.J. Barry, D. McAulay, S.S. Walker, W. Devlin, Edward Maunsell, Daniel Wilson, W. Wilson, John Wymerskirche, Claudius H. Horley, W. M. Sullivan, G.C. Borwell, T. Hall, F. Brown, George Maunsell, Archibald Hare, William Oliver, Patrick Burke, J.G. Stone, H. Nash, G. Kenley, Jos. Kenny, James Goree, M. Slevin."

20. Samuel Cartwright, whom he met later at Fort Walsh.

21. Insp. Wainwright Griffiths, the adjutant.

22. Likely T.T.A. Boys, noted orator, lawyer and author of a popular poem "Riders of the Plains." He later became town clerk for Calgary.

23. Although addressed from Fort Macleod, this letter and subsequent ones to June 6, 1877, were written from the wood camp several miles west of the barracks.

24. Lieutenant-Governor David Laird.

25. Lundbreck Falls, ten miles west of the present Pincher Creek.

26. John H. Ward, Reg. No. 282.

27. Sergeant-Major J.H. Bray, Reg. No. 17, was a member of "B" Division.

28. W.H. Lee had a trading post on the Oldman River, near the mouth of Pincher Creek.

29. Acting Const. F.N. Dobbs, Reg. No. 77, was a member of "D" Division.

30. This arrest was not kindly received by an irate correspondent to the *Saskatchewan Herald*, Battleford, January 12, 1880. "A very heartbreaking occurrence took place the other day between the Mounted Police and Mr. Alexander Cunningham, who had just arrived from Winnipeg with freight for the police," he wrote. "Immediately after his arrival in the barrack room, he [Cunningham], as a token of gratitude for the hospitable manner in which he had been received by the boys, placed a bottle of liquor on the table, and in total ignorance of the provisions of the North-West Territories' Act in the premises, asked them to partake of the luxury. He was then made a prisoner and tried next morning before the justice of the peace and to his great astonishment had to pay the enormous fine of sixty dollars. Now, notwithstanding that the action of the police in the matter was conformable to the regulations respecting liquor in the North-West Territories, don't you think it was rather harsh treatment? I do."

31. Const. Marmaduke Graburn was the first Mounted Policeman in the West to die by violence. A Blood Indian named Star Child was arrested for the crime but was acquitted.

32. The speculation was premature, for two years were to elapse before Regina barracks were established to become the new headquarters.

33. Sergt. Major Robert Belcher joined the Force in 1873, Reg. No. 13, and was promoted to inspector in 1893.

34. Rev. Canon Thomas Clarke was a teacher and Anglican lay missionary who took charge of Battleford in 1879 when Rev. J.A. Mackay was transferred to Prince Albert. Canon Clarke later studied for the ministry and was ordained.

35. "A young man named Rattlesnake Dog had a quarrel about the quantity of provisions he should get, and being dissatisfied made a knife thrust at Mr. [D.L.] Clink; and at the same time a squaw, commonly known as Mrs. Allen, broke in one of the windows with a club, also which she threatened to use on both Mr. and Mrs. Clink. Information was laid against the Indian, who was arrested and brought in on Saturday, and after a hearing of the case he was sentenced to two months' hard labour. A resolute attempt was made at the time of the arrest to rescue the Indian, but the police carried off their man. After pronouncing sentence the stipendiary magistrate remarked that it was the duty of the police to arrest and bring to punishment every one who in any way resisted them." *Saskatchewan Herald*, Battleford, February 14, 1881.

36. This was Jean Marie, who was arrested on February 22, 1881, but the charges were dismissed at his trial on March 4th.

37. This was the Walrond Ranch, directed by Dr. Duncan McEachran, Dominion Veterinary surgeon.

38. William McKay, Jr.

39. Corp. Stephen Wardin, Reg. No. 507.

Bibliography

Books and Periodicals

Annual Reports, North-West Mounted Police, 1874–1904. Ottawa.
Annual Reports, Department of Indian Affairs, 1879–97. Ottawa. Anonymous. "William Parker—'74 Original," in *RCMP Quarterly*, 2, 1: 43-57, July, 1945. Ottawa.
Boon, T.C.B. *These Men Went Out.* Ryerson Press, Toronto, 1970.
Cameron, W.B. *The War Trial of Big Bear.* Small, Maynard & Co., Boston, 1927.
D'Artigue, Jean. *Six Years in the Canadian North-West.* Hunter Rose & Co., Toronto, 1882.
Deane, R. Burton. *Mounted Police Life in Canada.* Cassell & Co., London, 1916.
Denny, Cecil. *The Riders of the Plains.* The Herald Co., Calgary, 1905.—. *The Law Marches West.* J.M. Dent & Sons, Toronto, 1939.
Haydon, A.L. *The Riders of the Plains.* M.G. Hurtig Ltd., Edmonton, 1971.
Hicks, Joseph. "With Hatton's Scouts in Pursuit of Big Bear," in *Alberta Historical Review*, 18, 3: 14-23, Summer, 1970.
Jamieson, F.C. *The Alberta Field Force of 1885.* Canadian North-West Historical Society, Battleford, 1931.
Jefferson, Robert. *Fifty Years on the Saskatchewan.* Canadian North-West Historical Society, Battleford, 1929.
Julien, Henri. "Expedition to the North-West," in *Alberta Historical Review*, 9, 1: 8-26, Winter, 1961.
Kelly, Nora. *The Men of the Mounted.* J.M. Dent & Sons, Toronto, 1949.
Klaus, J.F. "Fort Livingstone," in *Saskatchewan History*, 15, 3: 93-110, Autumn, 1962.
Longstreth, T. Morris. *The Silent Force.* The Century Co., New York, 1927.
Macoun, John. *Manitoba and the Great Northwest.* World Publishing Co., Guelph, Ont., 1882.
Maunsell, E.H. "With the North-West Mounted Police Force from 1874 to 1877," in *Scarlet and Gold*, 2: 50-59, 1920.
Morris, Alexander. *The Treaties of Canada with the Indians of Manitoba and the North-West Territories.* Willing & Williamson, Toronto, 1880.
Steele, Samuel B. *Forty Years in Canada.* Herbert Jenkins Ltd., London, 1915.
Strange, Thomas B. *Gunner Jingo's Jubilee.* Remington & Co., London, 1893.
Turner, John Peter. *The North-West Mounted Police.* 2 vols. King's Printer, Ottawa, 1950.
Walker, James. "My Life in the North-West Mounted Police," in *Alberta Historical Review*, 8, 1: 1-14, Winter, 1960.

Manuscripts

Bagley, Fred A. "The '74 Mounties," in Glenbow-Alberta Institute Archives, Calgary, No. A/B146.
Royal Canadian Mounted Police. Papers in Public Archives of Canada, Ottawa, RG-18.
William Parker. Papers in Glenbow-Alberta Institute Archives, Calgary, No. A/P 244.